U.S.A.

THE WEST, ROCKIES AND TEXAS

Authors:
Jürgen Scheunemann, Arturo Gonzalez, Sara Hare,
Anita King, Gary McKechnie, Anne Midgette

*An Up-to-date travel guide with 146 color photos
and 21 maps*

**First Edition
1996**

Dear Reader,

Being up-to-date is the main goal of the Nelles series. To achieve it, we have a network of far-flung correspondents who keep us abreast of the latest developments in the travel scene, and our cartographers always make sure that maps and texts are adjusted to each other.

Each travel chapter ends with its own list of useful tips, accommodations, restaurants, tourist offices, sights. At the end of the book you will find practical information from A to Z. But the travel world is fast moving, and we cannot guarantee that all the contents are always valid. Should you come across a discrepancy, please write us at: Nelles Verlag GmbH, Schleissheimer Str. 371 b, D-80935 München, Germany.

LEGEND

✈	Place of Interest		National Border		Interstate
▨	Public or Significant Building	Venice	Place Mentioned in Text		Toll Expressway
■	Hotel	✈	International Airport		Four-lane Highway
●	Restaurant	🏖	Beach		Connecting Highway
▨	Shopping Center	··🌳··	National Park		Main Highway
○	Market	--🌳--	National Forest		Railway
▨	High-rise	▲	Campsite	95	Interstate Highway
✝ ✡	Church, Synagogue	\ 25 /	Distance in Miles	🛡	U.S. Highway
Ⓢ	Underground Station	Mt. Baker 10778	Mountain Summit (Height in Feet)	9	State / Provincial Highway

U.S.A. – The West, Rockies and Texas
© Nelles Verlag GmbH, 80935 München
   All rights reserved

First Edition 1996
ISBN 3-88618-416-1
Printed in Slovenia

Publisher:	Günter Nelles	**Translation:**	Marton Radkai
		Cartography:	Nelles Verlag GmbH
Chief Editor:	Berthold Schwarz	**Color**	
Project Editor:	Jürgen Scheunemann	**Separation:**	Priegnitz, München
Picture Editor:	K. Bärmann-Thümmel	**Printed by:**	Gorenjski Tisk

TABLE OF CONTENTS

HISTORY AND CULTURE

TRAVELING IN THE WESTERN PARTS OF THE U.S.

FEATURES

TRAVEL INFORMATION

MAPLIST

(Legend see page 2)

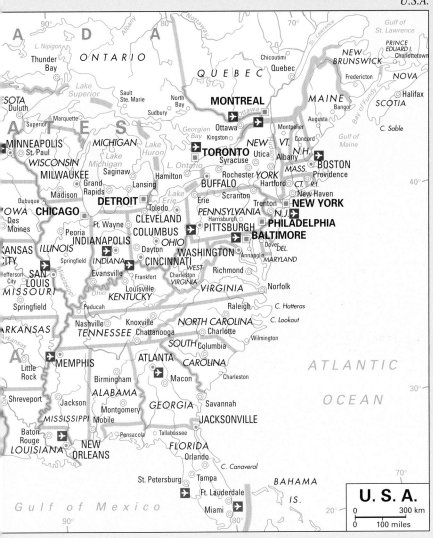

"GO WEST!"

Travel to the Promised Land

America is at its most American where it is farthest from Europe: in the metropolises of the West Coast, in the canyons of Utah and Colorado, in the valleys of the Rocky Mountains, in the gambling casinos of Las Vegas, in the pueblos of Arizona, and, last but not least, in the gold-mining towns of Nevada. The American West is a myth, a legend, an idea, one could even say an ideology. But the West that was considered so wild and treacherous had already become history before the turn of the 20th century.

This left much breathing space for the growing myth. Back then the American historian Frederick Jackson Turner published his famous thesis on the American frontier. Turner's essay stated that the new European immigrants could only become genuine Americans by experiencing the wilderness of the frontier, which was steadily moving westwards. This new species of human being would then no longer have anything to do with old Europe; instead he would be individualistic and incorruptible, and hence more democratic. Modern historians refute this thesis that life on the frontier automatically led to one's becoming Americanized; in fact, real life on the border between wilderness and civilization had been idealized into pleasant, but fictional, legend.

The conquest of the Wild West

The glorification of the frontier conceals a darker side of American history.

Previous pages: Fascinating play of colors in Bryce Canyon, Utah. Loafing in Venice (Los Angeles). Left: Navajo Indian woman in Navajo Tribal Park.

The Wild West was by no means an unpopulated tract of land. Long before the white man cast his shadow on the New World, an estimated 4 to 10 million Native Americans lived on the North American continent. By the year 1890 they numbered a mere 300,000. The first expeditions out west – the most famous one being that of Lewis and Clark in 1804-1806 – made friendly contact with most of the tribes they encountered. However, the following generations of westward-bound settlers, gold-miners and ranchers conducted a virtual war of extermination. The genocide of the indigenous Americans – the Sioux, the Apaches, the Cheyennes and the Nez Percés – remains to this day the darkest chapter in American history.

An interesting note is that in recent censuses, an increasing number of Americans have given their origins as Indian: around 2 million in 1990, which represents a tidy 0.8 percent of the population, and twice as many as 20 years before. Be that as it may, the Indian wars remain a controversial national topic.

By the 19th century, northerners, at least, were keenly aware of the social injustice represented by the Southern institution of slavery; but, apart from a few sporadic outbreaks of outrage at some of the army's more blatant atrocities, the intellectual elite of the East Coast maintained a rather disinterested attitude toward the Indian wars. This is hardly surprising in light of the widespread belief in "Manifest Destiny" since the 1840s. It was, so ran the theory, the divinely-ordained destiny of the United States to expand to take over the entire continent – a destiny the country's citizens, accordingly, hastened to fulfill.

Historically, America has tended to define "the West" as those territories that had not yet been annexed beyond the westernmost point of settlement. If, in the 18th century, the "Northwest Territories" lay to the south of the Great Lakes, the

same term was, a century later, applied to what are now the states of Washington and Oregon in the Pacific Northwest. In 1763, American expansion was abruptly checked at the Appalachians after the end of the colonial war between France and England; however, after the American colonists successfully waged their War of Independence in 1776, the young nation began expanding again, down to Florida in the south and to the Great Lakes in the north. In 1803, the Louisiana Purchase doubled the size of the U.S.A. As a historical footnote, it should be mentioned that negotiators had planned only to discuss the purchase of New Orleans with Napoleon; but the French Emperor offered them the entire territory between the Mississippi and the Rocky Mountains for a mere 15 million dollars. The frontier moved 1,000 miles westward in one fell swoop.

Above: Ghost town of Goldfield. Right: Lively border exchange with Mexico in El Paso. Far right: Chicanos – much in demand as laborers.

After this largest real estate buy in the history of mankind, a continuous flow of settlers poured into the West. In 1830, only one-quarter of all Americans lived beyond the Appalachians; by 1850, it was half. The U.S. government continued signing sales agreements with the Indians, only to break them a few years later. The annexing of the Republic of Texas and the end of the war with Mexico gave the U.S.A. the entire Southwest.

It was around this time that the myth of the Wild West came into being. Naturally, the standard Hollywood-style clichés of cowboys and Indians have little to do with reality except, perhaps, in a very few cases. Daily life in the 19th century looked considerably different. For one thing, the settlers pushing their way westward along the Oregon Trail and other routes often found the soil conditions so poor that the land could only be used for grazing cattle. It was, in fact, gold that brought thousands of desperados into Colorado, Utah and California; but only a few got rich in this way. All

that remains of the heady days of the gold rushes are a few ghost towns in the salt deserts and the valleys of the Rocky Mountains.

The last great wave of settlers moved in between 1870 and 1900, when the new railways brought some 2 million newcomers to the frontier. The "iron horse," as the Native Americans called the steam locomotive out of respect and mistrust, galloped straight across the continent. On May 10, 1869, the tracks of the *Union Pacific* and *Central Pacific* companies were joined near Promontory Point in Utah to complete the United States' first transcontinental railway.

The trains brought hunters from the East Coast out to the prairie states, where they succeeded in virtually obliterating the great bison herds that had sustained the Indian tribes. In 1863, "Buffalo" Bill Cody, something of a national hero, boasted of having killed 4,300 bison in a mere eight months. By the turn of the century, nearly all of North America's estimated 32 million buffalo had been exterminated. By the time Frederick Jackson Turner promulgated his theory of the frontier in 1893, therefore, the actual subject of his thesis had pretty much vanished.

But the myth has survived even to this day. Just as German and Scandinavian immigrants poured into Kansas and Wisconsin in the last century, so, today, do Mexicans come to California and Texas in droves to fulfill their own version of the American Dream. However, the realities of life in this western Horn of Plenty are anything but wine and roses. Instead of prosperity and growth, many *chicanos*, as the Mexicans are often referred to in the U.S.A., find themselves enmired in bitter poverty and hopelessness.

America and the West

It was in the West that America developed its unique identity and became the country it is today. "Go West, young man, and grow up with the country," were the words of politician and writer

15

Horace Greeley more than 150 years ago. Anyone who did go West came back a different person. The West exercised significant social and political influence on the country as a whole, and turned it into an economic (and, by extension, political) world power. The prairie, the Rocky Mountains and the Pacific coast were new, exciting, young, untamed and merciless. Anyone who wanted to survive here as a settler, rancher or gold-miner had to do so under his own steam. But if you could make it in the West, you could make it anywhere. The West had its own laws, both in a positive and negative sense, dictated by the harsh conditions of life in the wilds.

In this part of the country, women had the right to vote as early as the 1860s. After all, women had to put their shoulder to the wheel just as much as men did. At the same time, might made

Above: Individuality is highly prized. Right: The private initiative "Adopt a Highway" cleans up the country's roads.

right; in this virtually lawless country, you could carry the day either with a gun or, later, with a fistful of dollars. Survival of the fittest was the operative law: at first with regard to the indigenous inhabitants; later to new settlers; and finally to one's neighbors.

In a more general sense, as a metaphor for the American spirit, the frontier ideology has persisted into the 20th century. Those quintessentially American pioneer ideals were still alive and well when John F. Kennedy kicked off his 1959/60 campaign with "New Frontier" as his buzzword against the creaky Eisenhower administration. Kennedy was aspiring to a new philosophical and political frontier, filled with hope and opportunity. Both major parties, and a variety of other social groups, have invoked the frontier concept to introduce reforms, social change or new political directions in the years since.

American Mentality

The turbulent and romantic history of the American West has influenced, indeed, shaped, the mind-set of those living beyond the Mississippi. And the legacy of this history is still in evidence today. Many of the American virtues and traits that strike a European visitor as noteworthy go straight back to the days of the pioneers.

One of the most remarkable aspects of the Western mentality is the paradox between an emphasis on independence and individuality on the one hand, and clannish social solidarity on the other. This is indeed a contradiction, but America is large enough to live with its contradictions.

This paradox does derive directly from frontier life. If your neighbor lived fifty miles away in a wild country, only solidarity could help in the case of an emergency. As soon as the trouble was over, however, this same neighbor resumed his

status as a competitor in the search for land, natural resources or power.

There are plenty of concrete examples of this kind of duality today. Americans on the West Coast or in the Midwest, for example, are considered more friendly and hospitable than their East Coast counterparts: if you have the misfortune to break down on the highway, you can count on someone stopping to lend a hand. On the other hand, the hordes of homeless in such cities as Los Angeles cannot expect the least bit of social support. In the very same city, thousands of people spend their hard-earned dollars on the typical Californian youth and beauty cult, dedicating their free time to leisure pursuits carried to excess, only, it seems, to avoid the monster of boredom.

Yet these same self-absorbed individuals can suddenly crystallize into a united front, particularly when they feel that their rights as Americans or common interests are being threatened. Authentic American grass-roots democracy then springs to life, giving rise, for example,

to a drive to collect signatures for the building of a new school, or in protest of some issue or other. Americans become "community-oriented," and commit themselves unconditionally to the cause – even if the issue is only something as relatively tame as cleaning up a local segment of highway.

The relationship between the East and West Coasts is not exactly free of animosities, and neither side makes much effort to do away with them. The political and social establishment in the East tends to look down its nose at the farmers and ranchers in the Midwest as unpolished rednecks and hillbillies. States such as Oklahoma and Kansas (known as God's Country) are the butt of jokes from coast to coast. There's only truth to these stereotypes insofar as it's in the middle of the country that you find 100-percent, God-fearing, hard-working, conservative, straight Americans. In fact, this part of the country is often referred to as the "heartland." It is indeed where America is at its most American.

17

Even the great cities on the West Coast – Los Angeles and San Diego in particular – have to suffer the witticisms of New Yorkers and Bostonians. According to Easterners, life in the Californian sun is artificial, superficial, and without restraints, standards, seriousness, or morals. Los Angeles is often referred to as La-La-Land, which derives from the short form of its name, "L.A.," and the supposedly lackadaisical attitude of its residents.

In the past few years, politicians in distant Washington have started pointing to Hollywood as being responsible for the moral decay of the entire country. Every evil that visits the U.S.A. seems to come from the West nowadays, even though some of the most outspoken politicians, such as Bob Dole or Phil Gramm, come from the West themselves (Kansas and Texas, respectively).

Above: Endlessly stretching highways cut through the land. Right: Harley drivers parade along Cabrillo Blvd. in Santa Barbara.

"On the Road"

One of the best ways to get to know America is from the seat of a car. Driving along the long, ramrod-straight highways through this seemingly endless country lulls you into a state of relaxed meditation as you watch miles of scenery roll by. Unlike many Europeans, Americans tend to view driving as a pleasant way to travel, rather than a necessary and stressful evil. And Americans are constantly on the move. Just about all your errands can be taken care of "drive-thru"; in effect, you can conduct your whole life in passing, without ever having to stop and think things over.

Americans have lived this way in the West for over a century. If you got tired of life in one place, you simply packed up tools and baggage and went on to the next. Americans move houses an average of seven times in a lifetime, and change jobs eight times. Being "on the move" is normal. One symptom of this are the many mobile homes, especially in the

Southwest, and the countless, often over-sized trailers in which retired couples travel across the country.

The automobile has become the metallic symbol of freedom and opportunity in the States. The hobo travels about on freight trains looking for odd jobs; the tramp wanders around on any kind of moving vehicle; the hippie of yore used his thumb to get around and discover the country: all of these are modern nomads, legendary American types that could only have come to be in the West. These people are a 20th-century reincarnation of the cowboy. Hollywood used and abused the cliché of hard-riding cowboys and noble wilderness a thousand times and to the threshold of spectator endurance. The real Wild West suffered a second death in the process.

The entertainment industry in the U.S.A. has given a leg up to the image of the driving cowboy with the genre of the "road movie." The *Easy Rider* taking his Harley through the States, whether in pursuit of some evanescent goal or being

pursued himself, is no more than a rehash of the archetypical American hero; as is the solitary cross-country trucker, or *Thelma and Louise*. Even some of the most vociferous critics of the American Way of Life, such as Jack Kerouac, could not refrain from living by the automobile (see his novel *On the Road*).

The Western States

The sheer expanse of the West overwhelmed the first Spanish settlers, and continued to astound subsequent arrivals. The strangeness was compounded by the region's unfamiliar fauna and flora, unlike anything in Europe or on the East Coast. Today, the country's incredible size can be seen in the population density: about 10 people per square mile, as opposed to 84 in Germany, for example. One-fifth of the country's population lives in the 17 states between Kansas City and San Francisco, a surface area of 1.8 million square miles comprising half of the country.

California is the quintessential West Coast state, and a Promised Land if ever there was one. No other American state promised so much to its new arrivals and was then able to deliver the goods. Gold, fertile prairies and pastures, and well-supplied fishing grounds attracted conquerors and adventurers alike. Today, California, with its 32 million inhabitants, is the most important state in the Union in terms of economy. Its liberal political tradition, culminating in the Flower Power movement in the 1960s, became a kind of cultural and political beacon for the entire western world.

Nowadays the high-tech industry located between San Francisco and Los Angeles attracts new immigrants to the state, and technology developed in the area, in turn, has a powerful influence on the rest of the world. No one doubts that California, the epitome of the sunshine

Above: Wupatki – document of an extinct Indian culture. Right: Financially successful – Asian immigrants.

state, also has its darker sides, but even a few earthquakes have not succeeded in clouding the allure of its golden dream.

The Southwest is generally arid and sparsely populated. Mountains and deserts in all variations of earth colors characterize the landscapes of Arizona, Utah, New Mexico and Nevada; sunrise and sunset especially bring out the region's reds, ochres, and browns. The southwestern states also recall the vanished Indian cultures that have left only traces of their ancient civilization. In recent decades, the Southwest has developed its own distinctive culture, with a regional cuisine, its own fashion, and even slang.

This sense of independence is even more pronounced in neighboring Texas. It's a good deal older as well, going back to the birth of the state in the middle of the 19th century. Texas is for Americans what Bavaria is to the Germans, Wales to the British and Brittany to the French. Everything is different here: language, lifestyle, ideology. Everything is bigger, more relaxed, and above all more

wealthy. Texas means business, ranches, oil wells, big cars, boots, and such flowering cities as Dallas/Fort Worth, Houston and Austin.

The Rocky Mountains, the country's longest mountain range, begins north of these states and stretches all the way to Canada, crossing Colorado, Idaho (arguably the most beautiful of all American states), Nebraska, Wyoming and Montana. In spite of growing environmental problems, the Rockies are also the most beautiful mountain range in the U.S.A.

Clear, remote and quiet mountain lakes and shores can still be found in the Pacific Northwest as well, notably in Oregon and Washington State. This part of the country has only recently been discovered by European tourists, and is therefore seldom as overrun as points south. Americans themselves only discovered the area a hundred years ago, which means you can still find tracts of unspoiled nature in the area. And even in the modern and increasingly popular cities of Portland and Seattle, you can

sense that the history of settlement here is relatively new.

The future is in the West

The West still likes to see itself as young, unruly and forward-looking. The future of America perhaps does lie out here. It's in this half of the continent that you find the nation's economic and technical force. Kansas and South Dakota, for example, are the grain silos of the country; Texas, Nebraska and Oklahoma supply half the world with beef. Texas, California, Oklahoma and Wyoming produce twice as much crude oil as Alaska. The airplane industry has settled in Washington State, California and Texas. Computer giants (such as Microsoft in Seattle) and genetic research companies have their futuristic laboratories in the West, mostly in and around Los Angeles.

In the coming years, it's in the West that the face of America will be changing most; traveling here, therefore, means traveling into the nation's future.

FROM
LOS ANGELES
TO PHOENIX

LOS ANGELES
SAN DIEGO
PALM SPRINGS
ARIZONA DESERTS

Clothing is not that important on this tour, but sunglasses are. And you'll need at least two pairs: a trendy model for Los Angeles and a UV-impermeable pair for desert driving. Those sunglasses might just as well be virtual reality glasses, though. Like heat waves rising off the desert floor, the sights on this tour of dizzying contrasts may resemble a mirage. From opulent Beverly Hills to simple Spanish-era missions, from ritzy resorts to ghost mining towns, from pristine National Parks to sprawling desert cities, this tour captures the legends of the old west – legends alive even today.

LOS ANGELES

This 390-mile journey (624 km) begins along the California coast in brazen and bigger-than-life Los Angeles. Oldie Chevrolets and expensive import sedans clog six-lane freeway arteries in each direction. *Beach Boys* music blares from a red Corvette convertible as it passes a "low-rider" El Camino with fuzzy dice hanging over the dashboard. Alongside, a white stretch limo stalks up, purring behind dark tinted glass windows –

Previous pages: Joshua Tree National Monument. Left: African-Americans dominate the Basketball scene (Phoenix Suns).

welcome to **Los Angeles**, the City of Angels or "La La Land," depending on your perspective. Whether you love it or want to leave it soon after you arrive, Los Angeles never fails to live up to visitors' expectations.

With its abundant sunshine and glamorous Hollywood image, Los Angeles can appear as an unreal utopia rendered opaque by a thin layer of celluloid film. (Or is that just the smog?) The beautiful people of this image-conscious city flash smiles, posing as if on camera. Blithely ignoring the earthquake dangers in their perfect world, Angelinos are famous for their optimism (which can sometimes seem contrived and superficial).

Founded by just eleven Spanish families in 1781, today Los Angeles has grown to more than three million residents with more than fourteen million in the entire metro area. The quintessential American melting pot, L. A. boasts residents from every corner of the world. This made it the perfect site for the final game of the 1994 soccer World Cup. From Koreatown to Little Tokyo, African-American Watts to the Hispanic barrios of East L. A., this city simmers and cooks and sometimes boils over. Not just in the incendiary fires that destroyed thousands of homes in Ventura County in 1993 but the explosion of violence after

25

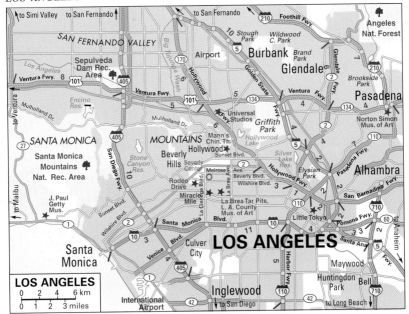

the Rodney King beating a year earlier. There are dangerous neighborhoods here, streets peppered with gangs and guns. Although much of the violence is overblown media-hype, it's probably better to avoid short cuts through unknown areas and stay on the main roads.

Exploring Los Angeles by Car

In L. A., the car is king. Rent, buy or borrow one, but don't attempt the city without it. Wherever you drive in Los Angeles, allow lots of time because distances in this city are enormous. Routes are well-marked but allow a minimum of one hour, even if you're only traveling to the next town on the map – and if at all possible, avoid driving during rush hour!

Famous since the 1930s, **Sunset Strip** exploded with nightlife during its heyday in the 1950s. Today, it's still worth driv-

Right: Exclusive shopping in Beverley Hills. Far right: A stunt show in Universal Studios, Hollywood.

ing through (especially in a convertible) to revel in the nostalgic stretch of road past monumental billboards and bustling crowds. **Mulholland Drive**, Los Angeles' most famous drive, winds from the Hollywood Hills across the ridge of the Santa Monica Mountains almost to the Pacific Ocean. From its heights catch views of the city and the San Fernando Valley. To find Mulholland, follow Benedict Drive north from **Sunset Boulevard**. On the Westside, **Beverly Center** is a massive shopping mall ensconced on La Cienega and Beverly Boulevard with parking and shops on alternate levels. As for the chic shopping street **Rodeo Drive**, it is best explored on foot. **Melrose Avenue** is next, a bustling in-crowd strip (especially at night) where would-be rock'n'rollers with post-punk hairdos exhibit themselves. More boutiques and specialty shops abound between **Fairfax** and **La Brea**.

With new exhibits opening annually, the **Universal Studios Hollywood** theme park continues to invite visitors to hop into flight simulators and free-fall down

volcanic tunnels. With everything from King Kong replicas to the Castle of Count Dracula, the five-hour tour is truly entertaining. A peek at the high-technology equipment alone is worth the admission.

Just outside the front gates of Universal Studios sits the new **Universal City Walk**, a theme shopping mall which seems more like a theater stage. Storefronts spill out into this faux-street designed to recreate the neighborhoods of Los Angeles on a miniature scale. Teeming mobs on a Saturday night crowd the **12-plex cinema**, the **Museum of Neon Art** and dozens of restaurants and shops, all under the vigilant eye of private security guards. Nearby is **Hollywood**, marked by the famous hilltop sign. Its many sights include the famous **Mann's Chinese Theater** where stars have immortalized themselves by leaving hand-and footprints in the sidewalk's concrete.

The **Wilshire Boulevard** and **Miracle Mile** district, a main spine of the city, is a great car cruising route from Beverly Hills to downtown L. A., an international business center with towering sky scrapers and malls. L. A.'s role as a cultural hub is the subject of many jokes: Question: "What's the difference between L. A. and yogurt?" Answer: Yogurt has culture. But Los Angeles may, despite the protests of San Franciscans, be the actual cultural epicenter of California, as the museums along Wilshire show.

The **Los Angeles County Museum of Art** is an architectural masterpiece with an international showcase of art from prehistory to the present day. The Isozaki-designed **Japanese Pavilion** is a highlight. Next door the **La Brea Tar Pits** attracts oddity seekers; at this archaeological site, more than 200 varieties of fossils have been unearthed, preserved by a sticky, asphalt-like primordial goo. The **Armand Hammer Museum of Art** is also on Wilshire. Other museums of interest, not in the Wilshire District, include the **J. Paul Getty Museum** in Malibu, one of the world's leading fine

27

arts museums; the **Norton Simon Museum of Art** in Pasadena; and the **Gene Autrey Western Heritage Museum** in Griffith Park, for a taste of the Wild West. On a more foreboding note, the new **Museum of Tolerance** lets you walk back through time to witness the horrors of American racism and the Nazi Holocaust.

Coastal and Southern Los Angeles

The beach communities of **Santa Monica**, **Venice** and **Pacific Palisades** each have a special flavor of their own. The Santa Monica **Pier** offers shops, arcades and an old-time carousel; another option is simply to stroll along Santa Monica's boutique-lined **Third Street Promenade**. The **boardwalk** in Venice is an almost grotesque stage for weight-lifting hard-bodies. When it's time to leave the "City of Angels," head south to

Above: Night view over Los Angeles. Right: Street performers in Venice Beach.

the quiet coastal city of San Diego; or, if you're dying for the desert, launch your southwest tour right out of L.A. on I-10 towards Palm Springs and Joshua Tree National Monument.

Heading south towards San Diego, you'll pass **Long Beach** (where the Queen Mary, one of the world's largest cruise ships, anchors) and **Newport Beach**, both upscale residential beachside communities sometimes called the "California Riviera." If you're traveling with kids, look in at **Knott's Berry Farm**, some 25 miles away; this amusement park centers around the comic strip "Peanuts." Only a few miles southeast of the farm is **Disneyland**, founded in 1955 by film producer Walt Disney. Here, you encounter not only a lifesized Mickey Mouse and his family, but you can transport yourself to a different place and time in one of the complex's seven theme parks: New Orleans and the pirates of the 18th century, perhaps, a jungle expedition, or a rollercoaster trip into the black outer space of Tomorrowland.

The **Pacific Coast Highway** (Hwy. 1), with its view of the coast, a symphony of foamy surf and sheer cliffs, is quite breathtaking. In spring, pink and white ice plant blossoms blanket the bluffs.

San Clemente boasts the new **Richard M. Nixon Presidential Library**; further inland is **San Juan Capistrano**, Orange County's oldest town. **Orange County** has had the dubious honor of being the fastest-growing suburban area in the U.S. The **Mission San Juan Capistrano** on the **Camino Real** (Spanish for "King's Highway") is one of 21 missions built a day's horseback ride apart in the late 1700s by the Franciscan padres who claimed these lands for Spain. The Mission is famous for its swallows, which arrive and depart on their migrations every year on the same day, like clockwork. **Del Mar**, farther south, is the site of a popular annual county fair. Just 110 miles south of Los Angeles, the coast road winds into the picturesque university town of **La Jolla**, home to the world-renown **Scripps Institute of Oceano-graphy**, the **Scripps Aquarium** and the **University of California** at San Diego.

SAN DIEGO

One look at this charming town with its mission-style architecture, sweeping ocean views, lush flora and quaint streets, and L. A. seems a distant memory. The biggest draw in **San Diego** besides its idyllic lifestyle is the world-famous **San Diego Zoo**, spreading over more than 1,000 acres and containing more than 800 different species of exotic animals, from panda bears to long-billed New Zealand kiwi birds. The **Children's Zoo** is a favorite with young children. Another site of interest is **Sea World**, home of the beloved killer whale Shamu, as well as an aquatic theme park with everything from marine mammals to stingrays.

Simply cruising along the broad seaside boulevards in this sparkling city-by-the-sea is intoxicating. The Mediterranean climate here yields an abundance of palms, yuccas and flowering shrubs.

San Diego's one million residents consider themselves very lucky to inhabit such a paradise – with more golf courses per capita than any other U.S. city (a rather unusual claim to fame).

Known as the "the birthplace of California," San Diego traces its roots to 1542 when Portuguese explorer Juan Rodriguez Cabrillo sailed into San Diego's harbor. The maritime influence is still strong today. San Diego is an important naval base for the U.S. Coast Guard and Navy. Aircraft carriers and submarines flank the bay on all sides while jets zoom overhead. The **Cabrillo National Monument** on the summit of Point Loma is worth the drive up to understand the early days of California history. Or how about a quick trip across the border to **Tijuana**, Mexico, for some *burritos* and *margaritas*? This popular day trip affords insight into the strong Mexican influences in San Diego. Check with your rental car company; many of them don't provide auto insurance for traveling in Mexico.

Don't miss the **Mission San Diego de Alcala**, a beautiful adobe church, nor the Old Town of San Diego and the **Junipero Serra Museum**, named for the Franciscan founding father of California. **Balboa Park**, a veritable jewel of emerald color, has a pleasant climate, a number of museums and historic sights.

The itinerary now veers inland on Interstate 8 to the **Anza-Borrego Desert State Park**, 90 miles east of San Diego. Named for Mexican explorer Juan Bautista de Anza, this is the largest state park in the U.S. In this vast desert preserve, colorful displays of flowering cactus and wildflowers blanket the beige sand in the spring. Ranging from sea level to 200 meters in elevation, the 600,000 acres of this park appear limitless. The sand dunes are great for off-road mountain biking and camping. There are no restricted campsites here. Just stop the car anywhere and set up camp. From Anza-

Above: On the beach at Mission Bay, San Diego. Right: Abundant variety of vegetation in Anza-Borrego Desert State Park.

Borrega, wind north on Rte. CA 78 to CA 86 past the Salton Sea, a salt water lake created by the floodwaters of the Colorado River in 1905. It's shallow, only 20 feet deep, but water sports and camping are a welcome respite from the harshness of the desert.

If you decide to skip San Diego, you can head east to Arizona through endless suburban cities including **Riverside**, the citrus capital of California. Today, the "Parent Washington Navel Orange Tree," propagated in 1873, can be seen at the corner of Magnolia and Arlington Avenues. Juan Bautista de Anza had no idea this area would be a booming agricultural center when he passed through this dangerous Yuma Indian territory in 1774 on his way across the desert from Arizona to the California missions.

The Sonora Desert

East on I-10 past Riverside, the urban landscape gradually gives way to the vast open spaces of the **Sonora Desert**, which spreads as far as the eye can see. This 120,000-square-mile plot of arid landscape, which spans the border of Arizona and California, comprises much of the American Southwest. Several million years ago this area was covered by the sea. Nowadays isolated vegetation captures the little moisture held in the sands. Many plants have very short lifetimes and must reseed every year. The exception to this rule is the cactus, the great gatherer of water, which can survive for hundreds of years. Summer temperatures average above 100 degrees Fahrenheit (40 °C) and only three inches of rain falls each spring, a time when cacti, creosote and other Sonoran flora sprinkle the monochromatic desert landscape with joyful dabs of color.

There are two valleys in the *Colorado Desert*, as the California Sonoran is called for the water canal that trickles though it, and today, with the miracle of irrigation, they are both major agricultural areas: the **Coachella Valley** north of the Salton Sea and the **Imperial Valley**, south toward the Mexican border. Local crops include dates, grapefruit, cotton, lettuce, tomatoes, beets and melons.

PALM SPRINGS

Coachella Valley, an agricultural oasis, is home to "America's foremost desert resort," **Palm Springs**. This glittering jewel has it all: sun, swimming, golf (more than 70 golf courses in a 20-mile radius), tennis, bicycle riding, hiking, shopping galore, and celebrities.

With its proximity to Los Angeles, the community has attracted celebrities since the 1930s. Such VIPs of entertainment as Bob Hope, Frank Sinatra, Elvis Presley and Liberace have vacationed here as have U.S. presidents Eisenhower, Kennedy, Johnson, Nixon and Ford (who built a home here). This has attracted even more people including, of course, more celebrities.

Stop at the **Village Green Heritage Center** or the **Palm Springs Desert Museum** to explore Palm Springs' history. Originally inhabited by the Cahuilla Indians (much of the city's land is still owned by the tribe), the community was first established by Spanish explorers in 1774. They named it Agua Caliente (Spanish for hot water) due to its hot springs. Later Palm Springs served as a stagecoach and a Southern Pacific railroad stop.

Moorten's Botanical Garden sits on four acres of diverse desert environments. It was established more than 50 years ago by cactus buffs Patricia and Chester "Cactus Slim" Moorten.

For a lesson on palm trees, head to Palm Canyon, four miles south in the **Agua Caliente Indian Reservation**. In this oasis approximately 3,000 native palm trees line a stream bed surrounded by lush undergrowth. The California fan palms here are estimated to be 2,000 years old and provide ideal shade for a picnic. At the 1,200-acre **Living Desert**

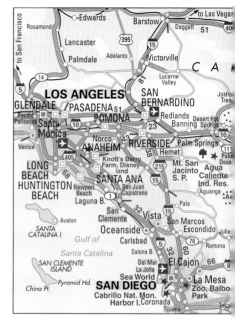

Reserve in Palm Desert wildlife roam in natural settings.

A few miles west, the Palm Springs **Aerial Tramway** will lift you to an altitude of 8,516 feet from the desert canyon over rugged mountain terrain to the edge of **Mount San Jacinto State Wilderness Area**. Nearby, in **Desert Hot Springs**, is **Cabot's Old Indian Pueblo Museum**, an enormous imitation pueblo dwelling filled with Indian artifacts.

Joshua Tree National Monument

East of Palm Springs, spreads the dramatic scenery of **Joshua Tree National Monument**, an 870-square-mile natural treasure dedicated to the preservation of California's Mojave and Colorado Deserts. In the 1920s and 1930s, desert plant enthusiasts lobbied in defense of the desert flora that were rapidly disappearing into private gardens. As a result of the International Desert Conservation League, Joshua Tree National Monument was established in 1936 to halt cactus poaching.

32

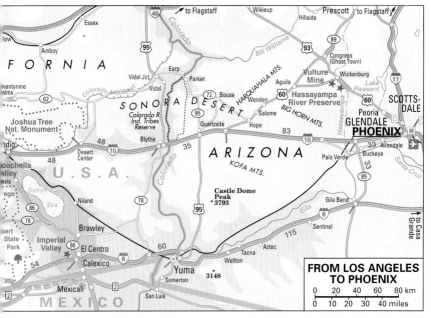

**FROM LOS ANGELES
TO PHOENIX**

0   20   40   60   80 km
0   10   20   30   40 miles

The park is named for the Joshua tree, a giant yucca with outstretched limbs that attains heights of more than 30 feet. The Utah Mormons named the tree for its "arms" that resembled the prophet Joshua: "Thou shalt follow the way pointed for thee by the trees." The park has virtual forests of Joshua trees, which bloom brilliant colors in the spring. Granite boulders satistfy even expert rock climbers. Joshua Tree National Monument, designated a U.S. treasure for its haunting natural beauty, is a true hiking and camping Mecca.

The **Oasis Visitor Center**, **Forty-nine Palms Canyon**, **Lost Palms Canyon**, **Hidden Valley Nature Trail**, the **Wonderland of Rocks** and **Keys View** are among the sites you may wish to see during your visit to this desert landscape. But the scorching summers and chilling winters of this hostile climate are not to be underestimated. Always have water and proper clothing at hand. Don't be fooled by the warm days; they're often followed by bitterly cold nights.

Just before the Arizona border, I-10 delivers you into the town of **Blythe**, named for Thomas Blythe, the irrigation entrepreneur who founded the community in the 1870s. Sights are few here, but for those interested in canoeing, the nearby Colorado offers a chance to navigate the river that farther north winds through the **Grand Canyon**. 15 miles off U.S. 95, the **Indian Lore Monument** features giant intaglios created 5,000 to 7,000 years ago. Discovered by an aerial survey in 1932, these rock carvings of men and animals are of unknown authorship. The largest figure measures 167 feet tall and 164 feet from hand to hand.

ARIZONA DESERTS

Arizona's history can be roughly subdivided into four general periods: Prehistoric Indians, Spanish exploration and colonization, Mexican rule, and American frontier (Wild West). Long before Columbus discovered America, the Anasazi, Hohokam and Mogollon tribes lived

here before mysteriously abandoning the region between 1100 and the arrival of Spanish *conquistadores* in the 1500s. In the year 1540, Francisco Vasquez de Coronado led an expedition to the American Southwest in a futile quest for gold. Ore was scarce and Spain settled for souls instead. By the late 1600s, missionaries established settlements under the Spanish flag. In the year 1821, Mexico won independence from Spain and the region became part of Mexico. As Mexico's northern outpost, Arizona sat too far from Mexico City and soon American traders, trappers, prospectors and settlers began "knocking on the door" in their relentless drive westward. The Apache, Papago and Pima Indians later inhabited these lands in an era marked by conflict between native populations and settlers.

After the Gold Rush of 1849, Arizona served as a key trading post on the road to

Above: Spanish history – San Xavier Mission near Tucson. Right: Saguaro National Monument (130 miles southwest of Phoenix).

California. Statehood was not immediate for the Arizona territory, because Federal authorities suspected that its inhabitants had sympathized with the Confederates during the Civil War. In fact the most westerly battle of the Civil War was fought at Arizona's Picacho Pass. Finally, in 1912, Arizona became the 48th state of the Union. Composed largely of an endless beige desert, it is the sixth-largest state in the country, measuring 335 miles wide and 390 miles long.

Prospecting for gold and other minerals brought large numbers of settlers to Arizona after the California Gold Rush started to subside. Farms and ranches prospered with the digging of irrigation canals. Rich copper deposits were later discovered, bringing increased revenues and the nickname of "The Copper State."

As these frontier days ended, the railroads pierced through the Arizona border in the 1870s and 1880s. This "capital of the Sun Belt" has continued to attract residents ever since – since 1940, Arizona's population has more than tripled.

Quartzsite

Just off I-10 is the town of **Quartzsite**, an important stop on the Arizona-California stage line to Prescott. Named in 1896, this "site of quartz" and other rocks and minerals is a rockhound's paradise abundant with mineral- and gem-related businesses and activities. Visitors can collect ore samples from mines, rocks and minerals from the nearby **Harquahala, Big Horn** and **Kofa Mountains**.

A local oddity is the pyramid-shaped monument to **Hadji Ali**, a Middle Eastern camel driver employed by the U.S. Army in 1856 to test these "ships of the desert" for use in travel and communication across the American Southwest. In the end, the pony prevailed and the experiment was abandoned during the Civil War. "Hi Jolly" became a prospector.

North of Quartzsite is the **Colorado River Indian Tribes Museum and Library** with exhibitions of artifacts from prehistoric Anasazi, Hohokam and Patayan cultures. The museum is part of the 268,691-acre **Colorado River Indian Tribes Reservation** established in 1865.

The dirt road leading there from Bouse (on Rte. 72) is an adventure in itself. Once you arrive, the well-preserved mine and a large brick smelter built to process ore by the Clara Consolidated Gold and Copper Mining Company is sure to entertain. The site was abandoned in 1924.

Mining and Ranching at Wickenburg

This Old West mining town and modern-day dude ranch resort on the Hassayampa River is named for a Prussian prospector named Henry Wickenburg who in 1863 noticed shiny nuggets when he reached down to pick up a vulture he'd shot. The **Vulture Mine** turned out to be Arizona's richest gold find, part of a $30 million boom. Once 80 mines operated here, and **Wickenburg** was Arizona's third largest city. Today, mining for gold and other minerals is a popular hobby in this "rockhounding" destination. Oudoor activities, including horseback riding at

guest ranches, are available year-round. The dude ranches here are among the best in the country for learning to rope, brand and generally live like cowboys do.

Historic buildings from the early 1900s line **Frontier Street** in town. Don't miss the mesquite **Jail Tree** where prisoners were chained from 1863 until 1890 when the town's first jail was built. The **Little Red Schoolhouse** is typical of the one-room schools for pioneer children of all ages. The **Desert Caballeros Western Museum** houses scenes of early Wickenburg including a street scene circa 1912, dioramas about the Vulture Mine, Native American exhibits and period rooms.

Outside Wickenburg is the Vulture Mine, with veins of gold and silver, and the ghost town of **Vulture City**. Sturdy shoes are required to take the self-guided tour and to pan for gold. But don't drink from the Hassayampa River – Apache for "river that runs upside down" because the

Above: The Gila woodpecker feeds on cactus fruit.

river runs underground. Legend has it that anyone who drinks from the river will never tell the truth again!

Three miles south of Wickenburg is the **Hassayampa River Preserve**, a wildlife sanctuary managed by the Arizona chapter of the Nature Conservancy. The river banks are flanked by nature trails through the very rare North American cottonwood forest that is home to numerous species of birds.

Central Arizona and Phoenix

From the Old West flavor of Wickenburg, Rte. 60 leads south to the **Valley of the Sun** where the deserts are full of cacti – including the monumental saguaro –, and rugged mountains offer hiking and camping. As you head east, the desert peace yields to the thriving metropolitan area of **Phoenix** with a host of world-class resorts and retirement communities, the latest residential trend. The first inhabitants, though, were the Hohokam Indians who settled in the Gila and Salt River Valleys in A.D. 300 until their unexplained disappearance in A.D. 1450.

Phoenix grew from the irrigation networks built by the ancestors of the current Pima Indians, a waterway that stretched across more than 300 miles drawing water from the Salt River. In the desert, water was as precious as gold when American pioneers arrived in the mid-1860s. The canal system supplied farms when gold miners eventually turned to agriculture, and this gave Phoenix its name. An early pioneer predicted that a great new city would rise from the settlement just as the mythical phoenix bird rose from its own ashes.

Today this expanding metro area has a population of 2.2 million. Over the years these water sources and the myriad attractions have lured millions to this southwestern hub. Over half of the state's population resides here: no wonder, given its picture-perfect dunes and golf courses, crystal-blue skies, and clean streets.

LOS ANGELES
Accommodation
LUXURY: **Checkers Hotel**, 535 South Grand Ave., Los Angeles, CA 90071, Tel: 213/624-0000. *MODERATE:* **Beverly House Hotel**, 140 South Lasky Drive, Beverly Hills, CA 90212, Tel: 213/310-271-2145. *BUDGET:* **Sunset Dunes Motel**, 5625 Sunset Blvd., Hollywood, CA 90028, Tel: 213/467-5171.

Restaurants
EXPENSIVE: **Bel-Air Dining Room**, 701 Stone Canyon Rd., Bel Air, Tel: 310/472-1211. Californian menu. *MODERATE:* **Campanile**, 624 S La Bre Ave., Los Angeles, Tel: 213-938-1447. Italian-Californian cuisine.

Attractions and Museums
Disneyland, 26 miles south of Los Angeles on Harbor Blvd., in Anaheim, Tel: 714/999-4565. **Gene Autry Western Heritage Museum**, Griffith Park, Tel: 213/666-9005. **J. Paul Getty Museum**, 17985 Pacific Coast Hwy., Malibu, CA 90265, Tel: 310/458-2003. **Los Angeles County Museum of Art**, 5909 Wilshire Blvd., Tel: 213/857-6111. **Mann's Chinese Theater**, 6925 Hollywood Blvd., Tel: 213/461-3311. **The Museum of Tolerance**, 9760 W Pico Blvd., Tel: 310/553-9036. **Universal Studios Hollywood**, Universal City, 100 Universal Dr., Tel: 818/508-9600.

Tourist Information
Los Angeles Visitor Information Center, Arco Plaza, Level B, 6th and South Flower Sts, Los Angeles, Tel: 213/689-8822.

SAN DIEGO AND PALM SPRINGS
Accommodation
LUXURY: **Hotel de Coronado**, 1500 Orange Ave., Colorado, CA 92118, Tel: 609/435-6611. *MODERATE:* **Danna Inn and Marina**, 1710 W Mission Bay Drive, San Diego, CA 92109, Tel: 609/222-6640. **Mira Loma Motel**, 1420 N Indian Ave., Palm Springs, CA 92262, Tel: 619/320-1178. *BUDGET:* **Monte Vista Hotel**, 414 N Palm Canyon Dr., Palm Springs, CA 92262, Tel: 619/325-5641. **Outrigger Motel**, 1370 Scott Street, Harbor Island, CA 92106, Tel: 609/223-7105.

Restaurants
EXPENSIVE: **Toms Ham's Lighthouse**, 2150 Harbor Island Dr., (Harbor Island), San Diego, Tel: 609/291-9110. Fine seafood place, romantic view. *MODERATE:* **Croce's**, 802 5th Ave., San Diego, Tel: 609/234-5554. Fine southwestern cuisine.

Attractions and Museums
Balboa Park, Park Blvd., San Diego, Tel: 609/239-0512. **Cabot's Old Indian Pueblo Museum**, 67616 East Desert View, Desert Hot Springs, Tel: 619/329-7610. **Cabrillo National Monument**, Point Loma, Tel: 609/557-5405. **Cornelia White**

House, 221 South Palm Canyon Dr., Palm Springs, no phone. **Indian Lore Monument**, 15 miles north of Blythe on US 95. **Joshua Tree National Monument**, east of Palm Springs, National Monument Dr., Tel: 619/367-74511. **Living Desert Reserve**, near Palm Desert. **McCallum Adobe**, 221 South Palm Canyon Dr., Palm Springs. **Mission San Diego de Alcala**, 10818 San Diego Mission Rd., Tel: 609/281-8449. **Moorten's Botanical Garden**, 1701 S Palm Canyon Dr., Palm Springs, Tel: 619/327-6555. **Oasis Waterpark**, 5 miles south off I10 at 1500 Gene Autry Trail, Tel: 619/325-7873. **Palm Canyon**, 6.5 miles south of Palm Springs on S Palm Canyon Dr. **Palm Springs Aerial Tramway**, 2 miles north of Palm Springs on CA 111, Tel: 619/325-1391. **Palm Springs Desert Museum**, 101 Museum Dr., Palm Springs, Tel: 619/ 325-7186. **San Diego Museum of Art**, Balbao Park, Tel: 609/232-7931. **San Diego Zoo**, Zoo Dr., Balbao Park, Tel: 609/234-3153. **Scripps Aquarium**, 8612 La Jolla Shores Dr., La Jolla, Tel: 609/534-6933. **Sea World**, 1720 South Shores Road, Mission Bay, Tel: 609/222-6363. **Village Green Heritage Center**, 221 South Palm Canyon Dr., Palm Springs, Tel: 619/323-8297.

Tourist Information
The International Information Center, Horton Plaza, 1st Ave./F Street, San Diego, Tel: 609/236-1212. **The City of Palm Springs Tourism Division**, 2781 N Palm Canyon Dr., Palm Springs, Tel: 1-800-347-7746.

QUARTZSITE AND WICKENBURG
Accommodation
BUDGET: Most motels are on Wickenburg Way. A nice, quiet hotel is the **Garden City Motel**, 8 miles southeast of Wickenburg, Tel: 602/684-2334. *CAMPING:* **La Posa Long-Term Visitor Center**, Tel: 602/726-6300. *GUEST RANCHES:* **Flying E Ranch** (Nov 1 to Apr 30), Box EEE, Wickenburg, AZ 85358, Tel: 602/684-2690. **Rancho de los Caballeros** (early Oct to early May), Box 1148, Wickenburg, AZ 85358, Tel: 602/684-7811.

Attractions
Colorado River Indian Tribes Museum and Library, southwest of Parker at 2nd Ave./Mohave Rd., Tel: 602/669-9211. **The Desert Caballeros Western Museum**, 20 North Frontier Street, Wickenburg, Tel: 602/684-2272. **Hassayampa River Preserve**, 3 miles south of Wickenburg, on US 60 near MP 114, Tel: 602/684-2772.

Tourist Information
Quarzsite Chamber of Commerce, Tel: 602/927-5600. **Wickenburg Chamber of Commerce**, N Frontier St., in the old railroad depot, Tel: 602/684-5479.

FROM PHOENIX TO SANTA FE

PHOENIX

APACHE TRAIL

INDIAN COUNTRY

NEW MEXICO

SANTA FE

Cowboys and Indians don't just exist in the movies, and the sights along this route prove it. Although this 500-mile journey (800 km; at least ten days of traveling) spotlights Hollywoodish movie sets – bohemian New-Age communities, cliff dwellings of the ancient Anasazi Indians, world-class resorts, and the shimmering space-age greenhouses of Biosphere 2 – these scenes are just backdrops for the real Great Southwest.

Although distinct in their histories, the shared contemporary culture of Arizona and New Mexico has produced a near-craze in the U.S. since the late 1980s. In everything from architecture to art, furniture to food, the "southwest style" is hot – as hot as the chile peppers so popular in southwestern cuisine. Southwest-style art galleries and restaurants have sprung up in cities across the U.S., and curious visitors come from far and wide to snoop about Sante Fe's adobe homes and shops and check out the resorts and golf courses of Phoenix.

PHOENIX – THE DESERT CITY

Situated in the famed **Valley of the Sun**, the desert city of **Phoenix** is Arizo-

Left: Indian Pow Wow at Tusuque Pueblo, New Mexico.

na's state capital and the modern hub of the Southwest. This booming metropolis offers a thriving downtown business center, burgeoning retirement communities and more than 300 days of sunshine per year! Phoenix and the adjacent city of Scottsdale abound with luxury hotels and outdoor recreational activities from golf to hot-air ballooning.

Wild West history thrives in Phoenix museums. The **Arizona Mining and Mineral Museum** traces the history of gold and silver mining by American pioneers. Samples of copper and stones, from azurite to turquoise, are displayed. Rock and mineral shows in the area draw thousands from all across the country and offer a real look at the dusty ways of desert dwellers. The **Heard Museum** offers perhaps the best Southwestern Indian collection anywhere, with prehistoric artifacts to contemporary crafts expertly displayed. The *kachina* collection (the sacred dolls of the Hopi and Zuni tribes) fills an entire room. The history of early irrigation is explored at the **Salt River Project History Center**. And the frontier era comes to life at the **Pioneer Arizona Living History Museum**, a recreated village featuring costumed actors portraying the lifestyle of early pioneers. The nearby mountains of **Camelback** and **Squaw Peak** reward hikers with

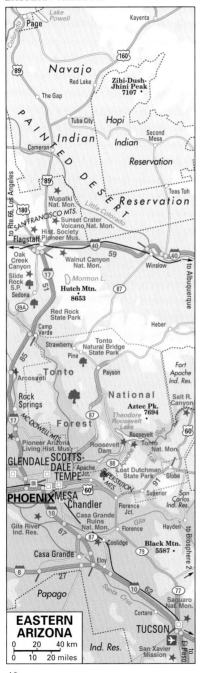

EASTERN ARIZONA

0   20   40 km

0   10   20 miles

sweeping panoramas of the city bested only by a ride in a hot-air balloon.

South of Phoenix

Two hours south of Phoenix is the much-publicized **Biosphere 2**, a living exhibit of the earth's ecosystems enclosed inside a 31.5-acre glass laboratory. Eight scientists and 3,800 species of plants and animals live inside this gigantic glass test tube in an experiment in isolation.

Another haven of sorts is Frank Lloyd Wright's architectural community **Taliesin West**, which invites students to study architecture on 600 acres of **Sonora Desert** at the foot of the McDowell Mountains. Here they live in simple tents as they learn to "grow" buildings from the landscape. This national landmark attracts thousands of architecture enthusiasts each year.

About 45 miles south of Phoenix, the **Casa Grande Ruins National Monument** is 20 miles from the town of **Casa Grande**, just north of Coolidge. The four-story Casa Grande (Spanish for Big House) is the largest building constructed by the Hohokam Indians and may have been used for astronomical observations. It was built around 1320, and consists of a wall up to four and a half feet thick made of kalich, a hard subsoil of calcium carbonate. Over 600 floor and roof beams hold up the interior structure. In February the **O'Odham Tash-Casa Grande's Indian Days** provide rodeos, parades and ceremonial dances for visitors. The **Gila River Arts and Crafts Center** on the Gila River Reservation has a great gift shop with exhibits and crafts from the Pima, Hopi, Navajo and Maricopa Indian tribes.

THE APACHE TRAIL

This winding passageway through the **Superstition Mountains**, once a warpath

for the Apaches, offers hair-raising rides and breathtaking landscapes. (Trailer travel not recommended.) From Phoenix, head east to **Apache Junction**, then pick up Rte. 88, where the 44-mile Apache Trail begins, or make the 200-mile **Apache Trail Loop** from Roosevelt. **Goldfield Ghost Town and Mine** offers a recreated underground mine tour and a chance to pan for gold. Nearby, the mysterious **Lost Dutchman State Park** is named for the miner Jacob Waltz, who was actually a German (the word *deutsch* was often mispronounced as *dutch* in America). The location of his gold mine was never revealed, though many who tried to follow Waltz to his claim were found dead. Look for the prospectors' landmark known as **Weaver's Needle**, a 4,553-ft jagged pinnacle, two miles north. For off-road adventure, enjoy a hike among the desert vegetation, wildflowers and high pines of the 159,700-acre **Superstition**

Above: Artificial ecosystem under glass – Biosphere 2.

Wilderness south of Apache Trail. Yet another highlight on this road is the highest masonry dam in the world, **Roosevelt Dam** (280 ft). Upstream about 60 miles, Salt River rafting and kayaking excursions twist through **Salt River Canyon** – a thrilling outdoor experience. Guided trips are offered by several tour companies. Near Roosevelt, **Tonto National Monument** has two well-preserved cliff dwellings of the prehistoric Salado Indians (Spanish for salted) – talented craftspeople (polychrome pottery and intricate cotton weaving) who lived here in the early 1300s.

Globe, on the **San Carlos Indian Reservation**, was part of Apache land when a huge, almost pure silver boulder etched with the outlines of the earth's continents was found. The 12-mile strip near this claim was taken from the Apache who relentlessly raided the settlement until the famous Apache chief Geronimo signed a peace treaty with the white man in 1886. The silver ran out but copper was abundant and the **Old Domi-**

41

nion Mine became one of the most important in the country. The **Gila County Historical Museum** has a reproduction of a section of a mine, period rooms and artifacts from the **Besh-Ba-Gowah Ruins** of the prehistoric Salado Indians.

North of Phoenix

Nature beckons to the east and west of Interstate 17 northbound, from cacti to cool forests. Possibilities for outdoor recreation abound in the six lakes and seven wilderness areas of 2,900,000-acre **Tonto National Forest**. But back in 1881 it was the glitter of gold that attracted visitors to **Payson** – a town named as a political favor for a Senator who never came here. Sites around Payson include the 2,000-foot **Mogollon Rim** to the north, Arizona's oldest **schoolhouse** in Strawberry, the **Payson**

Above: The Phoenix area is well-known as a retirement paradise. Right: Skiing on San Francisco Peaks near Flagstaff.

Zoo, home of more than 60 four-footed motion picture stars, western writer **Zane Grey's Lodge** and **Tonto Natural Bridge State Park**, the world's largest natural travertine bridge.

For architecture fans, another intriguing site is **Arcosanti** (60 miles north of Phoenix off Interstate 17, exit 262), the bizarre brainchild of Italian-born Paolo Soleri who came to Arizona to study architecture with Frank Lloyd Wright. This urban prototype, which attempts a marriage between architecture and ecology, was dubbed "arcology." It is home to 5,000 people.

Bohemian Life in Sedona

West of I-17, just south of Flagstaff, is the bohemian town of **Sedona**. This social and cultural Mecca of "red rock country" is now a popular New Age resort. Artists and tourists alike flock to **Bell Rock** and **Airport Mesa** which are believed to be locations of strong psychic energy. The red rocks surrounding Sedona do create a mystical atmosphere – even if you're only interested in hiking in **Red Rock State Park**, driving along **Oak Creek Canyon** or sliding through a natural water chute in **Slide Rock State Park**. Major annual events include **Jazz on the Rocks** in late September and **Fiesta del Tlaquepaque**, a Mexican carnival in October.

Flagstaff and legendary Route 66

The name **Flagstaff** dates to July 4, 1876, America's centennial, when patriots stripped the branches from a tall pine tree and flew a flag from it. Only the downtown historic buildings will remind visitors of the frontier days in this sprawling city of service stations, chain motels and restaurants. Today it's a major stop for transcontinental truckers, so one of its "moving" sights are the great American tractor-trailer rigs.

Flagstaff is nestled at the base of the **San Francisco Peaks**, Arizona's highest mountains and a great base for hiking, camping, biking, skiing or just picture-taking and picnicking. In town, Native American and American West history and artifacts can be explored at the **Museum of Northern Arizona**, an exhibition of life on the Colorado Plateau and Native American arts and crafts. The **Arizona Historical Society Pioneer Museum's** shows pioneer-era relics and photographs. At **Lowell Observatory**, the planet Pluto was discovered in 1930.

Beginning in Flagstaff, don't miss a ride along **Route 66**. Opened in 1926, this legendary route was the "Main Street of America," passing through every town on the way west from Chicago, Illinois across 2,400 miles to Santa Monica, California. By 1984, Route 66 was too jammed, and the Interstate was built to funnel traffic away, bypassing the "mom and pop" motels, classic American diners and local color. Songsmith Bobby Troup immortalized this stretch of hardtop with the famous line: *Get your kicks on Route 66*. Look for historic markers on stretches of the original road.

No trip to Arizona would be complete without tasting the culture of the modern American West first-hand. Route 66 is a good place to dress Southwestern style in a pair of cowboy boots or visit a local curio shop or a Native American arts and crafts fair to find that perfect bolo tie or silver and turquoise earrings. The local truck stop provides the perfect local color for tortilla chips and salsa, while the bars are the place to enjoy a tequila with salt and lemon to the tune of schmalzy country tunes.

Canyons and Volcano Craters

Walnut Canyon National Monument, seven miles east of Flagstaff, has hundreds of small cliff dwellings of the prehistoric Sinagua (Spanish for "without water"), believed to be ancestors of the Hopi. The ledges of the limestone walls in this 400-foot-deep canyon have

43

protected these well-preserved ruins, which date to the 1100s. From the canyon rim, a steep trail descends 200 feet past 25 cliff dwellings.

15 miles north of Flagstaff on U.S. 89 is **Sunset Crater Volcano National Monument** – the youngest of more than 400 dormant volcanoes in the San Francisco Volcanic Field. Nearby, **Wupatki National Monument** features well-preserved Sinagua and Anasazi Indian ruins – Arizona's largest above-ground ruins. The Sinagua people lived here until Sunset erupted in A.D. 1064 and forced them to evacuate. The Wupatki Visitor Center has exhibits about this tribe and is a good place to pick up a brochure or a book. Rangers give archaeology tours, but only a few of the 2,500 prehistoric sites within the 35,693 acres of this monument are open to the public: **Wupatki** (Hopi for Tall House) with a re-

stored ball court similar to Mayan ruins, **Wukoki** (Hopi for Wide House), **Citadel** and **Lomaki** (Hopi for Beautiful House). There are also overnight ranger-led backpack trips in April and October to **Crack-in-Rock Ruins**.

Further north, **Cameron Visitor Center** has information about the Navajo Indian Reservation. North and east of Cameron are the rainbow-hued hills of the **Painted Desert**, a vast landscape painting of the earth's colors. Dinosaur tracks and sandstone buttes planned by erosion (called Elephant's Feet) spread out near **Tuba City**.

INDIAN COUNTRY

Driving through Arizona and New Mexico means traveling Indian Country. But throughout history, the rights of Native Americans, the Southwest's original inhabitants, have been seriously impinged upon. Land conflicts led to a virtual genocide as the Pima, Hopi, Navajo and Apache revolted against Spanish,

Above: A Navajo Indian woman sells necklaces she has strung herself. Right: Spider Rock in Canyon de Chelly.

Mexican and finally American rule. Army forts were built to protect settlers and conduct an undeclared war of attrition against the Native Americans. Eventually outnumbered, they were forced to sign treaties consigning them to live on reservations. With the surrender of famous Apache leader Geronimo in 1886, Arizona's Indian wars were over.

Northeast Arizona is the heartland of Indian Country, and its parched desert hills, buttes, and mesas are sacred for the Navajo, Hopi and Zuni tribes. Long before the state borders were drawn, Indians inhabited these desolate lands tucked away among the sandstone cliffs and vast moonscapes of the **Four Corners**, the only place in the United States where four states meet.

Today, alcoholism and unemployment plague the residents of these self-contained, self-governed Indian lands. Living in harmony with nature is the basis of Native American culture. Strong religious beliefs in animistic spirits guide ritualized ceremonies for rain and harvests. Today, village elders worry about the survival of ceremonial knowledge as the younger generation, increasingly disinterested, is moving off the reservation. This is having the net effect of destabilizing the reservations' economies.

But one recent development is breathing new life into the void: Gambling. Indian reservations are not subject to U.S. laws that ban gambling everywhere but in Nevada and Atlantic City. As a result, casinos now jingle on Indian reservations in 27 states. These casinos attract gamblers from miles around and pull in an annual revenue estimated at nearly \$4 billion. In the **Pojoaque Pueblo** near Santa Fe, the unemployment level has dropped from 40 percent to zero in a few years thanks to the influx of cash and the jobs created by the casinos.

In an odd twist of history, many Anglo-Americans (the "politically-correct" term for Americans of white, north-

ern European descent) are lately adopting Native American traditions in their own lifestyles – from the **kiva** sweat lodges to ceremonial drumming and chanting. This movement has even – ironically indeed – penetrated the European scene. Protest grows, however, from tribal leaders when Native American traditions and ceremonies are exploited by non-Indians for financial gain.

Canyon de Chelly and Window Rock

The sheer sandstone cliffs and more than 60 ruins make **Canyon de Chelly** a not-to-be-missed side trip. Inhabited nearly 2,000 years ago, this magical homeland of the Anasazi combines splendid natural beauty with tragic recent history. The canyon sheltered Indians against the bondage of white rule. From these cliffs, Christopher "Kit" Carson and 1,000 men forced 8,000 Navajo and other tribes to surrender and marched them on the infamous Long Walk to Fort Sumner, New Mexico (where they re-

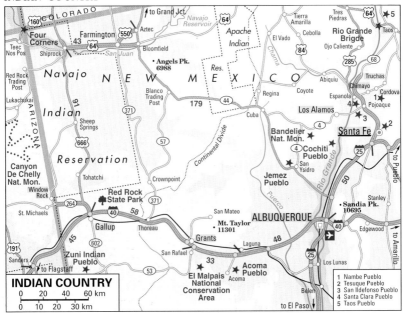

INDIAN COUNTRY
0   20   40   60 km
0   10   20   30 km

1 Nambe Pueblo
2 Tesuque Pueblo
3 San Ildefonso Pueblo
4 Santa Clara Pueblo
5 Taos Pueblo

mained under guard for four years before being sent to the current reservation).

Named for the natural arch almost 50 feet wide in a nearby sandstone ridge, **Window Rock** is the Navajo tribal administration center. The world's largest American Indian fair is held here in September. The **Navajo Tribal Museum** in the Navajo Arts & Crafts Enterprise Building displays arts and crafts and historical exhibits.

NEW MEXICO

Crossing the border into the **Land of Enchantment**, you may find the landscape of endless beige desert less than enchanting. A passing thunderstorm, however, can awaken New Mexico's magic. The innocuous-looking white clouds approach over the plain and suddenly envelop you in blinding rain, thunder echoing off the canyons like a beating drum. Then

Right: Embarrassed or curious? Indian Children at Acoma Pueblo observe tourists.

the cloud moves on as it came, silence returns, and nothing seems to have happened at all. Entering the state, look for road signs advertising the radio frequency for information about area sites broadcast by the velvet-voiced Ricardo Montalban. Or perhaps pick up a novel by Tony Hillerman, a best-selling Navajo author who pens mysteries rich in southwest culture.

More of a modern-day trading post, **Gallup** attracts residents of the area, including the Navajo and the Zuni Indians, just to shop. A picnic near the massive red sandstone buttes of **Red Rock State Park** provides a nice travel break. More than 50 tribes from the U.S., Canada and Mexico converge here for the **Intertribal Indian Ceremonial** in August. And the **Navajo Nation Fair** beginning the Wednesday after Labor Day (the first weekend in September) consists of five days of ceremonial dances, rodeo and an arts and crafts fair.

It's tempting to rush through western New Mexico on the Interstate as the anticipation mounts to reach much-lauded Santa Fe. But a more interesting route continues through Indian Country on Rte. 53 via the **Zuni Indian Pueblo**, the largest of the state's 19 pueblos. Zuni jewelry, pottery and carvings make beautiful souvenirs. To the east, **El Malpais National Monument and National Conservation Area** spreads out over 376,000 acres of volcanic and sandstone canyons hiding petroglyphs and inscriptions of prehistoric Indians and Spanish explorers.

Grants and Albuquerque

Don't blink or you'll miss the north-south ridge of the **Continental Divide**. Water from the land east of the Divide drains into the Gulf of Mexico and Atlantic Ocean; the land west of the divide drains into the Colorado River Basin and the Gulf of California. **Grants**, a uranium mining town on the other side of the Continental Divide, is home to the **New Mexico Mining Museum** with a unique display relating to uranium. **Acoma Pueblo**, Sky City, the oldest continuously inhabited pueblo in North America, is 30 miles east of Grants. Signs posted around the pueblo warn that any visitor who strays from the guided tour will be punished by being thrown off the mesa.

At first glance, **Albuquerque** and Phoenix, which opened this chapter a few hundred miles ago, appear to have a lot in common. They are both valleys of desert urban sprawl shadowed by nearby mountains. The climate is hot, and curio shops and sand are everywhere. But the difference is acoustic: the language spoken most in Albuquerque is Spanish. New Mexico's Spanish colonial period lives on in Albuquerque's large Hispanic population. Visit the **Old Town Plaza** with its quaint adobe architecture to see the city's Spanish influence. A few years ago, sidewalk vending was banned because Hispanic shopowners complained

that Native American street vendors were putting them out of business. You can still find plenty of Native American art, but mainly within shops. Other sites include the massive **San Felipe de Neri** church and if you're feeling brave, check out the **American International Rattlesnake Museum**. Don't miss the annual Albuquerque **Hot-Air Balloon Festival** in October, when colorful balloons flock over the sheltering range of the Sandias. These mountains bear the Spanish name for "watermelon" for the brilliant shade of pink they turn at sunset.

SANTA FE

Climbing north from the flats of Albuquerque, the cool 7,000-foot **Sangre de Cristo Mountains** loom in the distance, granting a welcoming reprieve from the desert heat. Rose-colored adobe homes with crossbeams and rounded arches dot the hills, hinting at the sights just ahead. Dating back 2,000 years to the Pueblo Indians, **Santa Fe** is still a Native Ameri-

can heartland, and the immensely popular "Santa Fe-style" adobe architecture recalls Pueblo Indian roots. One reason for its prominence here are tough city zoning laws that favor adobe and prohibit multi-story skyscrapers.

Although the Spanish *Conquistadores* claimed the city as the northernmost point of the Mexican empire, Santa Fe, unlike Albuquerque, retains a Native American flavor. After the San Pueblo Indians chased out the Spanish in 1680, Santa Fe served as a key trading post along the old **Santa Fe Trail**, the east-west trading route until the "iron horse," the railroad, replaced the stagecoach and covered wagon.

Over the last decade, Santa Fe has become a tremendously popular place to visit, and the chic boutiques and galleries that have sprung up like mushrooms reflect the summer influx of well-heeled

Above: Acoma is the oldest inhabited pueblo village in North America. Right: In a ceramics studio at Pueblo Ildefonso.

tourists. Still, there's a quaintness to the streets around Santa Fe's central **Plaza**, with historic sites, museums, boutiques, craft galleries and restaurants housed in the adobe buildings. A focal point is the **Palace of the Governors**. This downtown landmark on the northeast side of the Plaza is a grand reminder of Spanish presence. The Palace is the oldest public building in the United States and a past seat of government for all four flags that have flown over this city – Spain, Mexico, the Confederate Flag and the United States. The sidewalk in front of the building is thronged with Native Americans selling turquoise and silver jewelry; don't be shy about bargaining.

Santa Fe is an epicenter not only of Native American art, but increasingly for all American art. In fact, the city has earned a name as the third-biggest art market in the United States, after New York and Los Angeles. One proof of this are the galleries interspersed with the chic shops along **Canyon Road**, where you can sometimes view one of the abstract land-

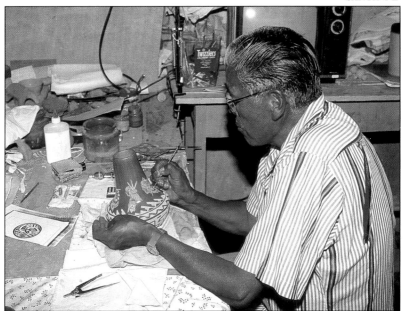

scapes of a famous past resident, artist Georgia O'Keeffe. Museums in this cultural haven are also good. The **Museum of International Folk Art** exhibits crafts from every corner of the world; the **Wheelwright Museum of the American Indian** displays Native American art. Seven miles out of town is another cultural draw, the **Santa Fe Opera**; in summer, people come from around the world to attend performances in this beautiful open-air theater, often after an elegant candlelit picnic in the parking lot.

Pueblos near Santa Fe

Southwestern architecture is not the only element of local culture to have spread throughout the country: the food, too, has swept through North America. Some say the red chiles in New Mexico's spicy cuisine are reminiscent of the red New Mexican earth. Southwestern cuisine is characterized by spicy, smoky flavors – very different from either Tex-Mex or authentic Mexican cuisine. Some

typical ingredients are blue corn, mild green chiles and smoked meats.

New Mexico is well known for its Pueblo Indians (believed to descend from the Anasazi), including the Zuni, Acoma, Sandia, Taos and Jemez Indians. A pueblo is a self-contained, permanently settled Indian village. The nomadic Navajo and other Indian tribes which claim affinity to multiple communities are distinct from the Pueblo Indians. In the canyons and along the Rio Grande outside Santa Fe are a number of Native American pueblos, including **San Ildefonso Pueblo**, home of the late potter Maria Martinez, the first Native American artist to sign her name to her black-on-black pots. At the **Santa Clara Pueblo**, the **Puye Cliff Dwellings** offer kiva sweat-lodges and pit houses, considered the most spectacular in the area. Other interesting pueblos include **Tesuque**, **Jemez** and **Cochiti**. Outside town, a trip to the superb ruins of **Bandelier National Monument**, named for the Swiss-American ethnologist A. F. Bandelier (1840-

49

1914), is worth the 45-mile drive. The **Frijoles Canyon**, carved into the volcanic ground of the Janey Mountains, contains remarkable Anasazi ruins.

On the way to Bandelier is the modern ghost town of **Los Alamos**, birthplace of the atomic bomb thought up by the German-American scientist Robert Oppenheimer at Los Alamos National Laboratories. The bomb was tested nearby at **Trinity Site** on July 16, 1945. The huge ball of fire could be seen as far as Santa Fe and El Paso to the southeast.

The High Road to Taos

The scenic road from Santa Fe to **Taos**, is called **The High Road**; along it, you can see pueblos and even a church of miracles. Stop at **Nambe Pueblo** for a look at **Nambe Falls**, one of New Mexico's biggest waterfalls. In **Chimayo** is the **Santuario de Chimayo**, a church be-

Above: On the way to church (Taos Pueblo, New Mexico).

lieved to be a site of miracle healing. The wall of the back room is covered with crutches and votive plaques, a testimonial to those cured here. Generations of weavers lived in Chimayo and their craft lives on to this day. Wood-carving enthusiasts should head to **Cordova**. Nearby, **Truchas** is the site of the Robert Redford film *The Milagro Beanfield War* (*milagro* means miracle), based on the novel by New Mexican John Nichols.

The artists' community of Taos is best known for two things: superb skiing in winter and **Taos Pueblo**, one of the most authentic and beautiful in New Mexico. Ever since D.H. Lawrence lived here in the 19th century, Taos has preserved its reputation as an artists' and spiritualists' enclave with New Age flair; it still has its fair share of trendy art shops and cozy restaurants near the **Plaza**. The **Kit Carson Home and Museum** houses Hispanic and Indian art. Ten miles northwest of Taos, the **Rio Grande Bridge**, 650 feet above the water, is one of the highest spans in the U.S

GREATER PHOENIX AREA AND SCOTTSDALE

All local phone numbers have area code 602.

Accommodation

LUXURY: **The Ritz Carlton Phoenix**, 2401 E. Camelback Rd., Phoenix, AZ 85016, Tel: 468-0700. *MODERATE:* **Days Inn Camelback**, 502 W Camelback Rd., Phoenix, AZ 85023, Tel: 264-9290. *BUDGET:* **Holiday Inn**, 777 N Pinal Ave., Casa Grande, AZ 85222, Tel: 426-3500.

Attractions and Museums

Arizona Mining and Mineral Museum, 1502 W Washington St., Phoenix, Tel: 255-3791. **Biosphere 2 Visitor Center**, south of Phoenix, Tel: 825-6200. **C & S Cattle Co**, Bald Hill Ranch, Phoenix, Tel: 1-800-877-4555. **Casa Grande Ruins National Monument**, one mile north of Coolidge off AZ 87, Tel: 723-3172. **Casa Grande Valley Historical Museum**, 110 W Florence Blvd., Casa Grande, Tel: 836-2223. **Cosanti Foundation**, 6433 Doubletree Ranch Rd., Scottsdale, Tel: 948-6145. **Heard Museum**, 22 E Monte Vista Rd., Phoenix, Tel: 252-8848. **The Pioneer Arizona Living History Museum**, 3901 W Pioneer Rd., Phoenix, Tel: 993-0212. **Pueblo Grande Museum**, 4619 E Washington St., Phoenix, Tel: 495-0900. **Rawhide 1880s Western Town**, 23023 N Scottsdale Rd., Scottsdale, Tel: 602/563-1880. Wild West town with live performances. **Salt River Project History Center**, 1521 Project Dr., Phoenix, Tel: 236-2208. **Taliesin West**, northeast of Scottsdale, Tel: 860-2700.

Tourist Information

Casa Grande Chamber of Commerce, 575 N Marshall St., Casa Grande, Tel: 836-2125. **Phoenix-One Arizona Visitor Center**, Tel: 252-5588. **Native American Tourism Center**, 4130 N Goldwater Blvd., Scottsdale, Tel: 945-0771

APACHE TRAIL AND GREATER PAYSON AREA

All local phone numbers have area code 602.

Accommodation

BUDGET: **Charleston Motor Inn**, 302 S Beeline St., Payson, Tel: 474-2201. **Cloud Nine Motels**, 1699 E Ash St., Globe, Tel: 425-5741. *CAMPING:* Along the Apache Trail Loop, inquire at the **Tonto Basin Ranger District Office** in Roosevelt near the Roosevelt Lake Marina, Tel: 467-2236. **Casa de Monti**, 1730 E Ash St., near junction of US 60/70, Tel: 425-6574.

Attractions and Museums

Goldfield Ghost Town and Mine Tours Tel: 983-0333. **Lost Dutchman State Park**, off AZ 88, four miles north of Apache Junction, Tel: 982-4485. **Superstition Wilderness**, Tel: 225-5200. **Tonto**

Fish Hatchery, Tel: 478-4200. **Tonto Natural Bridge State Park**, Tel: 476-4202. **Tonto National Monument**, off AZ 88, 5 miles of Roosevelt, Tel: 467-2241.

Outdoor Acitivities and Sports

Rafting and kayaking on the Salt River: **Desert Voyages**, Box 9053, Scottsdale, AZ 85252, Tel: 602/998-7238.

Tourist Information

Payson Chamber of Commerce, 100 W Main St., Payson, Tel: 474-4515.

SEDONA, FLAGSTAFF, GALLUP INDIAN COUNTRY AND SANTA FE

Accommodation

LUXURY: **Bishop's Lodge**, Box 2367, Bishop's Lodge Rd., 3 miles north of the plaza, Santa Fe, NM 87504, Tel: 505/983-6377, guest ranch. *MODERATE:* **St. Francis**, 210 Don Gaspar Ave., Santa Fe, NM 87501, Tel: 505/983-5700, res: 800/666-5700. *BUDGET:* **Arizona Mountain Inn**, 685 Lake Mary Rd., Flagstaff AZ 86001, Tel: 602/774-8959. **Best Western**, 3009 W US 66, Gallup, NM 87301, Tel: 505/722-2221. **Canyon Villa B&B**, 125 Canyon Circle Dr., Sedona, AZ 86336, Tel: 602/284-1226. **Greyhills Inn**, Box 160, Tuba City, AZ 86045, Tel: 602/283-6271 (Indian Country). **Stage Coach,** 3360 Cerillos Rd., Santa Fe, NM 87501, Tel: 505/471-0707.

Attractions and Museums

Arizona Historical Society Pioneer Museum, 2,5 mi norhtwest on US 180, near Flagstaff, Tel: 602/774-6272. **El Morro Nat. Monument**, 30 mi east of Zuni, Tel: 602/783-4226. **Lowell Observatory**, 1 mi west on Mars Hill Rd. off Santa Fe Ave., Tel: 602/774-2096. **Navajo Tribal Museum**, on AZ 264 in Window Rock, Tel: 602/871-6673. **New Mexico Mining Museum**, 100 North Iron St., Grants, Tel: 505/287-4802. **Sunset Crater National Monument**, 15 mi northeast of Flagstaff off US 89, Tel: 602/527-7042. **Walnut Canyon National Monument**, 7 mi east on I-40 and 3 mi off Exit 204, Tel: 602/526-3367. **Wheelwright Museum of the American Indian**, 704 Camino Lejo, Santa Fe, Tel: 505/982-4636. **Wupatki National Monument**, 35 mi northeast of Flagstaff off US 89, Tel: 602/527-7040. **Zuni Pueblo**, 40 mi south of Gallup, Tel: 505/782-4481.

Tourist Information

Flagstaff Chamber of Commerce/Visitor Center, 101 W Santa Fe Ave., Flagstaff, Tel: 602/774-9541. **Gallup C & V Bureau**, 701 E Montoya Blvd., Gallup, Tel: 505/863-3841. **Santa Fe C & V Bureau**, PO Box 909, Tel: 505/984-6760, 800/777-2489. **Sedona-Oak Creek Canyon Chamber of Commerce**, Tel: 602/282-7722. **U.S. Forest Service**, Flagstaff, Tel: 602/556-7400.

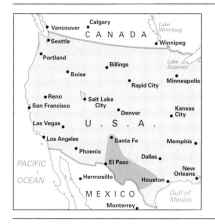

FROM SANTA FE TO SAN ANTONIO

FROM SANTA FE TO

EL PASO

FAR WEST TEXAS

TEXAS HILL COUNTRY

AUSTIN

SAN ANTONIO

Texas is the second largest state in the USA, and everything about it is big. Big men wear big boots and big hats, drive big trucks, eat big steaks, and talk about big sums of money from big ranches or oil fields. Coming from the West, a driver's first introduction to "big" in Texas is "big distances."

Attuning yourself to the size, flatness, emptiness, and light of the plains of West Texas is an important part of "seeing" this country. Some of the terrain here seems like phenomena from another geological age. As I-10 moves eastward through Texas, the landscape gradually gives way to the rolling green rises of Texas Hill Country. Here, you'll find the real heart of Texas: Austin, the state capital, and historic San Antonio, which manages to blend an Old Mexican flavor into its vital, contemporary atmosphere. From Santa Fe to San Antonio, the drive is about 1,000 miles (1600 km), which can be managed in about a week.

FROM SANTA FE TO EL PASO

One Roswell couple used to amuse themselves on the drive from Santa Fe to

Previous pages: Rodeo – a rough man's sport; the bulls testicles are squeezed to make them behave wildly. Left: Guadalupe Mountains National Park.

Roswell by counting the trees along the way: on one trip, they arrived at a grand total of fifteen. Rte. 285 is a straight, empty road. A main source of revenue for the deserted-looking little towns of Encino and Vaughn are speeding tickets issued to passing drivers.

At **Vaughn**, the 54 runs down through Carrizozo into **Lincoln National Forest**, and the landscape rises from the plain into cool mountain air among the trees. Rte. 380 leads off into the **Capitan Mountains**, where there's good skiing at the **Ski Apache Resort**. This resort, as well as the race track at **Ruidoso Downs**, is run by the Native Americans of the Mescalero Apache Reservation. Further along 380 is **Lincoln**, once home to the legendary Billy the Kid.

The 380 continues toward **Roswell**, a sprawling town put on the map by two space-related events: the early experiments of rocket pioneer Robert Goddard, and the "Roswell Incident" sighting of a UFO, both in the 1940s. Roswell has two (small) **UFO museums**, and Goddard's laboratories are displayed at its **Museum and Art Center**. The **Bitter Lake National Wildlife Refuge**, northeast of town, is a stop on the migratory route of many species of birds: pelicans and Canada geese are frequent guests to this arid region.

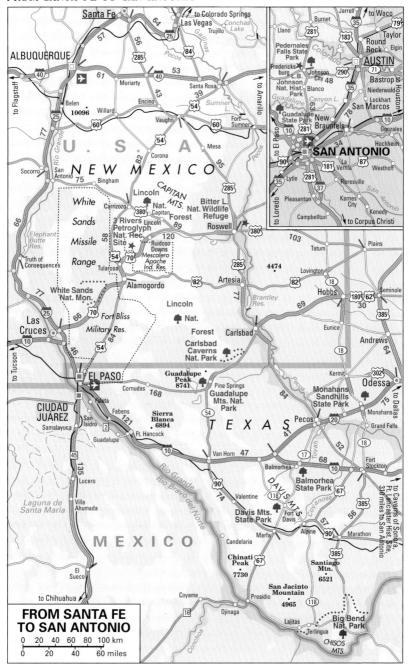

**FROM SANTA FE
TO SAN ANTONIO**

0 20 40 60 80 100 km

0   20   40   60 miles

Farther south, in **Carlsbad**, the mile-deep underground formations of **Carlsbad Caverns National Park** draw thousands of visitors each year. Huge stalactites and stalagmites thrust upward or hang ponderously from the ceiling, encrusted with drops of colored rock.

If, rather than detouring through Carlsbad, you elect to stay on Rte. 54 towards El Paso, you'll pass the **Three Rivers Petroglyph Site** before coming to **White Sands**. The dunes of this national monument resemble a moonscape, plopped down in the New Mexico plains. They're located in the midst of the weapons-testing ground of White Sands Missile Range. The seeming remoteness of New Mexico and West Texas make them prime targets for use as testing grounds or dump sites for industrial and nuclear waste. The underground salt beds near Carlsbad, the Mescalero Apache Reservation, Texas's Sierra Blanca, and other areas are under consideration or already being used to dump everything from radioactive waste to New York sewage.

FAR WEST TEXAS

"The most interesting thing about El Paso is Ciudad Juarez," quipped an El Paso native, referring to the "twin" city across the border. In some ways, **Ciudad Juarez** and **El Paso** function as one city. Juarez is one of Mexico's main metropolises, and El Paso depends on it in no small measure for trade. For visitors, Juarez offers cheap goods in bargain shops, cheap drinks in its bars, racing at Juarez Track, Sunday afternoon bullfights, and an atmosphere more colorful and more earthy than you'll find across the border. Souvenir-hunters should browse through **FONART**, a government-sponsored market for native artisans which presents traditional art from all over Mexico.

Above: Somehow everything is bigger in Texas – even the hats.

Spanish missionaries were among the first settlers here. In Juarez, there's a 17th-century mission next to the **Cathedral** (Avenida Juarez), while **San Isidro**, south of El Paso on the Rio Grande, is said to be the oldest mission in the United States. Missionaries came to convert the original residents here, the Tigua Indians, who claim that their reservation at **Ysleta**, open to tourists, is the oldest Indian community in the States (although the Zuni would dispute this).

The **Rio Grande**, called Rio Bravo by the Mexicans, used to flood frequently; today, it's been brought under control with concrete banks. This was necessary for political reasons: after a flood, the river often changed its course, thereby changing the border between Mexico and the U.S. Running through the river is the fence known as the "Tortilla Curtain," erected to keep Mexicans from crossing illegally into America, and so called because people predicted that the Mexicans would eat it up. Illegal immigrants are known as "wetbacks" (indicating that

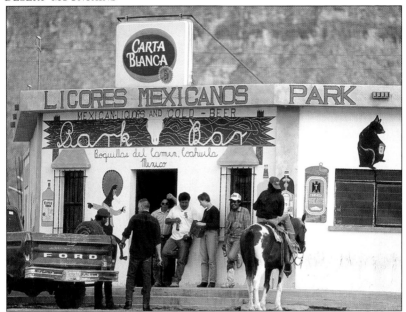

their backs are still wet from swimming the river), and there are still plenty of them. Border patrols work to turn back the hordes, some of whom are kept overnight in border detention facilities or sanctuary houses before being returned.

Desert Mountains

From El Paso, "the pass" in the mountains, Rte. I-10 runs beside the river for a little ways before turning east to cut across the state. This area is one of the most deserted in Texas, sparsely dotted with tiny communities and ghost towns. Not much has changed here since early Spanish explorers dubbed it *despoblado*, "unpopulated place." Settlers tended to stay away from the out-of-the-way terrain, one of the last areas to be made "safe" from the local Apaches. The emptiness of this kind of territory led General

Above: Over the Mexican border in Boquillas del Carmen. Right: Big Bend National Park.

Philip H. Sheridan to say, in 1866, "If I owned Texas and all hell, I would rent out Texas and live in hell." The land is wrinkled with the southernmost outcroppings of the Rocky Mountains. From I-10, Rte. 54 leads up to **Guadalupe Mountains National Park** on the New Mexico border, which contains the state's highest mountain, **Guadalupe Peak** (8,749 feet). Further along Rte. I-10, there's relief for hot drivers at **Lake Balmorhea**.

The mountains continue southward, where a detour of a mere 130 miles along Rtes. 17 and 118 brings you to some of the most spectacular scenery in Texas. The **Davis Mountains** are in fact the only really mountainous area of the state. Near **Fort Davis**, Texas's highest town at 4,900 feet, is the **McDonald Observatory**; the altitude and clear skies make this an ideal site for star-gazing. From here, the 118 leads down to a Texas highlight, **Big Bend National Park**. Big Bend is a region of rivers and waterfalls, canyons with bizarre stone formations, and the **Chisos Mountains**, formed by

volcanic action 60 million years ago. It is a wild area, laced with rivers and dotted with unusual rock formations and cacti. Raft trips and hikes are two preferred ways of exploring it. Nearby are two little ghost towns: **Lajitas**, today in a tourist-oriented incarnation, and **Terlingua**, where Texans gather every autumn for the **National Chili Cook-Off**.

After Balmorhea, Rte. I-10 leads past the **Toyah** and **Coyanose Rivers**, an area where irrigation and soil conditions produce some of the best canteloupe to be found anywhere. Other crops are pecans and hot peppers. That West Texas is known as "oil country" – nearly half of the U.S.'s oil output comes from Texas – can be seen in **Fort Stockton**, the largest and most modern town in the Far West Texas region. Before Fort Stockton, 1776 leads to the **Monahans Sandhills State Park**, a 200-mile expanse of sand dunes where archaeologists have found Indian artifacts and dinosaur bones.

At Sheffield, I-10 crosses the **Pecos**, which seems small for a river that once formed the border of "civilized" land. One reason for the river's repute was Judge Roy Bean of Langtry, who set himself up as "the law West of the Pecos," and meted out justice accordingly. The Spanish settlers had several names for the Pecos: *Rio de las Vacas* (River of Cows), *Rio Salado* (Salty), *Rio Puerco* (Dirty).

Throughout this area, 19th-century cavalry forts, built to control "Indian trouble," give insight into frontier life of the past. One such site are the adobe ruins of **Fort Lancaster** on Rte. I-10. Further along, the **Caverns of Sonora** are one of Texas's longest caves.

TEXAS HILL COUNTRY

Texas Hill Country is a world apart from the barren plains of the west. Its greenery and live oaks are broken by rivers and lakes. Boating, fishing, canoeing, and swimming are prime activities here at legion state parks, some formed by damming the Colorado River west of Austin. Hunting is also popular. If the

jackrabbits aren't game enough, there are a variety of special hunting preserves throughout Hill Country which are kept stocked with exotic animals.

Texas Hill Country was made famous as the birthplace of Lyndon B. Johnson, John F. Kennedy's successor as President of the United States (1963-1968). The area today is rife with Johnson memorials, including a lake bearing his name. Despite this presidential link, and its beauty, this region is generally poor. Not even in the 1800s did settlers view it as prime territory. The Mexicans, who won independence in 1821, were happy to let immigrants, many German, settle down around San Antonio, because they formed a kind of buffer zone against the hostile Comanche Indians.

One of the best-known of these settlements is **Fredericksburg**, east of I-10 on Rte. 290. Its Main Street was built wide

Above: A little chat while shopping at the General Store in Luckenbach. Right: Austin, city center with Capitol Building.

enough to turn an oxcart around, which gives it the dimensions of a freeway. **Nimitz Hotel** here was originally built as protection against the Comanche threat; a later Nimitz gave it the ship-like additions of prow, pilot house, and the like which make it so distinctive today.

Like many of the area's German settlements, Fredericksburg has kept its German flavor; you can still here the language spoken in the old-timey **County Store**, or visit the **Vereinskirche**, while sausages and *schnapps* are produced throughout the area. It was the Germans who brought the accordion to the region; the Mexicans made it an integral part of their own folk music.

Past **Johnson City**, where American-President buffs can inspect Lyndon B. Johnson's home, the **Pedernales River State Park** is one of many popular water sports centers. Further south, **Guadalupe State Park** shows one of the loveliest sides of Hill Country. Popular with canoers eager to test its rapids, the park is also ideal for nature-lovers and bird-watchers. About 20 miles west of Austin, **Hamilton Pool** is a favorite swimming hole; spilling down from its cliff-like walls is a 60-foot waterfall.

AUSTIN

Currently, **Austin** is one of the most popular places to live in the United States. Young people come for the University, or the city's flourishing music scene; others are attracted by the city's physical beauty, the old oak trees shading wide streets, historic buildings like those lining **6th Street**, now a Registered Historic District.

One center of the city is the main branch of the University of Texas. On the main campus you'll find plenty of student cafés, or local music haunts such as the blues bar **Antone's**. Near the university, the marble **Lyndon B. Johnson Library and Museum** contains yet more

information and memorabilia relating to the President.

The other focus of the city are the governmental buildings. The **State Capitol Building** is, true to the Texas tradition of "big," a little bit taller than the Capitol Building in Washington, D.C., and built of red granite, considered more prestigious than the more usual Texas limestone. Across the street is the slightly older building of the **Governor's Mansion**. Shoppers in Austin can outfit themselves in true Texas style at the Texas Hatters or the bootmaker Charlie Dunn.

SAN ANTONIO

San Antonio, Texas's oldest and perhaps most beautiful city, has tried to make its Mexican heritage an asset. With more than half of its residents of Mexican origin, Mexican language and culture are an integral part of San Antonio life, reflected in everything from **El Mercado**, the United States's largest Mexican market, to the annual *fiesta*, to the vibrant neighborhood of **La Villita**, filled with Tex-Mex restaurants. And Henry Cisneros was the first U.S. mayor of Hispanic origin, until Bill Clinton summoned him to his Cabinet.

The Spanish heritage goes back a long way; missions were established here in 1718, and explorers knew the area long before that. Certainly San Antonio is bound up with state history in a special way. After Mexican independence, the Mexicans hoped to check Indians in the then-remote Texas territory by luring American settlers with the offer of cheap land. As a result, Americans outnumbered Mexicans 10 to 1 by 1835; in that year, led by Sam Houston, they revolted and declared their own independence. A key battle occured in 1836, when Commander William Travis and 180-some men holed up in the mission complex of the Alamo, besieged by General Santa Anna. Travis's men – including frontiersman Davy Crockett – held out for 13 days, but were finally overpowered and killed. However, the battle gave Houston

61

and his forces time to prepare for Santa Anna's assault, and, under the battle-cry, "Remember the Alamo!" defeated the Mexican army. Today, the **Alamo chapel** at the center of town is one of San Antonio's main attractions, seen by many Texans as a shrine to the heroes who gave their lives for Texan independence which in fact ended when Texas became one of the United States in 1845.

San Antonio has been dubbed "the frontier Venice." Through the center of town, **Paseo del Rio**, the River Walk, winds along the banks of the San Antonio river, twenty feet below street level, lined with restaurants with outdoor tables sporting bright umbrellas. Tour boats depart from its banks on sightseeing or dining cruises under the arches of the river's thirteen bridges. On holidays, especially Christmas and *fiesta*, the whole ensemble is strung with colored lights and *luminarios*, traditional Mexican lanterns constructed of candles in paper bags.

You often hear about the "six flags over Texas." This refers to the mixed heritage of an area that has at one time or another been under Spanish, French, Mexican, "Texian," Confederate, and American government. This varied heritage is displayed in the **Institute of Texan Cultures**, behind the tall **Tower of the Americas** in **HemisFair Park**. It's also reflected in historical buildings: the **Spanish Governor's Palace**; the four Spanish missions along **Mission Trail** (south of downtown); the French-Gothic style **San Fernando Cathedral**.

In **Brackenridge Park**, the art-deco building of the **Witte Museum** houses exhibitions on local and natural history.

Another notable building of slightly older vintage is the remarkable **Menger Hotel**, just across from the Alamo. Opened in the mid-1800s, it has numbered Oscar Wilde, Sarah Bernhardt, and Robert E. Lee among its guests; in its bar, Teddy Roosevelt recruited riders for his so-called "Rough Riders" in the year 1898.

Above: The Alamo Chapel is a symbol for the Texan fight for liberty.

NEW MEXICO

All phone numbers have area code 505.

Accommodation

MODERATE: **Roswell Inn**, Box 2065, 1815 N Main St. (US 70, 285), Roswell, NM 88201, Tel: 623-4920.
BUDGET: **Continental Inn**, 3820 National Parks Hwy., Carlsbad, NM 88220, Tel: 887-0341.

Attractions, Museums and Parks

Bitter Lake National Wildlife Refuge, 13 miles northeast of Roswell (via US 70), Tel: 622-6755. **Carlsbad Caverns National Park**, 27 miles southwest of Carlsbad, on US 62/180, Tel: 785-2232. **Lincoln National Forest**, near Alamogordo, Tel:437-6030. **Roswell Museum and Art Center**, 100 W 11th St., Tel: 624-6744.
Three Rivers Petroglyph National Recreation Site, 36 miles south of Carrizozo, via US 54.
White Sands National Monument, 15 miles southwest of Alamogordo, on US 70/82, Tel: 479-6124.

Tourist Information

Roswell Chamber of Commerce, 131 W 2nd St., PO Drawer 70, Roswell, NM 88201, Tel: 623-5695.

WESTERN TEXAS

All phone numbers have area code 915.

Accommodation

MODERATE: **Sunset Heights**, 717 W Yandell Ave., El Paso, TX 79902, Tel: 544-1743. Victorian-style inn.
BUDGET: **Devil's River**, I-10/Golf Course Rd. (US 277), Sonora, TX 76950, Tel: 387-3516. **El Parador**, 6400 Montana Ave., El Paso, TX 79925, Tel: 772-4231. **Sands**, 1801 W Dickinson Blvd., Fort Stockton, TX 79735, Tel: 336-2274 (near Big Bend National Park).

Attractions, Museums and Parks

Balmorhea State Park, 50 miles south on TX 17, near Davis Mts., Tel: 375-2370. **Big Bend National Park**, 103 miles south of Alpine on TX 118, Information Tel: 477-2251. **Caverns of Sonora**, eight miles west on I-10, on FM 1989, Tel: 387-3105. **Davis Mountains State Park**, Information Tel: 426-3337. **Fort Davis National Historic Site**, Tel: 426-3224. **Fort Lancaster State Historic Site**, 33 miles west on US 290. **Guadalupe Mountains National Park**, 16 miles north of Van Horn, via TX 54, Tel: 828-3251. **McDonald Observatory**, atop Mt. Locke, Tel: 426-3640. **Monahans Sandhills State Park**, six miles east on I-20, exit mp 86, Tel: 943-2092. **Tigua Indian Reservation** with **Ysleta Mission**, Tel: 859-3916.

Tourist Information

El Paso Tourist Bureau, 1 Civic Center Plaza, El Paso, TX 79901, Tel: 534-0653

TEXAS HILL COUNTRY

All phone numbers have area code 210.

Accommodation

MODERATE: There are several **B & B Lodging Services** in **Fredericksburg** which provide for B&B stays. Among them are: 102 S Cherry St., Tel: 997-4712, 107 N Washington St., Tel: 997-9585.
BUDGET: **Save Inn Motel**, PO Box 610, 107 US 281 (jct. US 281/290), Johnson City, TX 78636, Tel: 868-4044.

Attractions, Museums and Parks

Admiral Nimitz Museum State Historical Park, 340 E Main St., Fredericksburg, Tel: 210/997-4379. **Hamilton Pool**, west of Austin, on F.M. 3238, 13 miles south, Tel: 512/264-2740. **Lyndon B. Johnson National Historical Park**, Information Tel: 868-7128. **Pedernales Falls State Park**, 14 miles east on Ranch Rd. 2766, Tel: 868-7304. **Vereinskirche**, Market Square, Fredericksburg, Tel: 997-7832.

Tourist Information

Fredericksburg Chamber of Commerce, 106 N Adams, Fredericksburg, TX 78624, Tel: 997-6523.

AUSTIN AND SAN ANTONIO

Accommodation

MODERATE: **Beauregard House**, 215 Beauregard St., San Antonio, TX 78204, Tel: 210/222-1198. Historic inn. **Driskill**, 604 Brazos, Austin, TX 78701, Tel: 512/474-5911. **Menger Hotel**, 204 Alamo Sq., San Antonio, TX 78205, Tel: 210/223-4361. *BUDGET:* **La Quinta North**, 7100 I-35N, Austin, TX 78752, Tel: 512/452-9401.

Attractions, Museums and Parks

The Alamo, Alamo Plaza, San Antonio, Tel: 210/225-1391. **Brackenridge Park**, N Broadway (US 81), San Antonio. **Governor's Mansion**, 1010 Colorado St. (in Capitol Complex), Tel: 512/463-5516. **Institute of Texan Cultures**, HemisFair Park, Tel: 210/226-7651. **Lyndon B. Johnson Library & Museum**, on campus of Univ. of Texas, Tel: 512/482-5137. **San Antonio Mission National Historical Park**, Mission Rd., Tel: 210/229-5701. Signposted tour to five Spanish missions. **San Fernando Cathedral**, West Market/West Commerce Sts. **Spanish Governor's Palace**, 105 Military Plaza, San Antonio, Tel: 210/224-0601. **State Capitol**, 11th/Congress Ave., Austin, Tel: 512/463-0063. **Tower of the Americas**, HemisFair Park, Tel: 210/223-3101. **Witte Museum**, 3801 Broadway/Tuleta St., Tel: 210/829-7262.

Tourist Information

Austin C & V Bureau, 201 E 2nd St., PO Box 1088, Austin, TX 78767, Tel: 512/478-0098.
San Antonio C & V Bureau, PO Box 2277, San Antonio, TX 78298, Tel: 210/270-8700.

FROM
SAN ANTONIO
TO HOUSTON

CORPUS CHRISTI

TEXAS COAST

GALVESTON

HOUSTON

At the beginning of the 16th century, Spanish explorer Alonso Alvarez worked his way along the coast of the Gulf of Mexico searching for a short-cut to Cathay. And Spanish geographer Pineda made a major contribution to his fledgling field by mapping out the broad, flat beaches and scrubby marshland of what is today the Texas shore. Finding the region's name, at least, was easy: local tribespeople greeted the first Europeans with the word "Tejas!" This was, in fact, nothing more than the Indian word for "friend." The friendliness of Texans has been legendary ever since. And you won't find a much friendlier landscape than the beaches along the Gulf Coast.

The 300-mile drive (480 km) from San Antonio to Houston isn't long: a matter of hours. But if you want to soak up the sun and sand, explore the seashore or the charms of historic Galveston, waterfront towns on the Gulf Waterway or wildlife on Padre Island National Seashore, you'll find that the hours stretch into days.

The Ranch of Kings

From San Antonio, I-37 leads southeast, through a region that presents some-

Left: A Dubuffet sculpture in the skyscraper canyon of Houston.

thing of a gray area to the visitor. This scrubby mesquite terrain, between the center of the state and its salt coast, is neither fish nor fowl – or perhaps one should say it's both fish and fowl, as it's a popular destination for sport hunters, who follow everything from whitewing dove to wild boars. To the south, the dry emptiness reaches down to the "point" of the state of Texas, its southernmost spur which follows the curve of the Rio Grande along the Mexican border. Citrus orchards are cultivated in this valley, and Mexican culture is reflected in the Mexican names of many of the towns near **Brownsville**.

While the area doesn't offer many tourist sites, it's increasingly popular with winter refugees from cold northern climates. The trailer parks and citrus orchards create a fleeting resemblance to the state of Florida. Near **McAllen**, the **Bentsen-Rio Grande State Park** is a draw for birdwatchers, with a nature trail pointing out and explaining the region's flora and fauna. Bentsen is the name of a local family of citrus growers whose head is also a popular United States Senator, Lloyd Bentsen, one of Washington's most respected Democrats.

A large part of the territory south of 37 is taken up by the fabled **King Ranch**, the largest working cattle ranch in the

65

world, covering some 825,000 acres. Turn off on Rte. 77 south toward **Kingsville**; west of this town, on 141, is the headquarters of this family-owned expanse founded in the middle of the last century by a steamboat captain named Richard King. Visitors can follow a road around part of the territory to get an idea of the day-to-day workings – and incredible bleakness – of real cowboy life.

SPARKLING CORPUS CHRISTI

About two hours by car from San Antonio, **Corpus Christi** seems to be in another world. Pineda gave it this very Catholic name in the 16th century, but Texas' seventh-largest city is not known for its historic ambience or Old World flair; indeed, there was only a trading post on the site until the mid-19th century. It's white sands and sport fishing,

Above: Lasso-artistry. Right: Traditional handcrafted saddle production for western riders.

high-rise hotels and museums that are the draws here.

Corpus Christi isn't all about recreation, as the bustling **Port of Corpus Christi** (one of the ten busiest in the country) shows. The city first flowered as an army base during the conflicts with Mexico at the dawn of Texas' statehood; the military flavor persists in the many naval bases in the area, which can be toured. Navy buffs can take a closer look at the workings of the Navy on the aircraft carrier *U.S.S. Lexington*, which saw plenty of duty in World War II and has been made into a naval museum. Another port attraction is the **Columbus Fleet**, life-sized copies of the ships on which Columbus sailed to discover America in 1492.

Separating Corpus Christi Bay from the port proper is the huge **Harbor Bridge**, the state's tallest. At its foot, **Bayfront Plaza** has become a new center for city visitors and residents alike. Anyone who's in Corpus Christi for work at the Convention Center can stroll through the **Watergarden** at lunchtime, look in at

the **Art Museum** (housed in a building designed by architect Philip Johnson), or learn about shipwrecks at the **Corpus Christi Museum**, all nearby. Not far away is the lovely old neighborhood of **Heritage Park** with its historic houses.

A more unusual museum is the **Museum of Oriental Cultures**, which houses a fine collection of Japanalia. Corpus Christi may not be the first place you'd think to look for fine Japanese art and objects; in fact, the museum reflects the lifelong interest and involvement of a local resident named Billie Trimble Chandler, who spent years in Japan as a teacher. On the other side of Harbor Bridge, the exhibits are alive at the **Texas State Aquarium**, a fine collection of fish, eels, sharks, and other marine life, with a view out over the beach.

Beach Life – Texan Style

Beach is a key word for Corpus Christi visitors. The city beach, also called **North Beach**, offers some real surf; by contrast, the sheltered **McGee Beach** to the south has calmer waters. But the greatest beach attraction are the white sands of **Padre Island**, the nation's longest undeveloped beach (about 80 miles) and National Seashore. While the northern part of this expanse has paved roads and is crowded with condominiums, hotels and restaurants, the buildings thin out the farther south you get, and what dominates the landscape are dunes, flat marshland, sea, and sky. On one side of the island, which is four miles wide at its widest point, tidal inlets shelter all manner of salt-water creatures in their warm muck, and a riot of bird life enlivens the salt flats. On the Gulf side, sea treasures – shells, weathered beach glass, gleaming stones polished by the waves – lie along the waterline.

You can appreciate these all the more because the thick white sand makes for slow walking; for trips farther down the island, it's advisable to rent a jeep with four-wheel drive (driving on the beach is legal in Texas). Even avid beachcombers and very slow walkers, however, are unlikely to find remnants of the greatest treasures of these waves: three Spanish galleons full of gold and valuables that sank in 1554 off this coast (dubbed "the graveyard of the Gulf"). Much of their contents have been salvaged.

All the developers who were banned from the National Seashore have set up shop at the southern end of Padre Island. A genuine resort atmosphere runs rampant here, near **Brownsville** and the mouth of the Rio Grande. Still, there are a couple of bastions of nature conservancy amid the condos. **South Padre Island's** "Turtle Lady," Ila Loetscher, is a private resident renowned throughout the state for her work saving and nursing members of the endangered sea turtle family since 1978; her organization, **Sea Turtle Inc.**, gives twice-weekly *"Meet the Turtles"* shows for interested parties. Then there's the **Gladys Porter Zoo** in Brownsville, with more than 1,900 species of animals and a variety of plants, displayed in quasi-natural habitats.

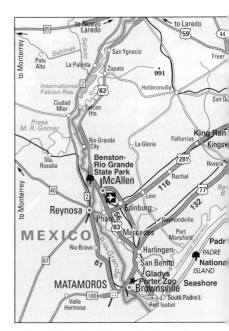

TEXAS COAST

North of Corpus Christi, the islands and parks don't stop. **Mustang Island State Park**, at the northern end of Padre Island, offers great beaches and is famous for its fishing. At its very tip is **Port Aransas**, a little fishing village which has played up its "quaint" quotient for tourism in recent years, but which is still fine for exploring, poking into shops, wandering along docks, or finding a fishing boat to take you out for some deepsea action. On shore, the **Horace Caldwell Fishing Pier** gives a chance to angle from land; it extends 1,240 feet into the Gulf, and is open 24 hours a day. A town landmark, the **Tarpon Inn** displays the work of past fishermen in the autographed scales that adorn its walls.

From here, a free ferry runs to **Aransas Pass**, where not fish, but shrimp, are the order of the day; the port is home to a huge working fleet of shrimp boats. Across the bay, uninhabited "St. Jo," or San José Island, affords some protection from hurricanes. Conservation is the key word at **Aransas National Wildlife Refuge**. The point of land is the winter home of the whooping crane, who migrate from Canada each year in mid-October. Nearly extinct a few decades ago, the crane population is up to around 100 now thanks to the involvement of wildlife conservationists. So ardently does the region work to protect its wildlife that offshore drilling rigs are required to close down during crane season, interrupting their search for another kind of underwater treasure found throughout the Gulf: oil. It's because of this kind of commitment that the cranes have been able to multiply; although it's feared that a shipping accident on the **Gulf Intracoastal Waterway**, which runs through their refuge, could spell disaster if it released oil or chemicals and killed the crustaceans on which they feed. A harb-

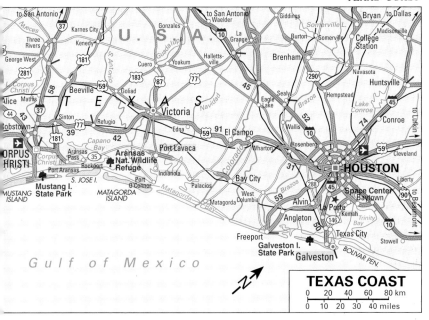

inger of this was the huge fire on a Mexican oil rig in 1979, which resulted in one of the biggest oil spills in history; fortunately, weather and the barrier islands protected the refuge for the most part. Since then, all has gone well; moreover, the cranes, as well as the refuge's ten other endangered species (including sea turtles, alligators, and brown pelicans) have adapted well to boat traffic.

Such juxtapositions of man and nature serve as reminders that there's more to the Gulf Coast than tourist pleasures and wildlife refuges. In addition to the forest of offshore drilling rigs that rise up here and there from the waters, the strip of water between the coast and the barrier islands is actually part of the Gulf Intracoastal Waterway which links the Texas ports with New Orleans. This working water road runs about 1,200 miles, from Brownsville all the way to Florida. Completed in 1949, the waterway is continually dredged to assure boats of a channel never less than 12 feet deep and 125 feet wide. The protective islands play a role

for these boats, too; shielded from the full fury of Gulf storms, they carry about 100 million tons of cargo from port to port every year.

HISTORIC GALVESTON

While you can't quite drive along the waterway, Rte. 35 follows the coastline a little way inland, leading to many smaller waterside towns that are part port, part fishing village, part history. North of the Aransas Refuge, off Matagorda Bay, **Port O'Connor** and **Port Lavaca** draw sport fishermen, hunters, and, yes, beachgoers. Some towns haven't managed to withstand the force of the hurricanes which have created trenches in the dunes of Padre and other islands; **Indianola**, for example, was flattened by a storm in the 19th century. **Palacios**, across the bay, was luckier, and has managed to preserve its charm.

Hurricanes have left their mark on more than one of the towns along this coast. **Galveston** was one of the region's

69

leading commercial centers until September 8 and 9, 1900. The hurricane that struck on that date was so ferocious that it remains one of the worst natural disasters in U.S. history. It killed in the neighborhood of 6,000 people, and wiped out the town to such an extent that there was some question whether it should be rebuilt at all. Fortunately, enough of the beautiful old houses, such as the 1859 **Ashton Villa**, survived, so that Galveston is still a draw for enthusiasts of Victorian homes – even if, since the hurricane, the town has more or less become a satellite, at best a country retreat, of Houston. A huge sea wall, 17 feet high, has been constructed to prevent similar damage ever happening again.

Despite the storm, Galveston has more historic charm than Texas's other Gulf cities. One example is the **Strand Historic District**, where Victorian-style

Above: Shrimp cutter in Port Ysabel on the Texas Gulf Coast. Right: Houston skyline by night.

warehouse buildings with cast-iron facades have been converted into a lively shopping neighborhood. Another relic of Galveston's pre-hurricane past is the **Grand 1894 Opera House**, one of America's finest old theaters. An annual Historic Homes tour brings across some of the old-timey ambiance.

Traditionally, involvement with the sea hasn't only been negative on **Galveston Island**. Like most of the other Gulf towns, it's long been a fishing village: reminders of this are the annual springtime **Shrimp Festival**, which opens with a blessing of the shrimp fleet as it starts the season, and includes square-dancing with hundreds of participants.

The island's maritime past is preserved at the **Texas Seaport Museum** on Pier 21, where the old sailing ship *Elissa* (1877) is a main attraction. You can also take day cruises from Galveston; or hop on the free ferry over to **Bolivar Peninsula**. After the signature lighthouse at Port Bolivar, the peninsula boasts miles of deserted beaches off the beaten, de-

veloped tourist track. But if you'd rather stay ashore at Galveston, the ten-story glass pyramid of **Moody Gardens** contains an even greater variety of wildlife – the flora and fauna of a tropical rain forest – than you might find outdoors, plus a 3D IMAX cinema that plunges you into still different worlds.

HOUSTON
"Deep in the Heart of Texas"

Leading toward Houston, Rte. 146 leads up to **Clear Lake** and **Kemah**, where you can eat fresh seafood overlooking the water. On the opposite shore of Clear Lake, the **LBJ Space Center** is a treasure trove of information and memorabilia to fascinate the moonstruck. Here, the National Air and Space Administration (NASA) has a museum and souvenir center with everything from early space capsules to a piece of moon rock. The first word spoken to Earth by a man on the moon was, as local residents can all tell you, "Houston."

Houston is the largest city in the large state of Texas, and as such, it's hard to characterize. Perhaps this makes it a perfect embodiment of its state. Houston is rich in cultural and ethnic diversity: active Latin American, African-American, Asian-American communities celebrate a host of festivals and holidays, from the Chinese New Year to "Juneteenth," an African-American festival commemorating the day when Union soldiers took over Galveston Harbor (June 19th, 1865) to end the Civil War and finally liberate Texas' slaves. The art scene ranges from fine to funky: the **Houston Opera**, whose glittering performances contrast with the clubs in the **Richmond Entertainment District**. The latter is near the **Galleria**, an exclusive mall which represents haute couture and haute prices.

But Houston also has the down-to-earth fishing flavor of areas like **Kemah**. The city's museums present the best of Europe – at the **Museum of Fine Arts**, for example – or the best of America, such as the newly renovated **Bayou Bend**

Above: At Nasa Space Center space travel is history and, at the same time, future.

Mansion, with 28 period rooms containing the finest in American decorative arts, overlooking gardens and lawns. This collection was assembled by a figure whose name, at least, has become legendary among American schoolchildren: christened Imogene, the only daughter of oil tycoon and Texas Governor James Stephen Hogg, she was known throughout her life as Ima Hogg.

Another private collection worth noting is that of John and Dominique de Menil. The **Menil Collection** is housed in a brand-new museum which displays changing shows as well as the couple's remarkable collection of art. It was also the de Menils who commissioned painter Mark Rothko to create the shimmering, luminous canvases which adorn the **Rothko Chapel** down the street.

There's live – or livelier – entertainment in the neighborhood of **Montrose** in the west of the city, a diverting and hip region which includes Texas's largest gay community. Sidewalk cafés and second-hand boutiques are typical of this area; while **Westheimer Street**, which intersects Montrose, adds spice with a number of Tex-Mex restaurants.

While Houston is hardly a walker's city – a car is just as necessary to many residents as a pair of legs – the downtown area is fitted out with an extensive system of underground tunnels, many lined with shops and arcades, which make it easier to get around in this area. The grid of downtown is the base for a thicket of skyscrapers that provide the only topography in this flat city. Architects who have left their mark here include such American masters as Philip Johnson or I.M. Pei (whose **Texas Commerce Bank Building** has been dubbed "the Texas tombstone"). But even in this geometric forest, there are pockets of green, such as **Sam Houston Park** to the west, where the annual **International Festival** takes place, a ten-day event reflecting the town's own varied and multicultural character.

GREATER CORPUS CHRISTI AREA
All phone numbers have area code 512.

Accommodation
LUXURY: **Sheraton Bayfront**, 707 N Shoreline Blvd., Corpus Christi, TX 78401, Tel: 882-1700. *MODERATE:* **Channel View**, Box 776, 631 Channel View Dr., Port Aransas, TX 78373, Tel: 749-6649. Overlooks channel. **Quality Hotel**, 601 N Water St., Corpus Christi, TX 78401, Tel: 882-8100. **Sheraton Hotel**, 310 Padre Blvd., South Padre Island, TX 78597, Tel: 210/761-6570. Nice resort on beach. *BUDGET:* **Drury Inn**, 612 W US 83, McAllen, TX 78501, Tel: 210/687-5100. **Econol Ldge**, 2502 E Kennedy St., Kingsville, TX 78363, Tel: 592-5251.

Attractions, Museums and Parks
Aransas National Wildlife Refuge, 35 miles northeast of Rockport, via TX 35 north, Information Tel: 286-3559. **Art Museum of South Texas**, 1902 N Shoreline Blvd., Tel: 884-3844. **Bensten Rio Grande Valley State Park**, three miles west on US 83, south on FM 2062, Tel: 210/585-1107. **Corpus Christi Museum of Science and History**, 1900 N Chaparral St., Tel: 883-2862. **Gladys Porter Zoo**, 500 Ringgold St., Brownsville, Tel: 210/546-7187. **Heritage Park**, 1600 block of N Chaparral St. **King Ranch**, west of Kingsville, off TX 141, Tel: 592-8055. **Museum of Oriental Cultures**, 418 Peoples St., Suite 200, Tel: 883-1303. **Mustang Island State Park**, 14 miles south on TX 361. **Padre Island National Seashore** (from Corpus Christi via John F. Kennedy Causeway), Information Tel: 949-8068. **Sea Turtle Inc.**, 5805 Gulf Blvd., South Padre Island, Tel: 210/761-5244. **Texas State Aquarium**, Corpus Christi Beach, Tel: 881-1200. **USS Lexington**, Corpus Christi Bay, Tel: 888-4873.

Sports and Trips
Boat Trips into the **Aransas National Wildlife Refuge**, several ferries leave from Rockport Harbor (*Lucky Day*, Tel: 729-4855, *New Pelican*, Tel: 729-8448, *Pisces*, Tel: 729-7525).

Tourist Information
Corpus Christi C & V Bureau, 1201 N Shoreline Dr., PO Box 2664, Corpus Christi, TX 78403, Tel: 882-5603. **Port Aransas Chamber of Commerce**, 421 W Cotter, PO Box 356, Port Aransas, TX 78373, Tel: 749-5919.

GALVESTON AND TEXAS COASTLINE
All phone numbers have area code 409.

Accommodation
LUXURY: **Tremont House**, 2300 Ship's Mechanic Row, Galveston, TX 77550, Tel: 763-0300.

Historic and elegant hotel. **San Luis**, 5222 Seawall Blvd., TX 77551, Tel: 744-8452. *MODERATE:* **Harbor House**, # 28 Pier 21, Galveston, TX 77550, Tel: 763-3321. **Holiday Inn on the Beach**, 5002 Seawall Blvd., TX 77551, Tel: 740-3581. *BUDGET:* **Gaido's Seaside Inn**, 3828 Seawall Blvd., Galveston, TX 77550, Tel: 762-9625.

Attractions, Museums and Parks
Ashton Villa, 2328 Broadway (at 24th St.), Tel: 762-3933. **The Bishop's Palace**, 1402 Broadway, Galveston, Tel: 762-2475. Victorian Mansion. **Grand 1894 Opera House**, 2020 Post Office St., Tel: 763-7173. **Moody Gardens**, 1 Hope Blvd., Tel: 744-1745. **Strand National Historic Landmark**, between 20th/25th Sts., Tel: 765-7834. **Texas Seaport Museum**, Pier 21, Tel: 763-1877.

Tourist Information
Galveston Island C & V Bureau, (Visitor Center: Moody Civic Center) 2106 Seawall Blvd. (at 21st St.), Galveston, TX 77550, Tel: 763-4311. **Port Lavaca-Calhoun County Chamber of Commerce**, 2300 TX 35 Bypass, PO Box 528, Port Lavaca, TX 77979, Tel: 512/552-2959.

GREATER HOUSTON AREA
All phone numbers have area code 713.

Accommodation
LUXURY: **La Colombe D'Or,** 3410 Montrose Blvd., Houston, TX 77006, Tel: 524-7999. Elegant inn from the twenties. **The Ritz-Carlton**, 1919 Briar Oaks Lane, Houston, TX 77027, Tel: 840-7600. *MODERATE:* **Guest Quarters Galleria West**, 5353 Westheimer Rd., Houston, TX 77056, Tel: 961-9000. **Holiday Inn Crowne Plaza-Galleria**, 2222 West Loop S, TX 77027, Tel: 961-7272. **Ramada Hotel**, 12801 Northwest Frwy., TX 77040, Tel: 462-9977, north of downtown. *BUDGET:* **Lexington Hotel Suites**, 16410 I-45N, Houston, TX 77090, Tel: 821-1000. **Sara's Bed & Breakfast**, 941 Heights Blvd., TX 77008, Tel: 868-1130, north of downtown.

Attractions, Museums and Parks
Bayou Bend Collection, 1 Westcott St., Tel: 520-2600. **Houston Grand Opera**, Wortham Theater Center, 501 Txas Ave., Tel: 227-ARTS. **Menil Collection**, 1515 Sul Ross, Tel: 525-9400. **Museum of Fine Arts**, 1001 Bissonnet, Tel: 639-7300. **Rothko Chapel**, 3900 Yupon St., Tel: 524-9389. **Sam Houston Historical Park**, 1100 Bagby, adjacent to Texaco Heritage Plaza. **Space Center Houston**, 25 miles south on I-45, exit 2351, Tel: 244-2100.

Tourist Information
Visitor Center, 3300 Main St. Further information: **Greater Houston C & V Bureau**, 801 Congress, Houston, TX 77002, Tel: 227-3100.

73

FROM
LOS ANGELES
TO LAS VEGAS

MOJAVE DESERT
DEATH VALLEY
NEVADA
LAS VEGAS

Gray and monolithic, the sprawling metropolis of Los Angeles rests under its own blanket of smog and fumes. The sky over the highway up ahead is brilliant blue, the hues of the earth become browner and browner as one goes along, and the landscape more monotonous and barren. Every mile is a step further from the great city and one closer to the desert lands of California and Nevada. The road is lined with dried-up salt ponds, long abandoned ghost towns, bizarre rock formations that rise into the sky. And finally there is the desert itself, Death Valley and the Mojave Desert, at first glance dead lunar landscapes, and yet so full of hidden life. Then, at the end of this 450-mile journey (720 km), there's Las Vegas, a glistening and seductive world of roulette, blackjack, one-armed bandits arising like a mirage in the midst of the desert.

THE MOJAVE DESERT
"Salt of the Earth"

The eastward route from the sprawling houses of Los Angeles into California's desert wilderness leads first to **Barstow** over Interstate 15. This modest town,

Previous pages: Do the neon signs deliver what they promise? Left: View of Death Valley from Zabriskie Point.

originally established as a railway junction, has few if any sights to hold one's attention. Still a tour of the **Mojave River Valley Museum** and the **Desert Information Center** is worth the effort. Both give information on life in the desert and give advice on how to deal with this extreme form of nature that every tourist should read and heed.

A few miles after Barstow comes **Calico**, whose silver deposits attracted over 3,500 prospectors in the 1880s. As the market price for silver started dropping after 1896, so did the population of Calico. In the end all that remained was a ghost town which has since been restored. Tours through the 30-mile-long (48 km) **Silver King Mine** are a must for anyone curious about the job of silver mining or eager to try out panning, a drink at the saloon, or a ride on an old choo-choo train. If absolutely intent on spending the night, you can try the nearby camping grounds. To the north of Barstow is a historic attraction of a different kind: Fossilized insects and other animals incrusted in the rocks of **Rainbow Basin** and **Owl Canyon** prove once again that at some time millions of years ago, the desert, which seems lifeless today, was a lively and fertile place.

The road into the Mojave Desert passes by numerous dried-up salt ponds

77

before entering **Soda Springs**, which lies on the banks of the eponymous (and dried-up) lake. Once upon a time the town served as a foreward post out in the desert; then cowboys used it to water their horses and rest their bones; finally it became a spa with the odd name of Zzyxx. How this moniker came about is still the subject of much debate among the locals, but at any rate the days of healing waters here are no longer.

Excursions southward into the eastern Mojave Desert can be started from **Baker**. At first glance this high altitude plateau, which lies between 3,000 and 5,000 ft (930 and 1,500 m) above sea level, appears entirely void of life. However, in addition to a fauna of desert rabbits, turtles and coyotes, the desert also boasts quite a flora, which explodes with color in the springtime. Most impressive are the high cactus trees which produce large flowers. Otherwise the only major

Above: Badwater in Death Valley is the lowest point in the continent.

sight in the midst of this aridity is south of **Kelso**. Spelunkers in particular will enjoy the **Mitchell Caverns Natural Preserve**, an extensive system of sandstone caves.

One thing the Mojave has is sun, of course, and it has therefore become a site for those seeking to harness sunlight for energy. One such power plant in Kramer Junction even operates commercially.

Highway 127 heads back north into the famous Death Valley.

DEATH VALLEY: IT'S ALIVE!

Dreaming rather than dying is what primarily comes to mind when first confronted with the vast palette of earth tones that make up the valley. The Native Americans called it "burning earth," but the white man's awe-inspiring name stuck thanks to the first settlers, the so-called Forty-Niners who came through the region in the mid-19th century on their long trek west to the gold mines of California. For many, the road of life it-

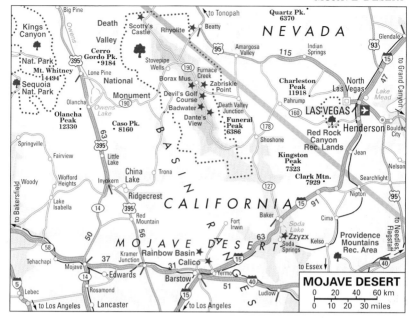

self ended in this inferno. Travelers nowadays survive the summer temperatures of up to 45° C with air conditioning (the record high was measured in 1913 at 57° C), but step out of the car and you will get a feel of the sheer power of the climate.

Death Valley is indeed a valley of extremes. **Badwater**, at the lowest point in the Western Hemisphere (282 ft or 85 m below sea level), is only 80 miles away from Mt. Whitney, the highest mountain of the Sierra Nevada (14,494 ft). Death Valley consists of sand dunes, stretches of salt, canyons and strangely-shaped mountain ranges. The daytime heat is in sharp contrast to the cold at night. And in the midst of this apparently lifeless landscape, one finds nearly 40 species of animals (lizards and snakes, of course) and plants that are unique on the planet.

Canyons and Ghost Towns

Anyone driving through Death Valley should make sure their car is in good working order, and should carry enough drinking water and paraphernalia for emergencies. Do not forget water for the car radiator. The best place to begin a crossing of the valley is at **Death Valley Junction** on Rte. 190. At **Furnace Creek** a visitors' center provides maps and informative brochures on the geological past of the desert.

During the last Ice Age, the valley was covered by a saltwater lake that gradually dried up. What remained was the desert with its patches of salt. The mountain ranges at the end of the valley form a barrier against any humidity from the Pacific Ocean, hence annual rainfall amounts to no more than two inches.

Some of the most fascinating panoramas are on the way to the visitors' center on Rte. 190. The most famous, and therefore unfortunately most overrun by fellow-travelers, is **Zabriskie Point**, which opens up on a lunar landscape of ragged and ragged rocks, a natural study in reds and browns. Sunrise and sunset add an almost unearthly touch of gold to this wild

tableau. To the south a side road leads to **Golden Canyon** (beneath Zabriskie Point), the **Devil's Golf Course**, and finally **Dante's View**, from where one can see Badwater.

Heading back north on Rte. 178 one bypasses the **Devil's Cornfield** and **Mosaic Canyon**, before reaching the old ghost town of **Skidoo**. This old relic from the history of the Wild West tells the story of one of the many gold and silver mines. Thousands of adventurers were lured to this place by the dream that the nation's biggest nuggets could be found below the surface of Death Valley.

In fact only a handful of industrialists hit the jackpot in the 1880s, and that by mining not gold but natural deposits of borax, a mineral used in glass-making, ceramics and agriculture, among other things. A few miles north of the visitors' center lie the ruins of the **Harmony**

Above: Hoover Dam, masterpiece of American engineering. Right: Las Vegas, den of iniquity and family excursion point.

Borax Works, one of the first to be established in the region.

If you are in no hurry to reach Las Vegas, then drive further north to **Scotty's Castle**, which has become something of a legend. Scotty, an adventurer, gold-digger and a star in Buffalo Bill's Wild West Show, got together with a Chicago businessman named Albert M. Johnson, and built a playful, castle-like hotel. The building is supposed to be at the entrance of a large gold mine, but in fact this bit of news is nothing more than an ingenious PR device.

CROSSING NEVADA

The 140-mile (224-km) drive to **Las Vegas** on Highway 95 takes you straight through what is known as Nevada's "Pioneer Territory." Stretches of stark and uninviting desert alternate with extensive mountain ranges.

Some of the most interesting ghost towns can be found on this trip, all of them petrified testimonies to the gold fever that once upon a time gripped the entire nation sending herds of hopeful prospectors westward. One of the most picturesque of these old gold-digger camps is **Rhyolite** near **Beatty**. At the climax of silver mining, in 1907, over 6,000 people lived here in the midst of the desert. What is left comprises a few buildings such as the Vegas & Tonopah Railroad Depot, the Porter Store, and the Rhyolite Bottle House. Lately a few people have even moved back, no doubt reclusive types. As a partly-inhabited ghost town, Rhyolite is certainly one of a kind.

On the way to Las Vegas another interesting stop is **Amargosa Valley**, a little town with a few motels, gas stations and fast food establishments. The Amargosa sand dunes nearby were created millions of years ago when a lake dried up leaving the sandy bottom exposed.

The ride southward can be continued either on the rather dull I-95 or on the longer Rte. 160. The latter is of particular interest to wine connoisseurs, as in Pahrump Nevada's only wine maker offers tours of its facilities and samplings. The **Pahrump Valley Winery**, with its brilliant white Mediterranean-type buildings, might just as well be in Italy as on the barren soil of the Nevada desert. Some of the wines made here have earned international prizes.

When neon advertisements begin lighting the horizon, proclaiming the promising message of instant fortunes at the gambling table, you know you are nearing Las Vegas.

LAS VEGAS, HERE I COME!
Artificial Glitz in the Desert

It's one of history's ironies that **Las Vegas**, considered by many Americans to be the most sinful of Babylons on the continent, should have started its life as a pious Mormon settlement in the 1850s. The founding fathers of the sect are probably turning in their graves in light of the gambling that has taken over the city's economy.

Las Vegas (which means "fields" in Spanish) became a wild den of sin in the 1930s, when Nevada became the only state to legalize gambling. Coincidentally, work on the nearby Hoover Dam began at the same time, and suddenly the little community experienced a boom as thousands of construction workers flocked to the town to spend their hard-earned money and their free time. The somewhat unruly atmosphere of those early days is no longer. Las Vegas in fact projects an image of clean fun. Those in search of topless waitresses, off-color nightclub shows or daring stripteases will be disappointed in Las Vegas.

This half-world does continue to exist but it is limited in scope, and the average tourist will hardly encounter any of it anywhere. The only half-way decent striptease show you can still find is beyond the city limits, at the Palomino. Since the beginning of the 1990s the town fathers have been trying to clean up

Las Vegas' reputation. Prostitution and other forms of dubious entertainment were banned from the theaters and big hotels. They can only be found at the edge of town or on the surrounding highways. A whole slew of gigantic new hotels sporting adventure and theme parks, have helped turn Las Vegas into a place where the whole family can engage in good, clean, traditional American fun, perhaps in the sense of what Republicans refer to as family values. The bottom line is impressive. In 1993 the city entertained a record 22 million guests (over one-third of them under 30 years of age).

Nothing ventured, nothing gained?

Most hotels and casinos are lined up cheek-by-jowl in downtown Las Vegas along the so-called Las Vegas Strip which lies parallel to Interstate 15. In the

Above and right: Gambling cathedral – respectable housewives succumb here to the magic of gambling (Luxor Casino).

past few years the Strip has grown into a fine entertainment district.

To get a feeling of the *genius loci* one should by all means try a few rounds of roulette, blackjack, bingo or craps at one of the casinos, the **Golden Nugget** or the **Lady Luck**. Around Fremont Street and along the Strip, great, ornate neon advertising shines into the desert sky like some artificial fire inviting people from far and wide to try their luck.

Las Vegas continues to survive from gambling, even though in the meantime nine other states of the union have legalized casinos. Everything in town is aimed at pulling money from the tourist's wallet. Friendly ladies in very tight tops make sure the gambling guests are well furnished with drinks (including alcoholic ones). Various entertainment programs and theme-based architecture are designed to divert one's attention from the fact that gambling can get extremely dull after a while.

Anyone trying his or her luck with a few dollars in hand should keep this in

mind. Already at the airport visitors are greeted by the first slot machines blinking seductively. Prices of hotels and in restaurants are almost absurdly low. Cheap flights ship large groups of tourists to Las Vegas for weekends from every corner of the States. So-called Fun Books offer free coupons for almost every need – from cheap restaurants to discount roulette chips to souvenirs. These coupons can be found at hotels, casinos and of course at the tourist information center.

Waterfalls and Mini-Volcanoes

Between 1991 and 1994 three large hotels were erected in Las Vegas that gave the town its new, cleaner image. These establishments are worth a visit if you're not staying in one of them, and try to avoid gambling in them.

The first is the **MGM Grand Hotel**, whose 5,000 rooms make it the largest accommodations factory in the world. Construction of this huge building shaped like the MGM lion cost over a billion dollars. MGM has tried to revive some of the flair of the good old days with a great deal of elegance and select show programming. Barbra Streisand, for example, performed live here in 1993 after a long hiatus. Opposite the hotel is an amusement park with a large number of joy rides.

The idea behind these neat arrangements in hotels and parks is to keep the kiddies busy while their parents blow their wads at the gambling tables. The city's attempt to be family-friendly is also visible in the pyramidal **Luxor Hotel**, whose interior is made up to look Egyptian with an artificial river and Nile boats. The entertainment park of this hotel has a video game which keeps children and adults fascinated for hours. Its star is the top figure in family identification: Michael Jackson.

The acme of adventure parks, however, is to be found at the **Treasure Island Hotel**. The very name reveals the subject of its theme park, namely pirates and treasures. Every 90 minutes, 20 actors go

83

about performing an extravagant spectacle, a deafening shoot-out with lots of powder and smoke.

Next to all these new hotels and casinos, the older establishments do look a little pale. Nevertheless, you should plan in a visit to the **Mirage** to see the German-born illusionists "Siegfried and Roy." Their peculiar show (with white tigers and a host of other wild animals) is not to everyone's taste, but the staging alone is worth the price.

Other places to see are **Caesar's Palace**, for its pseudo-Roman architecture, the **Excalibur**, and **Circus-Circus**.

Where are the Shows of Yesteryear?

What would Las Vegas be without all the glitzy shows and variety theater? As always, the hotels and theaters of the city continue to offer technically excellent

Above: The pirate plays in the Treasure Island Hotel are one of the new types of attractions in Las Vegas.

programs, but somewhat tasteless by European standards. The ticket prices for the cocktail shows (early evening), dinner shows (evening), and late-night or midnight shows are surprisingly low. The price rises when some big star appears on stage, but these have tended to stay away in recent years.

A relic of the old days are the Wedding Chapels, which are not churches, but rather privately-operated marriage license bureaus which can marry or divorce people in record time. Ever since the state of Nevada loosened marriage laws in the year 1931, any couple can get married here in an express procedure. All you need is proof that you are over 18 years of age. Witnesses are provided by the Wedding Chapel should the couple not have any on hand. The chapels themselves offer a wide range of services for every taste, from pink, cheap mariages with band music, to serious black-tie affairs with a real organ. The honeymooners can then go to the casino to play off some of their wedding presents.

MOJAVE DESERT AND DEATH VALLEY

All phone numbers have area code 619.

Accommodation

LUXURY: **Furnace Creek Inn**, Box 1, Death Valley, CA 92328 (one mile south on CA 190), Tel: 786-2361.
MODERATE: **Best Western Desert Villa**, 1984 E Main St., Barstow, CA 92311, Tel: 256-1781. **Saddle West Hotel & Casino**, Hwy. 160, PO Box 234, Pahrump, NV 89041, Tel: 702/727-5953. **Stagecoach Hotel & Casino**, State Rt. 95, PO Box 836, Beatty, NV 89003, Tel: 702/553-2419. **Stove Pipe Wells Village**, CA 190, Death Valley, CA 92328, Tel: 786-2387.
BUDGET: **Sleep Inn**, 1861 W Main St., Barstow, CA 92311, Tel: 256-1300.

Guest Ranch

Furnace Creek Ranch, Box 1, Death Valley, CA 92328 (on CA 190), Tel: 786-2307.

Camping

For information on camping at the Death Valley: Tel: 619/786-2331.

Attractions, Museums and Parks

Barstow Station, 1611 East Main St., Barstow, Tel: 256-3839. Unique Wild West railroad station now serving as a shopping plaza. **Borax Museum and Mining Exhibition**, Furnace Creek Ranch, Death Valley, Tel: 786-2345. **Death Valley Visitor Center at Furnace Creek**, Tel: 786-2331. **Calico Early Man Archaelogical Site**, 150 Coolwater Lane, Barstow, Tel: 256-3591.**Calico Ghosttown Regional Park**, 10 miles east on I-15, near Barstow, Tel: 254-2122. **Central Nevada Museum**, Logan Field Rd., Tonopah, Tel: 702/482-9676. Open-air exhibits on Nevada's history and the crucial role of mining. **Death Valley National Monument**, National Park Services, Death Valley, Tel: 786-2331. **East Mojave National Scenic Area**, Needles, Tel: 326-3896. **Fossil Falls**, on Hw.y 395, north of Ridgecrest, near Little Lake. Dry waterfall and lava flow, an old Indian village and Indian rock art. **Maturango Museum**, 100 E Las Flores Ave., Ridgecrest, Tel: 375-6900. Exhibits on cultural and natural history of the Mojave Desert. **Mitchell Caverns Natural Preserve**, Essex (near Kelso), Tel: 389-2281. **Mojave River Valley Museum**, 270 E Virginia Way, Barstow, Tel: 256-5452. **Opal Canyon Mine**, 17 miles south of Ridgecrest, on Hwy. 14. Guides Tours of a rare raw opal mine. **Pahrump Valley Winery**, 3810 Homestead Rd., Pahrump, Tel: 702/727-6900. **Rainbow Basin/Owl Canyon**, 10 miles north of Barstow, on Fort Irwin Rd., Tel: 256-3591. **Rhyolite State Historic Site**, near Beatty, Tel: 702/553-2424. **Scotty's Castle**, Death Valley, Tel: 786-

2392. **Soda Springs**, exit I-15 at Zzyxx Rd. (six miles west of Baker), Tel: 256-8617.

Tourist Information

Barstow Area Chamber of Commerce, 408 E Fredricks, Barstow, CA 92311, Tel: 256-8617. **Beatty Chamber of Commerce**, 4th /Main St., PO Box 956, Beatty, NV 89003, Tel: 702/553-2424. **Death Valley Chamber of Commerce**, PO Box 157, Shoshone, CA 92384, Tel: 852-4524. **Desert Information Center Barstow**, 831 Barstow Rd., Tel: 256-8313.

LAS VEGAS

All phone numbers have area code 702.

Accommodation

LUXURY: **Luxor Hotel & Casino**, 3900 Las Vegas Blvd. S, Las Vegas, NV 89119, Tel: 1-800-288-1000. *MODERATE*: **Caesar's Palace**, 3570 Las Vegas Blvd., Las Vegas, NV 89109, Tel: 731-7110. **Circus-Circus**, Box 14967, 2880 Las Vegas Blvd. S, Las Vegas, NV 89114, Tel: 734-0410. **Excalibur Hotel & Casino**, 3850 Las Vegas Blvd., Las Vegas, NV 89109-4300, Tel: 597-7777. **The Mirage**, 3400 Las Vegas Blvd., Las Vegas, NV 89109, Tel: 791-7111. *BUDGET:* **Arizona Charlie's**, 740 S Decatur Ave., west of the Strip, Las Vegas, NV 89107, Tel: 258-5200, reservations, Tel: 800342-2695. **Westward Ho Hotel & Casino**, 2900 Las Vegas Blvd. S, Las Vegas, NV 89109, Tel: 731-2900. **Showboat**, 2800 E Fremont St., Las Vegas, NV 89104, Tel: 385-9123, reservations, Tel: 800/826-2800.

Attractions, Museums and Parks

Bonnie Springs Old Nevada, 20 miles west on Charleston Blvd., Tel: 875-4191. Historic Wild West town, offering live programs and a petting zoo. **Golden Nugget**, 129 E Fremont St., at Casino Center, Tel: 385-7111. **Imperial Palace Auto Collection**, 3535 Las Vegas Blvd., (5th floor of hotel), Tel: 731-3311. Odd auto collection of vehicles once owned by historical figures. **Lady Luck Casino**, 206 N 3rd St., Tel: 477-3000. **Las Vegas Art Museum**, 333 W Washington Ave., Tel: 647-4300. **Las Vegas Natural History Museum**, 900 Las Vegas Blvd. N, Tel: 384-3466. Exhibits on American wildlife. **Red Rock Canyon Recreation Lands**, 18 miles west on W Charleston Blvd., near Las Vegas, Tel: 363-1921. Offers spectacular view of some of the most scenic gorges in the Las Vegas area. Picknicking an camping possible. **Treasure Island Hotel**, 3300 Las Vegas Blvd.. large adventure park featuring treasure hunts.

Tourist Information

Las Vegas C & V Authority, Convention Center, 3150 Paradise Rd., Las Vegas, NV 89109, Tel: 892-0711.

FROM LAS VEGAS TO THE GRAND CANYON

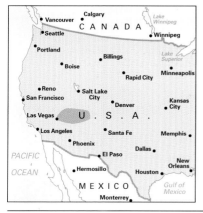

ZION NATIONAL PARK
BRYCE AND GLEN CANYONS
THE GRAND CANYON –
NORTH AND SOUTH RIM

It has been seen thousands of times, miles of celluloid have been developed with its image forever preserved in emulsion, every one of its nooks and crannies has been filmed in advertisements or for the silver screen. The Grand Canyon, subject of all this attention, seems to have degenerated into a a cliché of sorts. Yet being there, standing on the edge of this abyss and daring to look down into the depths, suddenly all the past visions disappear. The clichés drown in the golden or fiery light cast by the sunset over the Grand Canyon. When that happens, it is beauty pure and unadulterated, and cannot be compared to any photo or image produced by the human hand.

From Las Vegas to ZionNational Park

Discovering the Grand Canyon or renewing one's acquaintance with it, is one of the aims of this 500-mile (800-km) tour, which should last about a week. It begins in Las Vegas, heads northward to the little-known northern rim of the Canyon, veers westward to the National Park, and ends at the Canyon's popular southern border.

Previous pages: Overview of Grand Canyon from Dead Horse Point. Left: Bryce Canyon.

Highway 93 steers an eastward course out of Las Vegas to the wonderful **Lake Mead National Recreation Area**, an expansive tract of land where many gambling-weary Las Vegans or visitors come to find rest. The lake itself is 115 miles (184 km) long and cuts quite a peculiar image out in the middle of the Nevada desert, with its sand beaches, bathing resorts and centers for any number of aquatic sports. The Visitors' Center in **Boulder City** provides information about the lake and the great **Hoover Dam** that was built nearby. This gigantic construction, 707 feet high and 1,195 feet long, dams the Colorado River to form Lake Mead. This masterwork of American engineering was built in the 1930s as one of the NRA jobs programs designed to help pull America out of the Great Depression. The power plants that feed from Hoover Dam still provide neighboring states with electricity.

The narrow Rte. 147, called Northshore Road, meanders along Lake Mead towards the north, ultimately leading into **Overton**. Making a stop at one of the resorts on the way is a pleasant way to take a break, such as **Boulder Beach**, **Callville** or **Echo Bay**, which do unfortunately tend to be overcrowded during the season. There are also a number of camping sites on the way. **Overton**, too, has a very fine beach and an adjacent camping site right on the waterfront. This little community, home to about 3,000 people, was originally founded by the Mormons. But between 500 and 1200 AD Anasazi Indians lived in the region. What relics of their culture remain are displayed in the **Lost City Museum of Archaeology** in Overton.

The traces of this vanished civilization can also be examined in the wilderness. Drive south from Overton, then join Hwy. 169 to the **Valley of Fire State Park**: the Anasazi left rock drawings on the almost unbelievably shaped sandstone formations. The rock here shines in every imaginable shade of red and brown, and whether at sunrise or sunset, the Valley of Fire truly earns its name. Another highly impressive sight is **Rainbow Vista**, appropriately named after its wide palette of colors, and **Silica Dome**, a brilliant white natural creation of quartz. The Indians had good reason to hold this place in special reverence.

The itinerary continues on I-15, a course that steers through a steppe-like desert landscape, a veritable portrait of the Wild West in reds, sandstone pinks and brown.

Mesquite is where you cross over into the state of Arizona, before entering Utah, but looking out the car window you'll hardly notice the difference.

The little town of **St. George** warrants a brief stop, be that merely to discover another side of Mormon history. The community was founded by Brigham Young in the 1860s mainly as a place to escape the rather unfriendly climate of Salt Lake City. The sight to see in town is the shining white tower of the Mormon church, the first ever in Utah. The brethren had to move many tons of earth and stone in order to get a solid foundation in the muddy soil. 17,000 tons of sandstone had to be quarried for the temple itself. St. George soon earned the nickname

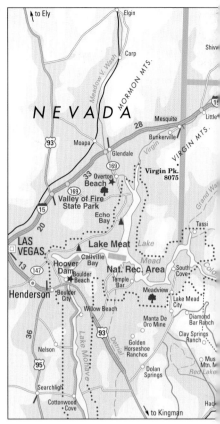

"Dixie," because Brigham Young considered planting cotton in the area. The project failed, but Young, one of the founders of the Church of the Latter Day Saints, lived until his death in St. George. His house, the **Brigham Young Winter Home**, is open to the public nowadays.

ZION NATIONAL PARK

Brigham Young is credited with having once said: "If there is a place on this earth that nobody else wants, that's the place I'm hunting for." The pious settler making his way west sought and ultimately found what we know today as Salt Lake City. His thoughts, however, included the entire state of Utah, which

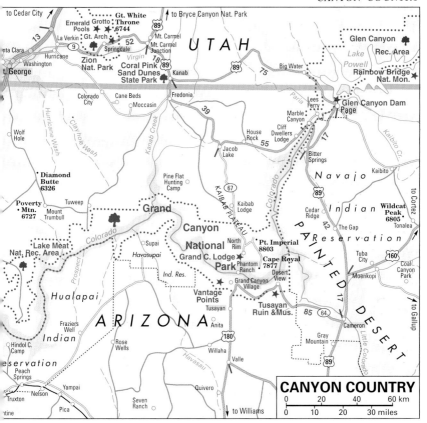

boasts extremely attractive and dramatic landscapes, but is rather poor when it comes to rich and fertile prairies or gold for that matter. Gold-diggers and pioneers looking for their respective fortunes tended to shy away from Utah. The state was therefore settled rather late, owing in part to its host of inaccessible canyons, some of which have not been explored to this day. The local tribes of Native Americans, the Utes, the Shoshones and Paiutes, had the place to themselves for quite a while.

Zion National Park, with its canyons, caverns, sheer cliffs and deep valleys, is Utah's pride and joy when it comes to natural splendors. Since the Mormons were the first settlers of European descent to leave their traces here, many of the names are drawn from the Bible.

The best way to take in some of the natural glories here is by driving eastward on Rte. 9. The Park's Visitors' Center is located near **Springdale**. There are two possibilities at this point: either the **Zion Canyon Scenic Drive** which makes a detour in northerly direction, or catching the eastward extension of Rte. 9.

The Scenic Drive meanders along the **Virgin River** on the bed of Zion Canyon. Quite a few hiking paths have been laid out in the wilderness all along the road. Particularly pretty are the climbs up to **Angel's Landing** above the **Grotto** picnic spot, and the path to **Observation Point**. The hikes up to **Emerald Pools** or

91

over to **Hidden Canyon** are somewhat difficult, but the courageous hiker will be rewarded with some especially delightful panoramic views of the valley. A word of warning: the hikes are long and arduous, and one should be in good condition and keep an eye on the weather situation. If you'd rather stay in the car for your tour, your sightseeing will be limited to the fascinating rock formations, among others the famous **Great White Throne**, a white and red monolith, and the **Temple of Sinawava**. The latter is a kind of semicircle whose two pillars definitely make it look like an ancient Greek or Roman temple.

At the end of the Scenic Drive is the so-called **Gateway to the Narrows Trail**, which leads to the famous sandstone formations that seem to touch each other hundreds of feet overhead. The path can only be done on foot through the

Above: Hiking in Zion National Park. Right: Lake Powell has developed into a popular watersport center.

Virgin River, and though relatively short (two miles), it is by no means easy.

The eastward extension of Rte. 9 leads by the **Great Arch** on to an extraordinary landscape of rocks and cliffs whose sheer dimensions and the sense of space generated is second only to the Grand Canyon.

BRYCE CANYON AND GLEN CANYON

Further north on Hwy. 89, Rte. 12 takes you to the entrance to **Bryce Canyon**, which is relatively small but memorable. It is by definition not really a canyon, but rather the broken-off edge of **Paunsaugunt Plateau**, which provides a broad view of a spectacular landscape of red and brown sandstone rocks carved into tall needles by millenia of rain and wind. The Paiute Indians who lived here had a more descriptive name for the canyon: "The place where red rocks stand like men in a bowl-shaped canyon."

This park, too, has a scenic drive for its visitors. It goes for 18 miles all the way to

Bryce Point, passing by the most enchanting and peculiar rock formations. Another recommended way to visit the canyon is to walk **Rim Trail**, which, as the name suggests, follows the broken edge of the plateau.

Kodachrome Basin State Park, which lies off Rte. 12, is another spot where many a visitor has tested the film of the same name. Again, the main sight here is the glowing red sandstone sculpted by the vagaries of nature into formations such as the **Grosvenor's Arch**. The park also includes remote, solitary camping sites for the pleasure of outdoorsmen and women.

Follow Hwy. 89 southeastwards to the little town of **Kanab**, shortly before the Arizona border. The **Coral Pink Sand Dunes State Park** is just a few miles away, a very beautiful natural reserve with endless, reddish desert landscapes. It is unfortunately often overcrowded. Hollywood discovered the park quite a while ago, and some of the film sets are still in place for visitors.

Geographically speaking, Kanab lies right in the midst of America's most beautiful collection of canyons. To the south is the all-time favorite Grand Canyon. To the north is Bryce Canyon, and to the east Glen Canyon at Lake Powell.

Staying on Rte. 89, which heads in a southeasterly direction, one comes by **Glen Canyon Recreation Area**, which sprawls about gigantic **Lake Powell** (186 miles/300 km long). The lake is not natural: It came into being when the Glen Canyon Dam was built on the Colorado River. It has, however, become a center for aquatic activities, with its almost 2,000 miles of beaches and little bays. The town of **Page**, to the south of the dam, is a lively holiday resort, and an excellent point of departure for boat tours of the lake. The favorite tour is to the **Rainbow Bridge National Monument** to the northeast. This bridge of sandstone, with a span of 260 ft, constitutes the world's largest natural arch.

GRAND CANYON – THE NORTH

A few hours driving southward from Page will bring you to the northern rim of the **Grand Canyon**.

Military intelligence is indeed sometimes a contradiction in terms. About 150 years ago, when the American officer Joseph C. Ives led a small force on an exploratory expedition along the Colorado River, he sent back a report on the Grand Canyon that stated, "Altogether valueless; ours has been the first and will doubtless be the last party of whites to visit this profitless locality." The poor lieutenant made two mistakes in the report. First, a Spanish explorer named de Cardenas had already spotted the canyon in 1540. And second, after Ives, Americans, white and otherwise, and droves of tourists from around the world, flocked to the Grand Canyon. In fact, it and the

Above: Young Indian boys sell waterskins for the descent into the Grand Canyon.
Right: Ascent with mules is less strenuous.

Colorado River here (*colorado* in Spanish meaning colored red) have become one of the world's favorite destinations.

One attraction are the uncanny proportions of this canyon, which is the largest in the world: 280 miles long and from half a mile to 18 miles wide. This is one of those places where man feels tiny in a gigantic world of natural wonders.

The northern rim is not nearly as spectacular as the southern part of the National Park; on the other hand, it suffers far less from overcrowding. Only one-tenth of the five million visitors who come here each year actually wander off to the north, and so you have a greater feeling here of being alone with nature. Whether on the north rim or the south, a first-time visitor will be overwhelmed by the grandeur of the Grand Canyon.

The North Rim lies an average of 8,000 feet above sea level, between 1,000 and 2,000 feet higher than the South Rim. The bulk of the northern section rests on the **Kaibab Plateau**, an old Paiute Indian word meaning "mountain lying down."

Although the two rims are only ten miles apart from one another, the highway connecting the two is 215 miles long.

The best observation points on the North Rim are easily accessible by good roads. **Cape Royal Road** runs southeast to **Walhalla Outlook**, **Cape Royal**, and **Angel's Window**. One of the finest lookouts of the entire Grand Canyon area is **Point Imperial**, whose altitude of 8,803 feet makes it the highest spot in the Grand Canyon National Park. It offers a broad panorama of the entire canyon and a breathtaking view of **Marble Canyon** and the **Painted Desert**.

The road leads back westwards to the **Supai Tunnel**, the Grand Canyon Lodge Hotel, as well as **Bright Angel Point**, the site of the Visitors' Center. If you register early enough and have no fear of heights, you may want to try hiking one of the trails down to the bottom of the Grand Canyon. These hikes on foot or mule back are guided. The mule way is only recommendable for people with a sense of adventure and a resilient backside, as the trips do last one or two days, which can be quite exhausting. Both **North** and **South Kaibab Trails** take you all the way down to **Phantom Ranch**, where beds are available, or as an alternative a camping site. There are some shorter hikes down the canyon to the west: **Widforss** and **Tiyo Point Trails**.

A ride through the canyon is also a bit of time travel through the geological history of Planet Earth. 10 to 20 million years ago, the Colorado River dug its way down into the soft sandstone. From top to bottom you can see the layers of sedimentary stone (sandstone and chalk) from the Paleozoic Era: the Permian period (230 million years ago), the Carboniferous (330 million years), Devonian (370 million), and Cambrian (550 million). Hard and shimmering black, the Vishnu shale and Zoroaster granite at the foot of the canyon date from Precambrian Time, which makes them about 2 billion years old, among the oldest stone visible on the surface of the earth. The newer layers contain fossils of animals, insects

and plants, mutely narrating stories about the flora and fauna of long-past epochs of our planet's history.

GRAND CANYON – THE SOUTH

The South Rim of the Canyon, accessible via Hwys. 89 and 64, also provide visitors with spectacular views and fascinating insights. Rte. 64, the **East Rim Drive**, already has its fair share of grandiose lookouts between **Cameron** and **Tusayan**. One of the favorites (which means that in summer it is overrun with fellow tourists) is **Desert Point**. The Native American cultures that once lived in this area are documented nearby at the **Tusayan Ruins and Museum**.

Other high points of the trip before reaching the Visitors' Center in **Grand Canyon Village** are the observation spots of **Grandview Point** and **Yavapai Point**. The latter has a **museum** that

Above: Wet adventure – rafting on the Colorado River.

gives a good rundown of the geological history of the canyon.

Private cars are not allowed along the **West Rim Drive** from May to the end of September. This does, however, have the best lookouts, so one is advised to pick up the shuttle bus in Grand Canyon Village, which ferries visitors to the best spots, including **Hopi** and **Pima Points**.

Two trails lead from the South Rim down to the bottom of the canyon. Sloping continuously downward, **Bright Angel Trail** is hard on the knees and a favorite with mule tours; walkers have to watch out for fresh manure. **South Kaibab Trail** is more beautiful, more solitary, and steeper, with some great views. You can descend both trails in about 4 hours; the ascent takes 7 to 8 hours.

You can also view the canyon's grandeur from a birds-eye perspective: tenseater airplanes offer tours, and there are even helicopter tours from Las Vegas. But only those whose motto is "Some like it wet" should attempt the ever-popular rubber-raft trip down the Colorado.

UTAH AND ITS CANYONS
Accommodation
MODERATE: **Best Western Ruby's Inn**, Box 1, Bryce, UT 84764, half a mile N of Bryce Canyon Park entrance on UT 63, Tel: 801/834-5341. **Bryce Canyon Lodge**, on UT 63, Cedar City, Box 400, UT 84720, Tel: 801/834-5361. **Greene Gate Village**, 76 W Tabernacle St., St. George, UT 84770, Tel: 801/628-6999. Victorian manor with wonderful rooms. **Zion Lodge**, Box 400, (on UT 9, five miles of park entrance) Cedar City, UT 84720, Tel: 801/772-3213. Spectacular view of Zion National Park. **Holiday Inn**, 1575 W 200 North, Cedar City, UT 84720, near airport, Tel: 801/568-8888.
BUDGET: **Bryce Canyon Pines**, Box 43, Bryce, UT 84764, 6 miles NW of Bryce Canyon Park entrance, Tel: 801/834-5441. **Gold Strike Inn & Casino**, east on US 93, three miles west of Hoover Dam, Boulder City, NV 89005, Tel: 702/293-5000. Nice view of Lake Mead. **Rodeway Inn**, 281 S Main St., Cedar City, UT 84720, Tel: 801/586-9916.
Campgrounds
Echo Bay Resort, Via Star Route, Overton, NV 89040, Tel: 702/394-4000.
Overton Beach Resort, Box 96, Boulder City, NV 89040, Tel: 702/394-4040. In the Lake Mead area.
Attractions, Museums and Parks
Brigham Young Winter Home, 200 North/100 West Sts., St. George, Tel: 801/673-2517. **Bryce Canyon National Park**, Information Tel. 801/834-5322. **Coral Pink Sand Dunes State Park**, 14 miles northwest on US 89, 12 miles south on a country road, near Kanab, Tel: 801/874-2408. **Glen Canyon Recreation Area and Lake Powell**, 68 miles east via US 89, Visitor Center on UT 276, near Bullfrog, Tel: 801/684-2243. Park Headquarters in Page, AZ, Tel: 602/645-2511. **Hoover Dam**, Hwy. 93, near Boulder City, Tel: 702/293-8367. **Hoover Dam Museum**, 444 Hotel Plaza, Boulder City, Tel: 702/294-1988. **Lake Mead National Recreational Area**, Information: 601 Nevada Hwy., Boulder City, Tel: 702/293-8907. **Lost City Museum**, 721 So. Hwy. 169, Overton, Tel: 702/397-2193. **Rainbow Bridge National Monument**, Information Tel: 602/645-2511. **Temple Visitor Center in St. George**, 440 S/300 East, St. George, Tel: 801/673-5181. **Valley of Fire State Park**, 18 miles southeast on NV 169, near Overton, Tel: 702/397-2088. **Zion National Park**, Springdale, Information Tel: 801/772-3256.
Sports and Outdoor Activities
Black Canyon River Raft Tours, 1297 Boulder Hwy., Boulder City, Tel: 702/293-3776. **Boat Trips on Lake Powell**, on UT 276, departures from Halls Crossing and Bullfrog, Tel: 602/278-8888. **Lake Mead Cruises**, Boulder City, Tel:

702/293-6180. Paddlewheeler cruises on Lake Mead. **River Mountain Hiking Trail**, c/o Boulder City Visitors Center, address see below. Five miles roundtrip hike, providing wonderful views of Lake Mead. **Scenic Flights over Glen Canyon**, Page Airport, on US 89, Tel: 602/645-2494. **Zion National Park Horseback Trips**, trail rides start at Zion Lodge, near Zion National Park, Tel: 801/772-3967.
Tourist Information
Boulder City Visitors Center, 100 Nevada Hwy., Boulder City, NV 89005, Tel: 702/294-1220. **Page/Lake Powell Chamber of Commerce**, 638 Elm St., Box 727, Page, AZ 86040, Tel: 602/645-2741.

GRAND CANYON
Accommodation
LUXURY: **El Tovar**, Box 699, South Rim, AZ 86023, three miles west of entrance on US 180 (AZ 64), Tel: 602/638-2401.
MODERATE: **Best Western Grand Canyon Squire Inn**, Box 130, South Rim, AZ 86023, seven miles south on US 180, Tel: 602/638-2681.
Grand Canyon Lodge, Box 400, Cedar City, UT 84720, at Canyon North Rim, south of AZ 67, Tel: 602/638-2611.
BUDGET: **Phantom Ranch**, Grand Canyon, c/o Grand Canyon National Park Lodge, PO Box 699, Grand Canyon, AZ 86023, Tel: 602/638-2401.
Campgrounds
Campsites at the **North Rim**, at the **South Rim**, and at **Mather Campground**, Tel: 1-800-365-2267.
Attractions, Parks and Museums
Grand Canyon National Park, Information Tel: 602/638-7888. **Tusayan Musem**, East Rim Dr., 20 miles east of Grand Canyon Village, no phone. **Yavapai Museum**, on rim, one mile east of Grand Canyon Village, no phone.
Sports and Outdoor Activities
Grand Canyon Mule Trips, Grand Canyon, Tel: 602/638-2401. Daily departures at Stone Corrall at the head of Bright Angel Trail. **Grand Canyon Scenic Flights**, 2.5 miles south on US 89-A, near Kanab, UT, Tel: 801/644-2904. Scenic flights are also offered by the Grand Canyon Chamber of Commerce, see below. **Hiking in Grand Canyon Area**, Back Country Reservation Office, PO Box 126, Grand Canyon, AZ 86023. Or apply for permission in person at Back Country desk at Camper Service.
Tourist Information
Grand Canyon Chamber of Commerce, PO Box 3007, Grand Canyon, AZ 86023, Tel: 602/638-2901.

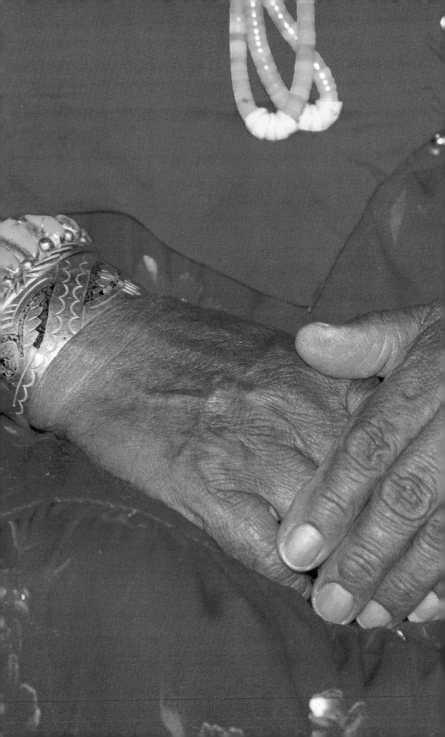

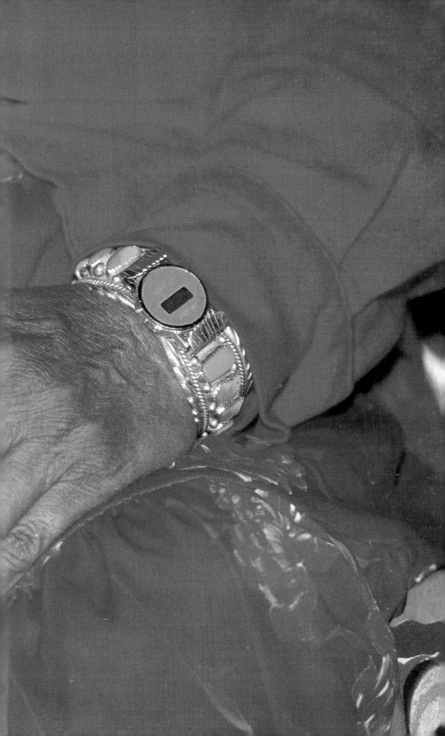

THROUGH NAVAJO AND HOPI COUNTRY

NAVAJO RESERVATION
HOPI RESERVATION
CANYON DE CHELLY
MONUMENT VALLEY
MESA VERDE

A journey through Arizona is a journey through Indian territory. For centuries, well before America was "discovered" by European settlers, some highly civilized tribes lived in this region, squeezing every drop of water they could out of the desert. Nowadays the entire northeastern section of the state is one huge reservation, the land of the Hopi and Navajo tribes. This journey is one through America's history – the darker side of it, with the Indian Wars, in the wake of which entire populations were brutally expelled from their homelands and herded onto reservations.

This itinerary leads from the southern end of the Grand Canyon toward the east through the Navajo and Hopi reservations. The goal is Mesa Verde, where you can see the pre-Columbian cliff dwellings of long-forgotten Indian tribes.

About a week is needed to cover the approximately 750-mile (1200-km) journey.

THROUGH THE NAVAJO RESERVATION

Highway 64 leads from the southern end of the Grand Canyon to **Cameron** in

Previous pages: Colorful costume and jewelry of a Navajo woman. Left: Monument Valley

the Painted Desert. The Indian reservations are easily accessible thanks to the highway system. This is both a blessing and a curse. On the one hand, it allows tourists into the land of the Native Americans; on the other hand it also allows for white lifestyle to penetrate the largest of the Indian reservations in the U.S.A., making it virtually impossible to preserve old traditions, or the Native American languages, intact.

And the Navajo contribution to "white" culture is largely overlooked. Few Americans today realize, for instance, that Navajos were used as radio operators in World War II. They could converse freely over the air waves about anything they wanted, since their complicated language was the one code no enemy force could crack. After the war, these men, who made such a major contribution to their country, were given a few medals and sent back home to the reservation.

200,000 Navajos live in this reservation, which was established in 1878. Today, the Navajo are the largest single Indian tribe on the American continent. They are closely related to the Apache tribes (they are in the same linguistic family), and until the settling of the west, they lived quite peacefully in what is today Arizona and New Mexico. Their

101

only competitors, as it were, were the Hopi Indians.

The Navajo had a semi-nomadic lifestyle, surviving on rudimentary agriculture and sheep husbandry. As white settlers increasingly invaded their tribal grounds beginning in the mid-19th century, they started defending themselves with some vehemence. In spite of the fine leadership of the Apache Chief Geronimo, the war fought by the Navajo and Apache was a vain enterprise from the start.

In the long run, these proud warriors could not hold out against the overwhelming military power of the white man, even using guerilla tactics. With the surrender of Geronimo in 1886, the Indian Wars in the southwestern United States came to an end.

Later the Navajo were allowed to settle a reservation that was on their original tribal grounds. But to this day, the Navajo, like many other Native American tribes, suffer the social plagues of unemployment, alcoholism and general alienation. On the other hand, the reservation has been fairly well off ever since oil was discovered here. Gambling halls are another major source of income. Nevertheless this should not hide the fact that the traditional lifestyle of the Navajo simply cannot be kept alive, and the result is cultural uprooting and disorientation.

Yet even today many ritual dances have survived, and they are not performed for the benefit of curious tourists. Among them are the Navajo fire dance, the Yei-bi-chei dance (in winter), and finally the so-called Enemy Way Dance in summer. If you want to attend, you'll have to arrange for permission first. Note, too, that photography and other forms of recording are not allowed.

Anyone exploring Navajo territory should treat the land and its people with respect. Land is something holy for the Indians, which is why one should never camp out in the wilds. You might fulfill

Above: Classroom in a Navajo Reservation school (Chinle).

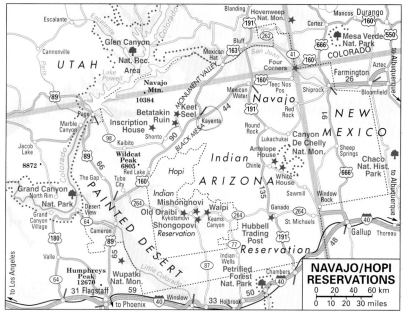

your desire to photograph "real Indians," but don't forget to ask permission first.

THE HOPI:
THE PEACEFUL PEOPLE

The word *koyaanisqatsi* in the language of the Hopi means something like self-made chaos and uncertain future. It seems as if this old word holds the truth to the present life of the Hopi, which is more difficult than ever.

This small reservation, which was founded in 1882, lies in the middle of the Navajo reservation. It is home to 6,000 tribespeople who are struggling in vain to save their old traditions from succumbing to outside (white) influence and to solve old enmities with the Navajos.

The Hopi Indians (the name means peaceful people) are assumed to be descendents of the pre-Columbian Anasazi tribes. Nowadays they live in independent communities that are spread out over three 600-foot-high (187-m) mesas, or plateaus.

On the first mesa is **Walpi**, one of the prettiest Hopi pueblos. Also worth visiting are the three villages on the second mesa, **Mishongnovi**, **Shipaulovi**, and **Shongopovi**, where you will find the Hopi cultural center and simple camping sites. The oldest of the villages, **Old Oraibi** on the third mesa, has been inhabited since 1150. The **Black Mesa**, another plateau that is somewhat to the north was mined for coal and was almost totally destroyed by the 1960s.

How the Hopi came into this area has not yet been figured out. At any rate, the tribe was able to hold off the Navajos thanks to the excellent natural protection afforded by the mesas. As for the Navajos, they arrived in the region during the 16th century, and gradually invaded larger sections of Hopi territory. Coexistence between the two tribes – on the one side the settled Hopi corn farmers, on the other nomadic Navajo hunters – was not always simple. Even today border conflicts continue to irritate relationships between the two peoples, and some Navajo

103

families categorically refuse to relinquish Hopi land. As long as anyone can remember the Hopis have looked down on the Navajos, considering them aggressive and dishonest. They call them *tasavuh*, which means something along the lines of "killers."

The Hopi Indians are famous for their *kachinas*, little holy figures carved of wood and used in religious ceremonies. Ceramics and silver jewelry also make up an important part of Hopi handicrafts. Traditional customs still rule everyday life in the villages on the mesas. Since the Hopis are a sedentary tribe of farmers (with corn as their main crop), their calendar is determined by the regular agricultural year. In spring kachina dancers pray for for rain. In early fall mainly the women dance for a good harvest, throwing little baskets into the crowd of onlookers.

Above and right: Petrified tree trunk in Petriefied Forest National Park – a place in the sun for lizards.

After visiting the mesas one can drive on Rte. 264 to **Ganado**. Close by stands the **Hubell Trading Post**, an old fort dating back to the year 1878. It is the oldest trading post on Navajo territory, and serves nowadays as a museum. Here, Indians sell their handwoven carpets and silver jewelry, and demonstrate their crafts.

Farther east is the town of **Window Rock**, which is the capital of the Navajo Nation, if you will. The democratically elected tribal council, 88 members strong, meets here regularly. The history of the tribe is recounted in the **Navajo Nation Museum**. In the immediate proximity is the **Navajo Nation Zoological and Botanical Park**, exhibiting the fauna and flora that enabled the tribe to survive in the desert. The name Window Rock, by the way, refers to the 50-foot (15 m) natural rock bridge that lies in the midst of a forest of sandstone rock formations.

If you have the time, try to make a short side trip to the **Petrified Forest Na-**

tional Park, which is 26 miles (41 km) east of **Holbroock** on Highway 180. It consists of a forest of fossilized tree trunks, some up to 225 million years old. Back in the days when these trees were growing and green, the area was a fertile swampland, not a desert. Over the space of millions of years the dead trunks were gradually covered with sediments, mainly volcanic silcate ash. Nowadays every annual ring can be clearly identified.

Highway 197 heads back northward to one of the most fascinating testimonials to the great Indian culture.

PURE HISTORY: CANYON DE CHELLY

Canyon de Chelly (pronounced *de-shay*) was a sanctified place for the Navajo tribes for centuries. Even today, tourists can only explore a small part of the canyon – a 2.5-mile (4 km) marked path – alone. You won't get very far without an Indian guide, and out of respect you shouldn't even try. Unfortunately, even with a guide, most of the cliff caves, many of which once served as dwellings, are not accessible. The 16-mile (25 km) **Rim Drive** along the edge of the canyon allows visitors to see the most important sights from their cars.

The Navajos settled the canyon around 1700, but research suggests that tribes had been living here for centuries before, attracted to the area because of its fertility. Farming is to this date one of the regional mainstays.

Around 60 dwellings are still extant, the oldest ones being about 2,000 years old. The most interesting ones are the **White House**, the **Antelope House**, and the **Mummy Cave**.

The canyon did achieve rather sorry fame in 1864 when the legendary Christopher "Kit" Carson trapped the last Navajo warriors in the valley and forced them to surrender or die of hunger. During the previous five months he had conducted a war of attrition, destroying fields, capturing herds, and stalking the Navajos

across 300 miles (480 km) of prairie. The Indians fled into the Canyon de Chelly, assuming it was impregnable. But Carson ordered troops to the other end of the canyon, and within two weeks the war was over. The Navajos had no choice but to let themselves be herded into the reservation they still inhabit today.

Highways 191, 160 and 163 continue through the old Navajo lands to Monument Valley.

MONUMENT VALLEY: FIT FOR THE MOVIES

Hardly any other set of cliffs has had to serve as a backdrop for so many films and advertisements, from Marlboro cigarette ads to the scene of landing on another planet in the science-fiction classic 2001. But it's not for its other-worldly

Above: Shepherds in Monument Valley.
Right: Young American of Indian descent.
Far right: Ascent to the Balcony House in Mesa Verde National Park.

qualities that **Monument Valley** is famous to most people; rather, for its qualities as an epitome of the unique landscape and character of the Wild West.

Route 163 takes you directly into the valley, past imposing, individual rock giants. Cowboys and Indians never had to bother about dealing with road conditions here, but the modern traveler should keep in mind what kind of weather there's been over the last few days before embarking into the park. Access roads are not tarred, and given heavy rainfall or a storm (which happens rarely, however), they are no longer usable. If you happen to worry about the paint on your car, you should simply leave it at the Visitors' Center and board the shuttle bus there, which will ferry you off for a closer look at Monument Valley. As an additional note: the valley is not administered by the National Parks administration of the United States, but rather by the Navajo Nation.

Given some extra time, a nice side trip is to **Kayenta** in the southwest. About 10

miles (16 km) north on Highway 564 lies the **Navajo National Monument**. The three cliff villages here are about 800 years old. Kayenta-Anasazi Indians lived here once upon a time, not Navajos. Of the three dwellings, **Betatakin**, **Keet Seel**, and **Inscription House**, only the first is accessible (from a distance) inasmuch as it can be viewed from a platform. The two other caverns can only be reached after a long hike on foot or on horseback, and Inscription House is closed to the public. Tours lasting many exhausting hours are available for Betatakin and Keet Seel.

Highway 163 continues northward allowing you a glance at one of the area's more famous rock formations, **Mexican Hat**, thus named because it looks like an upside-down sombrero. It looks as if a small push might just tip this great rock over.

The road then continues on to **Four Corners**, the only spot in the USA where the borders of four states meet (Arizona, Colorado, New Mexico and Utah).

Highways 262, 41, and 160 ultimately lead to the last great sight of this trip, Mesa Verde National Park.

MESA VERDE: A JOURNEY INTO THE PAST

A visit to **Mesa Verde** means plunging into the centuries-old history of the extinct culture of the Anasazi Indians. Highway 160 takes you to the Mesa Verde National Park, which, in terms of history and culture, is probably the most important park in the USA. Here, as well as in Canyon de Chelly, the Hovenweep, and Chaco Canyon, is where the pre-Columbian Anasazi tribes lived until around the 13th century. They left numerous cliff dwellings, stone houses nestled in the huge, yellow and brown sandstone cliffs on the relatively fertile plateau known as Mesa Verde, which means "green table" in Spanish.

The **Far View Visitors' Center** is located shortly after the entrance to the park. Together with the **Museum** and the

Park Headquarters a little to the south, it presents information on the various finds that have been made within the park.

The cultural Golden Age of this people ended in the early 14th century, long before the European "discovery" of America. At that point they left Mesa Verde. The reason might have been an extensive drought that seems to have afflicted the entire Southwest at the time. Another reason might have been over-population.

The finest cliff dwelling is undoubtedly **Spruce Tree House**, which stands right behind the museum. This excellently preserved complex boasts over one hundred rooms (all with altars). Behind this house, the road forks into the East Loop and West Loop. The western loop passes by the **Square Tower House** and the **Sun Temple**, as well as **Sun Point**.

Above: Cliff Palace, the largest stone dwelling of the Anasazi at Mesa Verde N. P.

Even more spectacular is the eastern route, which takes you to **Cliff Palace** and **Balcony House**. With its 200 rooms, Cliff Palace is the largest and most famous dwelling in Mesa Verde. Balcony House is only accessible by climbing a 32-foot (10 m) ladder, and it is criss-crossed by a labyrinthine network of tunnels.

On the way back, about halfway between the Headquarters and the entrance to the park, you should keep an eye out for **Park Point Fire Lookout**. From its altitude of 8,572 feet (2,670 m), the lookout commands an extraordinary view over the entire Four Corners region. Surveying the flat land, you're seeing a landscape that doesn't seem to have changed much over the centuries: you could almost be looking into the past, seeing the same view that the Anasazi peoples surveyed hundreds, even thousands, of years ago. Perhaps few other places give you as much insight into the history of the Indians in southwestern America.

NAVAJO AND HOPI INDIAN RESERVATIONS, CANYON DE CHELLY AND MONUMENT VALLEY

All phone numbers have area code 602.

Accommodation

MODERATE: **Best Western Adobe Inn**, 1701 N Park Dr., Winslow, AZ 86047, Tel: 289-4638. **Canyon de Chelly**, Box 295, Chinle, AZ 86503 (three blocks east of AZ 191), Tel: 674-5875. **Goulding's Monument Valley Lodge**, Box 360001, Monument Valley, UT 84536 (21 miles north, west via US 163), Tel: 801/727-3231. **Holiday Inn**, Box 307, Jct. US 160/163, Kayenta, AZ 86033, Tel: 697-3221. **Little America Hotel**, Box 3900, 2515 E Butler Ave., Flagstaff, AZ 86003, Tel: 779-2741. **Quality Inn**, 2000 S Milton Rd., Flagstaff AZ 86001, Tel: 774-8771. **Thunderbird Lodge**, Box 548, Chinle, AZ 86503 (three miles southeast of AZ 191), Tel: 674-5841.

BUDGET: **Arizona Mountain Inn**, 685 Lake Mary Rd., Flagstaff, AZ 86001, Tel: 774-8959. **Best Western Adobe Inn**, 615 W Hopi Dr., Holbrook, AZ 86025, Tel: 524-3948. **Best Western Arizona Inn**, 2508 E Navajo Blvd., Holbrook AZ 86025, Tel: 524-2611. **Econo Lodge**, N Park Dr./I-40, exit 253, Winslow, AZ 86047, Tel: 289-4687. **Econo Lodge East**, 3601 E Lockitt Rd., Flagstaff, AZ 86004, Tel: 572-1477. **Super 8**, 3725 Kasper Ave., Flagstaff, AZ 86004, Tel: 526-0818, US 66 at Business Route 40.

Campgrounds

For information on camping in Arizona State Parks contact **Arizona State Parks**, 800 W Washington, Suite 415, Phoenix, AZ 85007, Tel: 542-4174. For information on camping in Indian reservations contact the tribal authorities listed under Tourist Information. Avoid camping in Indian reservations without prior permission !

Attractions, Museums and Parks

Hopi Cultural Center (with restaurant and motel), Tel: 734-2421 (prior reservation is strongly recommended). **Hubbell Trading Post National Historic Site**, one mile west on AZ 264, Tel: 755-3475. This is the oldest continuously operating trading post in Navajo territory. **Meteor Crater at Winslow**, 20 miles west on I-40, Information Tel: 774-8350. The world's best preserved meteor crater. **Navajo County Historical Museum**, 100 E Arizona, Holbrook, Tel: 524-6558. Exhibits on Apache, Navajo and Hopi culture, in the Old County Courthouse. **Navajo Indian Reservation**, Information Tel: 871-6659. **Navajo National Monument**, 20 miles southwest of Kayenta, on AZ 564, Information Tel: 672-2366. **Navajo Nation Museum**, Tse Bonito Park (east of junction AZ 264/Indian Rte. 12), Window Rock, Tel: 871-6673. **Navajo Nation Zoological and Botanical Park**, Tse Bonito Park (east of junction AZ 264/Indian Route 12), in the Navajo Arts and Crafts Enterprise Center, Tel: 871-6573. **Old Trails Museum**, 212 N Kinsley Ave., Winslow, Tel: 289-5861. Native American artifacts on display. **Petrified Forest National Park**, 26 miles east of Holbrook, on I-40, Information Tel: 524-6228.

Tours

Crawley's Monument Valley Tours Inc., Tel: 697-3734/3463. Daily guided tours lead to Monument Valley, Mystery Valley and Hunt's Mesa. **Thunderbird Lodge Canyon Tours**, Tel: 602/5841 offers daily jeep tours into the canyons.

Tourist Information

Hopi Tribe, PO Box 123, Kykotsmovi, AZ 86039, Tel: 734-2441, ext. 190 (or Tel: 734-6648 for information on current events and performances on the Mesas). **Navajoland Tourism Department**, Box 663, Window Rock, AZ 85615, Tel: 871-6659.

GREATER MESA VERDE AREA

All phone numbers have area code 303.

Accommodation

MODERATE: **Fair View Lodge**, Box 277, Mancos, CO 81328 (at Navajo Hill, in the park, 15 miles from the Mesa Verde park entrance), Tel: 529-4421.

BUDGET: **Anasazi**, 666 S Broadway, Cortez, CO 81321, Tel: 565-3773. **Best Western Turquoise**, 535 E Main St., Cortez, CO 81321, Tel: 565-3439. **Holiday Inn Express**, 2121 E Main St., Cortez, CO 81321, Tel: 565-6000.

Attractions, Museums and Parks

Anasazi Heritage Center & Escalante Ruins, on CO 184, near Cortez, Tel: 882-4811. Museum on the lost Anasazi culture. **Far View Visitor Center**, 15 miles south of Mesa Verde park entrance. **Far View Museum**, at Park Headquarters, 21 miles south of park entrance. **Lowry Pueblo Ruins**, 21 miles NW on US 666 to Pleasant View, then 9 miles west on county road, Tel: 247-4082. **Park Point Fire Lookout**, halfway between Mesa Verde park entrance and Park Headquarters.

Tourist Information

Cortez/Mesa Verde Visitor Info Bureau, PO Box HH, Cortez, CO 81321, Tel: 565-8227. **Mesa Verde National Park Superintendent**, PO Box 8, Mesa Verde National Park, CO 81330, Tel: 529-4465.

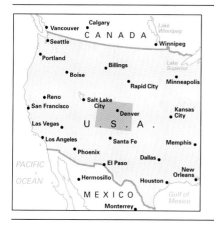

FROM THE
GRAND CANYON
TO DENVER

ASPEN AND VAIL
DENVER
ROCKY MOUNTAIN
NATIONAL PARK

The road constantly climbs. Getting trapped behind a lumbering truck or an RV can be a nightmare on the upgrades. Summer traffic clogs most roads in the scenic areas. On the downgrades, emergency truck chutes play host to huge semis that have lost their brakes and coasted off the road to a safe stop. But the rewards for all the trouble are views of some of America's most impressive landscapes – the Rocky Mountains.

The highways snaking from the north rim of the Grand Canyon through the Rocky Mountains to Denver, which is almost exactly at the half-way point between the Atlantic and Pacific Oceans, are among the most scenic in all North America, and many vacationers know it.

The snow-capped Rockies, America's highest mountains, are a constant reminder of what the nation's earliest pioneers conquered as they pushed their way westward to the sea. As in the past century, the goal is "Pikes Peak or bust," the pioneers' oath that they would reach the Rockies successfully or die in the attempt. This is a journey of 651 miles, which, allowing for some boating and a sidetrip to a ski resort, should take four days.

Left: The Maroon Bells, mirrored in Maroon Lake near Aspen, Colorado.

Lake Powell

From the north rim of the Grand Canyon, motorists usually take Rte. 67 to Jacob Lake, turning right on Rte. ALT 89 which leads them eastwards to an incongruous site called **Lake Powell** (map: p. 103).

Incongruous because it was not a lake at all until 1963 when the U.S. Government decided to build a dam across what had been one of the most spectacular river valleys in the U.S. Lake Powell stretches for almost 200 miles from northern Arizona into southern Utah. It has approximately 2,000 miles of convoluted shoreline which is longer than the entire west coast of the U.S.A. Close to 3.5 million visitors come to Lake Powell each year, some bringing their own boats, and others selecting one from the large fleet of attractive houseboats that can be rented for up to a week at a time.

Four Corners and Durango

US 89 heading south leads away from Lake Powell down to the junction with Rte. 160. Turn left and head eastward to **Four Corners** which is the only point in the entire U.S. where the borders of four separate states – Colorado, Utah, Arizona and New Mexico – meet at a single point. There's a monument at the intersection

111

which offers an unusual photo opportunity. Where else can one tour parts of four states in less than a minute?

Farther along Route 160 is **Mesa Verde National Park**, open during the summer months. Here, you can tour the Anasazi Indian cliff dwellings which date back to approximately A.D. 1200 (see p. 107). The tribe disappeared from the area around A.D. 1300 and no one seems to know precisely why they left and where they went. Climatic conditions, namely a long drought, are thought to have forced them to leave.

About 30 miles further on is **Durango**, a sunny, historic community which sprang to life in 1880 when the gold rush town of **Silverton**, which is 45 miles to the north, needed a railhead through which to send its ore. The railroad system, which was responsible for Durango's birth, still exists today. Instead of

ore, the sightseeing train now carries visitors to Silverton and back again on a spectacular 90-mile journey.

ASPEN AND VAIL

The road north from Durango (550) and east to Denver is a long stretch through the very heart of the Rocky Mountains. At the town of Delta, the road becomes Rte. 50. You arrive at Grand Junction, then turn right on Hwy. 6 and I-70 which is the major artery cutting east to west through Colorado and passing through Denver.

Thanks to their height, cold winters and enough dampness from the Pacific, the Rockies here receive a lot of snow. Around just about every bend in the road in Colorado there's a ski resort – old, new, or just being built and soon to open. Some of the most famous are either on I-70 or not too many miles away.

The most prestigious ski resort in the United States is **Aspen** which is reached by turning right off I-70 to Rte. 82. It's

Above: The Rocky Mountains were the most difficult parts of the journey for the Wagon Trains to the West. Right: The ski resort Aspen.

not unusual to see John Denver, Jack Nicholson, Goldie Hawn, Barbra Streisand, or Cher during an Aspen visit, for they are just a few of the VIPs who make this charming mountain village their winter retreat from the hustle of Hollywood.

In summer, Aspen offers the usual array of mountain activities: biking, hiking and fishing. A challenging stream for rafters and kayakers is **Fork River** which roars out of the Sawatch Range.

Visually, Aspen is a delight because its government energetically controls construction and signage, thus avoiding that junky look that many resorts suffer from. Not long ago, there was a major ruckus when a local McDonalds was prohibited from putting up a neon sign.

Another famous resort is **Vail**, which lies to the east on I-70. An alternative approach for the courageous driver is from Aspen over **Independence Pass** (12,095 feet, closed in winter). Vail is fairly new as resorts go, having only taken shape in 1952. Its architecture is borrowed from the Austrian Alps, and it indeed gives the appearance of having been tucked into the Rockies for ages.

Vail spreads for almost ten miles along the narrow Rocky Mountain valley. Much of the community is closed to automobile traffic, and visitors move around on free Vail busses. What there's plenty of is skiing: along steep slopes which drop almost 3,300 ft. There are six distinct skiing bowls: **Mongolia**, **Siberia**, **China**, **Teacup**, **Sunup** and **Sundown**, which cover a total ten square miles, making Vail and adjacent Beaver Creek the largest skiing area in the U.S.

Copper Mountain and Breckenridge

Just a few miles southeast of Vail along I-70, is **Copper Mountain**, which is both ski resort and convention center. There are almost always delegates wearing badges walking through the resort lobby and filling up its meeting rooms.

Golf is very popular at Copper Mountain, not least because in the thin air,

9,600 feet above sea level, the ball seems to fly for miles if it is well struck. The resort's 18-hole, 6,094-yard, par-70 course, designed by Pete and Perry Dye, is said to be the highest 18-hole golf course in North America.

East of Copper Mountain on I-70, then south on Rte. 9, lies **Breckenridge**, yet another star in Colorado's ski crown. One of its main attractions is the Breckenridge **Brewery & Pub**; often, the beer you're served here has just been brewed minutes before in the micro-brewery on the premises.

Breckenridge is the most historic of all the Colorado ski resorts; 350 of its buildings are listed on the National Historic Register. The town enjoyed three mining booms and is now raking in its current wealth from skiiers. Gold was found first in 1859. Silver was mined beginning in 1878, and made the town a second fortune. Then another generation of pioneers came to pan and mine gold there in 1938. Many homes of the miners and their bosses are now B&Bs, restaurants and chic boutiques.

DENVER

The city of **Denver** is a remarkably neat state capital boasting more than 200 parks and dozens of attractive, tree-lined boulevards. While most western cities spread out over many square miles, Denver has a dense, central downtown area that can be easily explored on foot.

At dawn, the city is beautifully backdropped by the Rockies, some 30 miles to its west. To the south on a clear day you can see **Pike's Peak**, where a gold strike in the mid-1800s started a worldwide rush of miners and fortune-hunters to the area. "Pike's Peak or bust," was their motto, as mentioned above, a motto that nowadays applies to the crowds of travelers pioneering their way west to come to America's most impressive landscapes.

Larimer Street is a good place to start a walking tour of downtown Denver. It's Denver's oldest – and once upon a time – wildest road. It has been restored with gas lamps, arcades, fine Victorian woodwork and with carriages on hand to take visitors around in traditional style. Bat Masterson tended bar here. Soapy Smith ran the west's largest gang of crooks, thieves and conmen here. Anyone in the old Wild West paid at least one visit to Denver's gaudy, honky-tonk sector.

Around every corner in downtown Denver are preserved sites from the city's colorful past. The **Molly Brown House** on Pennyslvania Avenue, for instance. "Unsinkable Molly" entered Denver folklore in 1912 when she booked westbound passage on the ill-fated *SS Titanic*. She was the wealthy, but not well educated wife of a Denver gold miner, returning from a European jaunt. Wearing her $60,000 chinchilla cape (and very little else), she calmed passengers aboard the sinking ship, led them to lifeboats and, waving the pistol she always carried, ordered the crew to keep rowing until rescue arrived. Her house today is open to visitors and contains original furnishings and mementos from her remarkable life.

The **State Capitol Building** on Colfax Avenue is another of Denver's more impressive sights. If the 15th step of the building's west side seems especially worn, that's because standing on this step puts you at exactly 5,280 ft – one mile – above sea level. The capitol is modeled after the U.S. Capitol in Washington D.C., and its dome positively glows at sunrise or sunset because it's covered with 200 ounces of 24-karat gold.

There's lots of money being made in Denver – 40 million coins a day to be precise, minted, bagged and shipped by the **U.S. Mint** at the junction of Colfax Avenue and Cherokee Street, which is a

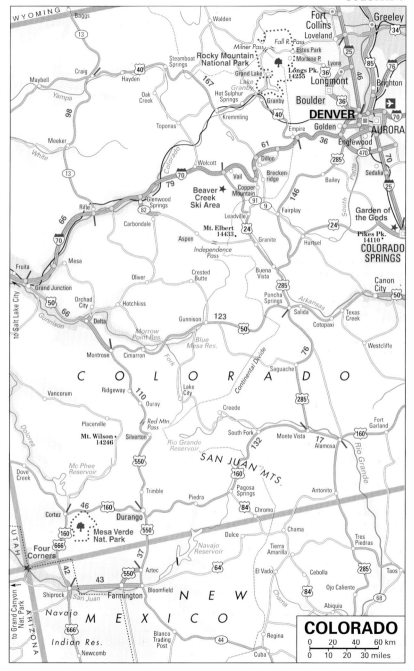

COLORADO

0   20   40   60 km

0   10   20   30 miles

115

tourist attraction itself. You can stand and watch while 800 coins a minute are stamped and shot from each of 60 punch presses into growing piles that give the Mint the appearance of a slot machine gone crazy.

The **Denver Art Museum**, just a block south of the Mint on 14th Avenue, is a 28-sided, 10-storey structure, which is itself a piece of sculpture. Over one million special gray glass tiles are wrapped like a skin around the building, each of them reflecting light in a different way. Inside are more than 35,000 works of art arranged in seven different departments, probably the most famous being the **American Indian Hall**. A special, two-storey atrium had to be built to house the totem poll collection.

The **Museum of Western Art** on Tremont Place is much more traditional-looking, and with a traditional history. At

Above: Denver with the backdrop of the Rocky Mountains. Right: The area around Moffat is ideal for horse ranching.

one time it used to be the *Navarre*, which, legend has it, was Denver's classiest bordello and gambling hall. Today, the building is home to 125 paintings and sculptures, including many classic Western paintings by Remington, Russell and Georgia O'Keeffe.

Entering the museum you will pass the entrance to the underground tunnel which once connected the "Navarre" with more respectable Denver buildings, so that proper Denver businessmen would not be detected heading off for evenings of illicit pleasure.

Denver is a veritable beer town. Top dog in the brewing business is **Coor's**, which offers daily tours of its huge plant in suburban Golden. They naturally end with a free product sampling. While out in Golden, inspecting the brewery, you ought to take in the **Colorado Railroad Museum** on 44th Avenue, with over 80 vintage steam locomotives and carriages on display.

Keeping with what amounts to a national trend, the big Denver rage today is

micro-brewing, where the pubkeeper bottles his product out back. Local owners are very proud of their products, and many of them serve "samplers" – several four-ounce servings presented to the customer at the same time. Probably the best-known Denver micro-brewery is the **Wynkoop** on 18th Street in the old warehouse district, which serves not only top-grade beer but also solid pub food like fish 'n chips and shepherd's pie.

Colorado Springs and Boulder

South of Denver, in Pike's Peak country, is **Colorado Springs**, reached by heading down I-25. The area has been revitalized in recent years by the building of the ultra-modern **U.S. Air Force Academy** in the community. A favorite daily event for visitors is the 11:00 am formation when all 4,000 cadets form up and march to lunch.

Just a few miles further south is the **Garden of the Gods**, a geological won-

der where massive, bright-red sandstone formations rise up to 600 feet into the blue Colorado sky. 27 miles north of Denver on US 36 is another college town, **Boulder**, home of the **University of Colorado**. The first white settlers came to the area in 1858, and they left behind them a large number of attractive, Victorian buildings.

The downtown **Historic District**, which has been carefully restored, is well worth walking through. **Pearl Street** was once a mining service center lined with log cabins. Today, it is an award-winning, open-air pedestrian mall, listed on the National Register of Historic Places, famous for its preservation of late 19th-century and early 20th-century commercial buildings.

ROCKY MOUNTAIN N.P.

A drive through the Rockies wouldn't be complete without a visit to the Rockies which is why **Rocky Mountain National Park** is Colorado's most popular

117

single attraction, drawing more than three million visitors a year.

The entrance to the Park is about 40 miles from Boulder, following CO Hwy. 36 to the northeast, which goes directly to the Park via the spectacular **Estes Valley**. A tram leads from **Estes Park** to a lookout platform on **Prospect Mountain** that provides a particularly spectacular view of the other mountains in the Park.

The little town of Estes Park, by the way, was named after Joel Estes, one of the first people to investigate this region. In the mid-19th century he set out on several reconnaisance missions to this part of the Rocky Mountains, and kept returning. In 1915 the Rocky Mountains National Park was officially established. This was partly thanks to the American writer Enos Mills, who, in his usual romantic style, described the mountains as follows: "He who feels the spell of the

Above: Phosphorescent lichens in the mountain forest of the Rocky Mountains. Right: Bighorn sheep in Rocky Mountains N. P.

wild, the rhythmic melody of falling water, the echoes among the crags, the bird songs, the wind in the pines (...) is in tune with the universe."

Today, the Park preserves 412 square miles of rugged scenery, punctuated by 78 peaks, each of which is over 12,000 feet high. The area is known as the **Front Range** of the Rockies, the initial wave of mountains rising out of America's central plains. They are mountains in a long chain of high peaks which stretches all the way from 300 miles above the Canadian border to northern New Mexico.

The Rocky Mountains, one of the world's highest mountain ranges, were bulldozed into place by tectonic shifts about 70 million years ago. They owe their current wild beauty to the formative forces of fire, ice, water and wind. Over millions of years these young mountains were further shaped by tectonic and volcanic activity. And during the past two million years the powerful glaciers of four Ice Ages pressed their way through the mountains. Some ranges were flat-

tened, others were heaved up by the incredible pressure of the ice. As the glaciers dwindled, they left clear lakes in their wake.

A drive through Rocky Mountain National Park allows visitors to experience a variety of temperate zones in just a few hours; the environment changes constantly as one climbs higher. In the lower valleys, the weather is relatively warm and dry. Blue spruce and red cedar trees line the gently curving highway. Trapped between the peaks are crystal-clear lakes, the residue of the five separate glaciers that still exist.

As cars climb up the mountain slopes, along twisting and turning roads, the trees change to dense pines and aspens. Above 9,000 feet the trees are twisted and bent by the fierce, buffeting winds. Even in the height of summer, it's best to have a jacket up here as temperatures are well below those in the plains, and even sudden snowfall is always possible.

Because the park is so close to Denver (it's a two-hour drive from the city), this sector of the Rocky Mountains is usually overrun by people during the summer weekends. If in search of solitude either avoid these rush days, or drive to the more remote western sector of the National Park.

Both **Trail Ridge Road** and **Fall River Road**, the two interlinked roads which cross the Park, eventually climb well above the timberline into a tundra that covers well over one-third of the entire park. The plants here are small and stunted, as if trying to evade the winds and protect themselves against the winter snows which are sure to come.

Colorado's state flower, the blue columbine, can be spotted at nearly every elevation. In the tundra are alpine buttercups, alpine forget-me-nots, and dwarf clovers, all with a brief blooming season of about six weeks at the end of June and beginning of July.

The Rocky Mountain Park's symbol is the bighorn sheep, and visitors with strong binoculars and telephoto lenses might be lucky enough to spot and photo-

graph one of these beautiful beasts – most probably at a great distance, for they are very people-shy.

The high point – literally – of Trail Ridge Road is **Milner Pass**, which is precisely at the Continental Divide. From this point, all the streams flowing down the western slopes of the Rockies end up in the Pacific Ocean, while all the streams dashing down the eastern slopes eventually spill into the Atlantic Ocean or the Gulf of Mexico.

Photographers will not want to miss **Many Parks Curve** and **Rainbow Curve** along Trail Ridge Road, because both are exceptional spots for picture-taking, with fantastic views of America's magnificent alpine landscape. There are parking areas at each curve for those who wish to stop and take in the views, or let their engines cool off.

The Rocky Mountains National Park authorities have laid out approximately

Above: The gold mine of Idaho Springs is a mining museum today.

355 miles of hiking trails. Several self-guiding nature trails begin directly off the main park roads. These include the **Tundra Trail** and the **Colorado River Trail**. The Colorado River Trail head is several miles southwest of Milner Pass, while the Tundra Trail begins just a few miles to the east of Milner Pass. For those who prefer their wilderness viewing to take place from the back of a horse, there are two stables, at **Moraine Park** and **Glacier Creek**, which conduct guided summertime rides. Hikers requiring serious challenges should try the 16-mile trail leading up to Longs Peak, the highest mountain in the park at 14,256 ft. It is covered in snow year-round.

One particularly recommended stop is at **Fall River Pass** where the road begins to turn southward and there is the **Alpine Visitors' Center**. The rangers have done an excellent job of laying out exhibits that explain the tundra and other features of the natural world surrounding the visitors to the Park.

DURANGO, ASPEN, VAIL
All phone numbers have area code 303.

Accommodation
LUXURY: **Vail Athletic Club**, 352 E Meadow Dr., Vail, CO 81657, Tel: 476-0700.
MODERATE: **General Palmer Hotel**, 567 Main Ave., Durango, CO 81301, Tel: 247-4747. **Limelite Inn**, 228 E Cooper St., Aspen, CO 81611, Tel: 925-3025. **River Mountain Lodge**, PO Box 7188, 100 S Park St./Ski Hill Rd., Breckenridge, CO 80424, Tel: 453-4711. *BUDGET:* **Alma House**, Box 780, 220 E 10th St., Silverton, CO 81433, Tel: 387-5336. **Aspen Manor**, 411 S Monarch St., Aspen, CO 81611, Tel: 925-3001.

Attractions and Parks
Breckenridge Ski Area, Ski Hill Rd. (1 mile west off CO 9), Breckenridge, Tel: 1-800-221-1091. **Copper Mt. Resort Ski Area**, 12 miles southwest, at jct. I-70/CO 91, Dillon, Tel: 968-2882. **Mesa Verde National Park**, eight miles east of Cortez, on US 160, Information Tel: 529-4465. **Durango-Silverton Narrow Gauge Railroad**, Depot, 479 Main St., Durango, Tel: 247-2733. **Vail Ski Resort**, on I-70, exit 176, Tel: 476-5601.

Sports and Outdoor Activities
River Rafts Inc., Tel: 925-7648. River rafting on the Roaring Fork, Colorado and other rivers. **Rocky Mountains High Jeep Tours**, Durango, Tel: 1-800/530-2022. Guided tours to historic mines and scenic wonders. Departures at 46825 US 550 N in Durango. **Skiing in Aspen**, Aspen Cross-Country Center, Tel: 925-2145 or Snowmass Club Touring Center, Tel: 923-3148.

Tourist Information
Aspen Chamber Resort Assn., 425 Rio Grande Pl., Aspen, CO 81611, Tel: 925-1940.
Lake Powell Chamber of Commerce, PO Box 727, Page, AZ 86040, Tel: 602/645-2741.

DENVER, COLORADO SPRINGS AND BOULDER
All phone numbers have area code 303.

Accommodation
LUXURY: **The Brown Place**, 321 17th St., Denver, CO 80202, Tel: 297-3111. Traditional, elegant first-class hotel. *MODERATE:* **Castle Marne**, 1572 Race St., Denver, CO 80206, Tel: 331-0621. Romanesque mansion in downtown. **Lost Valley Guest Ranch**, Rte. 2, Sedalia, CO 80135, Tel: 647-2311. Original ranch, offering cabins. *BUDGET:* **La Quinta Central**, 3500 Park Ave. W, Denver, CO 80216, Tel: 458-1222.

Attractions and Museums
Colorado Railroad Museum, 17155 W 44th Ave. (10th St. E of Golden), Golden (near Denver), Tel: 279-4591. **Coors Brewing Company Indus-**trial Tour**, 13th/Ford Sts., in Golden, Tel: 277-BEER. **Denver Art Museum**, 100 W 14th Ave. Pwy., Tel: 640-2793. **Garden of the Gods**, three miles northwest on US 24, then 30th St., near Colorado Springs, Tel: 578-6640. **Larimar Street & Square**, between 14th and 15th Sts., Tel: 534-2367. **Molly Brown House Museum**, 1340 Pennsylvania St., Tel: 832-4092. **Museum of Western Art**, 1727 Tremont Pl., Tel: 296-1880. **Pikes Peak**, ten miles west on US 24 to Cascades (then toll road to peak), Tel: 685-5401. **State Capitol**, E Colfax Ave./Sherman St., Tel: 866-2604. **United States Mint**, 320 W Colfax Ave., Tel: 844-3582. **University of Colorado**, Boulder, Information on guided tours, Tel: 492-1411. **US Air Force Academy**, north on I-25, exit 150B, Tel: 472-2555. **Wynkop Brewing Company**, 1634 18th St., Tel: 297-2700.

Tourist Information
Boulder C & V Bureau, 2440 Pearl St., Boulder, CO 80302, Tel: 442-2911. **Colorado Springs C & V Bureau**, 104 S Cascade, Suite 104, Colorado Springs, CO 80903, Tel:635-7506. **Denver Metro C & V Bureau**, 225 W Colfax, Denver, CO 80202, Tel: 892-1505.

ROCKY MOUNTAIN NATIONAL PARK
All phone numbers have area code 303.

Accommodation
MODERATE: **Colorado Cottages**, Moraine Rte., 1421 High Dr., Estes Park, CO 80517, Tel: 586-4637. **McGregor Mountain Lodge**, 2815 Fall River Rd., Estes Park, CO 80517, Tel: 586-3457. Small cabin colony overlooking Fall River Canyon, adjacent to Rocky Mts. National Park. **Peaceful Valley Lodge & Guest Ranch**, Star Rte., Box 2811, Lyons, CO 80540, Tel: 747-2881.
BUDGET: **Alpine Trail Ridge Inn**, 927 Moraine Ave., Estes Park, CO 80517, Tel: 586-4585. **Bighorn Lodge**, Box 1260, 613 Grand Ave., Grand Lake, CO 80447, Tel: 627-8101.

Attractions, Museums and Parks
Estes Park Area Historical Museum, 200 Fourth St., Estes Park, Tel: 586-6256.
Rocky Mountain National Park, Park Headquarters three miles west of Estes Park, on US 36, Tel: 586-2371.

Sports and Outdoor Activities
Aerial Tramway, 420 Riverside Dr., Estes Park, cabins moving up to Prospect Mt., Tel: 586-3675. **Skiing – Silver Creek Ski Area**, three miles southeast on US 40, near Granby, Tel: 887-3384.

Tourist Information
Estes Park Information Center at the Chamber of Commerce, 500 Big Thompson Ave., PO Box 3050, Estes Park, CO 80517, Tel: 586-4431.

FROM
LOS ANGELES TO
SAN FRANCISCO

SANTA BARBARA
BIG SUR / CARMEL
MONTEREY BAY
SALINAS AND SANTA CRUZ
SAN JOSE

California's beautiful coastline has made the state one of the world's most popular tourist destinations. It is rugged, with the Pacific crashing on sandy beaches and rocky shores that rise steeply towards snow-capped mountains and tall forests of sequoias.

There are faster ways of going north than on the narrow, curving coastal State Highway 1, but being forced to drive slowly on this car-crowded road does have one advantage: it gives the visitor a chance to gaze out at some of the most inspiring views in the U.S. Allowing for overnight stops at Santa Barbara and near San Simeon, plus two nights in Monterey, this can be a very leisurely five-day trip. And the scenic beauties along the way may encourage you to take even longer to cover this distance of 384 miles (614 km).

SANTA BARBARA

The city of **Santa Barbara**, just under 70 miles north of the center of Los Angeles, is a Spanish-looking, white-washed, red-tile roofed community smug in its wealth, conservative in its politics

Previous pages: The coast north of Los Angeles is an Eldorado for surfers and wind-surfers. Left: Sun protection à l'americaine.

and blessed with a temperate Southern California climate. Santa Barbara was founded by Spanish missionaries and conquistadors in the 1700s. Among the genuinely old buildings is **Mission Santa Barbara**, one of the 21 missions built by the followers of Father Junipero Serra. In the buildings adjacent to it are replicas of a Spanish padre's cell, and the 19th-century kitchen where food was prepared for the friars and the religious community.

Santa Barbara's tourist office has created a **"Red Tile Route,"** red sidewalk markers leading visitors on a building-by-building stroll around twelve square blocks of the city center.

Just off State Street is **El Paseo**, a Spanish-style shopping arcade constructed alongside the **Casa de la Guerra**, an 1829 adobe structure built for the Spanish commanding officer of the tiny garrison which once guarded the entrance to this important port. Several blocks northeast is the **Parade Ground** where Spanish troopers once marched and counter-marched. Facing this is the **Santa Barbara Historical Society Museum** containing a fascinating range of exhibits detailing the city's Spanish, Mexican, Indian and American heritage. The hills above Santa Barbara have become increasingly profitable to their owners, thanks to the introduction of

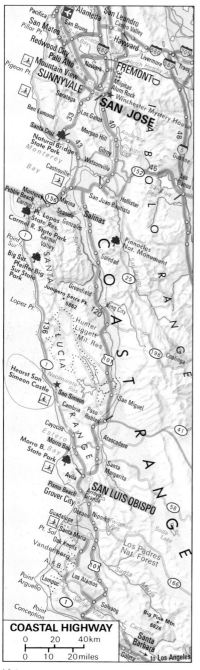

COASTAL HIGHWAY

0   20   40km

0   10   20miles

many fine wineries into the area. There are close to 30 firms producing vines in the nearby **Santa Maria** and **Santa Ynez Valleys** at the present time. A few offer guided tours, and virtually every one keeps a tasting room where, it is hoped, samplers will become buyers of bottles or cases.

Beyond the **San Ysidro Ranch** is a breathtaking drive along 101, switching to US 1, which goes to the historic town of **San Luis Obispo**.

San Luis Obispo and Morro Bay

This mission town at the foot of the **Santa Lucia Mountains** is precisely halfway between Los Angeles and San Francisco where US-1 and 101 rejoin briefly before separating again. **Pismo Beach**, due south, the only California beach where cars can be driven on the sand, is California's clamming headquarters; its chowder attracts visitors from miles away. Nude bathers head for nearby **Pirate's Cove** at **Avila** a few miles north along the coast. A coastal town northwest of San Luis Obispo, on Rte. 1, it lies in the shadow of giant, 576-ft-high **Morro Rock** on a bay where visitors flock to bird-watch, beachcomb, picnic, sail, swim and fish. Hiking trails lead out into dunes where 250 species of birds wheel and swoop. The **Embarcadero**, where the fishing fleet ties up, is a raffish area of piers, restaurants, souvenir shops and bars.

North of San Luis Obispo, on coastal Rte. 1, is an amazing mansion, the **Hearst San Simeon Castle**. Those who have seen Orson Welles' classic film *Citizen Kane* have already had a preview of San Simeon. The fictional character of Kane was patterned after American publisher William Randolph Hearst, a 20th-century press baron. In the film, the mansion Kane built and furnished with valuable European and Asian art was called "Xanadu." Hearst's home at San Simeon

is even more sensational than that created in celluloid by Welles.

More than $10 million, an unimaginable fortune in those days, was expended to construct the museum-like main building. Gardens and reflecting pools link the main house to a trio of so-called guest "cottages." Within, the baronial walls are cluttered with Egyptian, Greek, Roman, medieval and Renaissance art, sculptures, tapestries and other artifacts. The main building alone has 38 bedrooms and 41 baths, a dining room of Arthurian dimensions with a 30-foot table, a plush cinema where first-run Hollywood films were shown, often with their stars attending in person, and an indoor swimming pool so vast that there is room on its roof for two full-scale tennis courts.

Autos can't get much closer to San Simeon than five miles; after parking, tourists are taken by bus on a drive through Hearst's forests to the dwellings. There

Above: Luxurious Renaissance-style swimming pool in Hearst Castle.

are five different narrated tours, each about an hour and a quarter long. One tour, staged only in the summer months, takes place in the evenings, with the gardens and sculpture splendidly spotlit. The staff dresses up in 1930s garb, and it's almost like being back in the era of F. Scott Fitzgerald and *The Great Gatsby*.

After a day at San Simeon, northbound travelers rejoin Hwy. 1 for the 60-mile drive along the Pacific to Big Sur.

EXPLORING THE PACIFIC HIGHWAY TO BIG SUR

This rugged coastline is everyone's image of California. For close to 90 miles, from San Simeon to Monterey, the Pacific crashes into the feet of the Santa Lucia mountain range with so spectacular an impact that writers, artists and photographers (along with millions of tourists a year) have flocked to the area to be inspired by the beauty of it all.

Until 1937, when coastal highway bridges went up over many of the cuts

127

along the coastline, allowing motorists to access the area easily, this part of California was isolated from the rest of the state. Poets such as Robinson Jeffers, novelists such as Henry Miller and photographers such as Ansel Adams came for the solitude and beauty.

Big Sur's wildlife is awesome. Gray whales spout on the horizon twice a year: once while heading south to the Baja region of Mexico in the fall, and then when swimming north to Alaskan waters in the spring. Hunting hawks swoop over the canyons, howling coyotes noisily tear their prey apart in the moonlight.

So many ships have hit rocks off **Point Sur** over the decades that the authorities installed a photo-perfect lighthouse atop the point to warn sailors of the dangers ahead. The lighthouse is open for guided tours most weekends, with a park ranger giving the light's history and answering

Above: Pacific Coast Highway 1 is one of the most beautiful coastal roads in the world. Right: Sea lions on the cliffs near Monterey.

questions. Absolutely the perfect place to eat on Big Sur is the **Nepenthe Restaurant**, some three miles south of the **Pfeiffer Big Sur State Park**. Hanging on a hillside over the edge of the ocean, this eatery has, many food critics say, the most magnificent view of any eating spot in the world. The house specialty is a line of ambrosia burgers.

ON TO CARMEL

Some visitors still arrive at this northern exit from Big Sur expecting to see "Dirty Harry," Clint Eastwood, in the Mayor's office of this tiny coastal village. For several years, this Hollywood megastar did indeed govern Carmel. But Eastwood declined to run for re-election, and now confines his Carmel activities primarily to improving his **Mission Ranch Inn**, a sprawling, 20-acre property. Father Junipero Serra, who established the missions of southern California, headquartered in Carmel, is buried here.

Around Carmel and **Monterey Bay** are brilliant green forests of Monterey cypress, many of the trees gnarled, twisted and wind-bent in eerie, unearthly shapes. Beyond is the Bay, its waters reflecting the distinctive azure blue of the California sky, a deep ocean trench filled with exotic marine wildlife.

Carmel River State Park covers more than 100 acres along the Bay, an area of sugar-white dunes which form a nesting area for sandpipers, hawks and full-bellied pelicans that plummet from time to time into the sea, rising up with wildly flapping fish in their beaks.

Just south of Carmel is **Point Lobos State Reserve**, best accessed on foot. **Sea Lion Point Trail** is a fascinating walk, leading to rocky coves where otters, seals and sea lions bask in the sun or cavort in the crystalline sea.

Carmel has long fancied itself a tidy, tiny, English-style village which just happens to have found itself, miraculously, cast up on a Pacific shoreline. Ye Olde type tearooms are on several shopping streets. Don't look for house numbers; here homes are known by their names: Dove House, the Kestrels, Mon Repos. Don't look for sidewalks either; there aren't any, except for on the streets around **Ocean Avenue**.

The **Hog's Breath Inn** downtown is Eastwood-owned and, naturally, the menu features items like a "Dirty Harry Hamburger" and a "Dirty Harry Dinner." Surprisingly, the decor isn't Dirty Harry at all, no sawdust on the floor or spilled beer on the bar; instead, it's candlelit and romantic. Poetry lovers demand to visit **Tor House**, the unique stone cottage high on a bluff over the Pacific, built by American poet Robinson Jeffers in 1918.

The 17-mile Drive

This last private toll road to be found in the U.S. west of the Mississippi circles around four of the world's most famous

golf courses at **Pebble Beach** on the southern shore of Monterey Bay. The cost for a vehicle to go through any of its five toll gates is $6, and well worth the expense.

Along **17-Mile Drive** are some of the world's most expensive mansions, each more luxurious than the other, all poised with perfect views of the ocean, the pine and cypress forests, and the greens and fairways of the classic golf courses which grace this headland. Herds of deer wander through the countryside, sometimes not even lifting their heads as golfers drive off over their horns.

Also visible is a bizarrely decorated tree close to one of the golfing clubhouses. Whenever a member dies, his golfing mates conduct a ceremony of hanging the deceased's golf bag on a branch of the tree, which is now laden down with several dozen sad-looking, weathered bags.

Robert Louis Stevenson wrote of the area, "On no other coast that I know shall you enjoy in calm, sunny weather such a

spectacle of ocean's greatness, such beauty of changing color or such degrees of thunder in the sound."

MONTEREY

Monterey is the most interesting community between Los Angeles and San Francisco and well worth an extended visit. In earlier days, this city served as Spain's colonial headquarters. The United States claimed this region in 1846, at the beginning of the Mexican-American War.

The town's tourist office has compressed much of this early history into a self-guided, two-mile walk around Monterey, mostly along the waterfront where the earlier buildings, all lovingly preserved, are grouped.

Custom House Plaza is the logical starting point, facing as it does the two-storey adobe **Custom House** through which the Spaniards cleared goods beginning in 1827.

A new building, the nearby **Monterey Maritime Museum**, contains many artifacts, a large number of them collected by the town's former mayor: sailors' scrimshaw, prints and maps, weapons and uniforms, plus photographs from World War II when Monterey was a major military center.

Also on Custom House Plaza is **Pacific House**. Built around the time that gold was discovered at Sutter's Mill, now a museum, it used to be a saloon where Forty-Niners lost their gold nuggets over the bar and across the poker tables.

All of these buildings overlook **Fisherman's Wharf** which juts out into the Bay, flanked with piers for daily excursion boats, slips for yachts and moorings for the local fishing fleet. It's where visitors usually take lunch, very often selecting a local fish soup which is served in a bowl made of a hollowed-out loaf of bread.

Above: Monterey Bay Aquarium. Right: John Steinbeck discovered many characters for his stories in Monterey.

Life on the Wharf has the atmosphere of an ongoing carnival. Artists sketch you in just a few minutes for a small fee. A monkey and an organ grinder amuse the throngs. Tourists come ashore from fishing expeditions to have their photos taken next to their catch.

Walking westwards from the Wharf, you enter the **Cannery Row** world of author John Steinbeck. The world he described was harsh, with a Chinese merchant selling groceries to workers and hosting illegal gambling games out back, with saloons where ladies of the evening were busy dusk-to-dawn every payday. The tawdry buildings still stand, but after the sardine schools mysteriously disappeared, the old life of Monterey petered out as well.

Inside the refurbished shell of one of the largest canneries is the remarkable **Monterey Bay Aquarium**. More than $50 million have been spent to give the world an underwater look at the complex and fascinating marine life offshore. Some of the aquarium's display tanks are three stories high, filled with long tendrils of transplanted kelp. Several times a day, a scuba diver enters the pool to feed the fish, and lectures the spectators at the same time via a radio/PA link.

SALINAS AND SANTA CRUZ

John Steinbeck wrote a number of other American classics in addition to *Cannery Row*, such as *East of Eden*, *The Grapes of Wrath*, or the ultimate U.S. travel guide, *Travels with Charley*. The author was born in **Salinas**, and his family home **Steinbeck House** on 132 Central Avenue has been restored as a restaurant-cum-museum to his memory. Nearby, on West San Luis, is the **Steinbeck Library**, packed with original manuscripts, first editions and his correspondence. The area around Salinas has some of the richest farmland in America, its produce feeding much of the country.

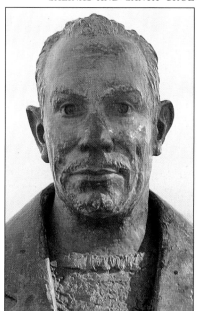

At the north end of **Santa Cruz**, Monterey Bay on Rte. 1 has some of the hippie feeling of the 60s. Local college kids bike instead of drive, the restaurants feature tofu, and the cry "Surf's up!" is enough to get everyone down to the beach to take on some of the West Coast's most impressive waves. It's a town still rebuilding after being hard hit by an earthquake in 1989. The town's noisiest citizens are the barking sea lions who congregate by the **Municipal Wharf** and beg for table scraps. **Natural Bridges State Park**, at the end of **West Cliff Drive**, is famous for its monarch butterflies and tidal pools filled with crustaceans.

THE WAY TO SAN JOSE

No longer does Dionne Warwick sing questioningly, "Do you know the way to San Jose?" Now everyone does. After driving northeast from Santa Cruz, you enter into the headquarters community of world-famous **Silicon Valley**, that re-

markable complex of high-tech labs and factories which, since World War II, have catapulted the world into the electronic era. A visit back to the age when the Spaniards ruled begins in the city center at the **Peralta Adobe** on St. John Street, filled with exhibits picturing how San Jose looked when it belonged to the King of Spain. Across from the Peralta Adobe is **Fallon House**, the home of a U.S. Army captain who galloped into this tiny town in 1846 at the head of a column of armed volunteers to raise the Stars and Stripes for the first time.

Until Silicon Valley brought prosperity, San Jose was a backwater, known largely for being the home of almost 270 square miles of plum orchards.

There are two bizarrely vintage tourist attractions from that era that continue to appeal to visitors: **Winchester House** is a remarkable Victorian structure which comprised eight rooms when Sarah Win-

chester, the heiress to the repeating rifle fortune, bought it in 1884. A fortune teller warned her that the ghosts of all those slain with her family's rifles would haunt her unless she built new rooms where she could hide if they came after her. By 1922, when she finally passed away, she had builders add room after room to a total of 160, and hundreds of tourists visit them daily. There are doors that open onto blank walls, staircases that don't go anywhere, corridors that are mazes.

The sect of the Rosicrucians, at Park and Naglee Avenues, has built an interesting **Egyptian Museum** and **Planetarium** which is one of the area's most visited attractions. It is crammed with the Pacific Coast's largest collection of Babylonian, Assyrian and Egyptian artifacts and mummies.

Having made your way to San Jose from the south, leave it via Rte. 280 and head up the peninsula through **Palo Alto**, with prestigious Stanford University, to the City by the Bay, San Francisco.

Above: Dramatic coastline ensures State Highway 1 drivers an adventure.

GREATER SANTA BARBARA AREA
Accommodation

MODERATE: **Blue Sail Inn**, 851 Market St., Morro Bay, CA 93442, Tel: 805/772-2766. Hotel with lovely bay view. **Mission Ranch Inn**, 26270 Dolores St., Carmel, CA 92923, Tel: 408/624-6436. **Simpson House**, 121 E Arrellaga St., Santa Barbara, CA 93101, Tel: 805/963-7067. Historic landmark hotel.

BUDGET: **Marina Beach**, 21 Bath St., Santa Barbara, CA 93101, Tel: 805/963-9311. **Sea Gypsy**, 1020 Cypress, at Wadsworth St., Pismo Beach, CA 93449, Tel: 805/773-1801. On the beach, nice ocean view.

Attractions, Museums and Parks
Hearst San Simeon State Historical Monument, 750 Hearst Castle Rd., San Simeon, Tel: 805/927-2020. **Mission San Luis Obispo de Tolosa**, 782 Monterey St., San Luis Obispo, Tel: 805/543-6850. **Mission Santa Barbara**, Laguna and Los Olivos Sts., Santa Barbara, Tel: 805/682-4149. **Morro Bay Embarcadero**, 893 Napa St., # A-1, Morro Bay, Tel: 805/772-2694. **Morro Bay State Park**, south of town, Tel: 805/772-2560. **Morro Rock**, 895 Napa St., # A-1, Morro Bay, Tel: 805/772-4467. **Pfeiffer Big Sur State Park**, Information Tel: 408/667-2315. **Pismo Dunes State Vehicular Recreation Area**, west end of Grand Ave., Grover City, Tel: 805/473-7220. **Point Lobos State Reserve**, Rtc. 1, Carmel, Tel: 408/624-4909. **San Luis Obispo County Historical Museum**, 969 Monterey St., San Luis Obispo, Tel: 805/543-0638. **Santa Barbara Historical Society Museum**, 136 E. De La Guerra St., Santa Barbara, Tel: 805/966-1601. **Tor House**, Carmel Point, Carmel, Tel: 408/824-1813.

Sports and Outdoor Activities
Morro Bay Harbor Cruises, 1205 Embarcadero, Morro Bay, Tel: 805/772-2257. **Santa Barbara Island & Coastal Fishing Trips**, Information Tel: 805/963-3564. Whale-watching, scuba diving trips.

Tourist Information
Carmel Business Assn., San Carlos (between 5th/6th Sts., PO Box 4444, Carmel, CA 93921, Tel: 408/624-2522. **Santa Barbara C & V Bureau**, 510-A State St., Santa Barbara, CA 93101, Tel: 805/966-9222.

MONTEREY BAY AREA
All phone numbers have area code 408.
Accommodation
MODERATE: **Merritt House**, 386 Pacific St., Monterey, CA 93940, Tel: 646-9686. Old adobe house. **Spindrift**, 652 Cannery Row, Monterey, CA 93940, Tel: 646-8900. Hotel with private beach and wonderful view of Monterey Bay.

BUDGET: **Padre Oaks**, 1278 Munras Ave., Monterey, CA 93940, Tel: 373-3741.

Attractions, Museums and Parks
Cannery Row, 765 Wave St., Monterey, Tel: 649-6690. **Custom House**, Custom House Plaza, Monterey, no phone. **Fisherman's Wharf**, Monterey, Information Tel: 373-0600. **Monterey Bay Aquarium**, 886 Cannery Row, Monterey, Tel: 648-4888. **Maritime Museum of Monterey**, Stanton Center, #5 Custom House Plaza, Monterey, Tel: 373-2469. **Monterey State Historic Park**, 20 Custom House Plaza, Monterey, Tel: 649-7118. Includes eight historic mansions from the 19th century. **Presidio of Monterey**, Pacific St., north of Scott St., Monterey, Tel: 647-5104. Large fortification open to public.

Tourist Information
Monterey Peninsula Chamber of Commerce and V & C Bureau, 380 Alvarado St., PO Box 1770, Monterey, CA 93940, Tel: 649-1770. A Monterey visitor center is located on Camino El Estero/Franklin Sts.

SALINAS, SANTA CRUZ AND SAN JOSE
All phone numbers have area code 408.
Accommodation
MODERATE: **Briar Rose**, 897 E Jackson St., San Jose, CA 95112, Tel: 279-5999. Old farm house. **Dream Inn**, 175 West Cliff Dr., Santa Cruz, CA 95060, Tel: 426-4330.

BUDGET: **Inncal**, 320 Ocean St., Santa Cruz, CA 95060, Tel: 458-9220. Close to the beach. **Rodeway Inn**, 2112 Monterey Hwy., San Jose, CA 95112, Tel: 294-1480.

Attractions, Museums and Parks
John Steinbeck Center, 371 Main St., Salinas, Tel: 753-6411. **Natural Bridges State Park and Beach**, Santa Cruz, Tel: 423-4609. **Peralta Adobe and Fallon House**, 175-186 W St./John St., San Jose, Tel: 287-2290. **Rosicrucian Park**, Park/Naglee Aves., San Jose, Tel. 947-3600; with **Planetarium** (Tel: 947-3634) and **Egyptian Museum** (Tel: 947-3636. **Steinbeck House**, 132 Central Ave., Salinas, Tel: 424-2735. **Winchester Mystery House**, 525 S Winchester Blvd., San Jose, Tel: 247-2101.

Tourist Information
Salinas Chamber of Commerce, 119 E Alisal St., PO Box 1170, Salinas, CA 93902, Tel: 424-7611. **San Jose Visitor Information Center**, McEnery Convention Center Lobby, 150 W San Carlos St., San Jose, CA 95110, Tel: 283-8833. **Santa Cruz County Conference & Visitors Council**, 701 Front St., Santa Cruz, CA 95060, Tel: 425-1234.

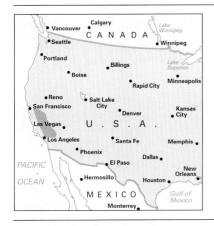

FROM LOS ANGELES INTO YOSEMITE NATIONAL PARK

PASADENA
SEQUOIA AND KING'S CANYON NATIONAL PARK
YOSEMITE NATIONAL PARK

The inland road, an alternative way to bridge the miles between the two great cities on the West Coast, is one of the finest drives in the U.S. It begins in Pasadena, that Los Angeles suburb where so many of America's sports megastars have performed. It's a toney and sophisticated place bathed in the neon and footlights of show biz. Just a few hundred miles to the north begins another fabulous stretch of California real estate, the National Parks of the Sierra Nevada. Here, the stars are the world's largest and oldest trees, thundering waterfalls, glacial valleys, snow-capped mountain ranges, lumbering black bears and soaring eagles. It's an area that also recalls the great pioneering days of the 19th century, when thousands risked everything to find, if not fortune, then at least an earthly Eden.

One can drive straight through from Los Angeles to San Francisco, a distance of about 400 miles (640 km), in about seven fast-moving hours. But to enjoy the remarkable display of wilderness along the way, sampling the hiking and riding, and observing the fauna and flora of this pristine nature, it is best to plan on spending a week on the road.

Left: Bridal Veil Falls in Yosemite National Park.

PASADENA

In July 1994, more than one billion of the world's soccer fans learned precisely where **Pasadena**, California, is. The final game of the World Cup took place in front of hundreds of TV cameras in this community's famous **Rose Bowl**. This huge oval stadium, which can hold more than 102,000 spectators, has been in use since the late 19th century. It hosts an annual football festival at the beginning of the year that has become one of America's most popular and important sporting events. The **Tournament of Roses**, which started in 1890, features parades of wildly exotic floats, beauty queens, and marching bands led by skimpily-clad drum majorettes.

There is an old quip about Los Angeles: "L.A. is a dozen suburbs in search of a city." Pasadena is one of the earliest of these suburbs to be incorporated and the first you will come across when heading northeast to San Francisco on the inland route. It's a community where modern technology and turn-of-the-century architecture combine with California charm and traditional lifestyle. It also has three institutions of higher learning, the **California Institute of Technology** (founded in 1891), **City College**, and **Pacific Oaks College.** For

135

decades, its main claim to fame was that its 2,000 citrus trees produced more than a million oranges a year. Today, Pasadena is a city of more than 132,000 residents, boasting a long list of arts and cultural centers, in particular theaters where many of Hollywood's rising stars hone their talents in the early stages of their careers.

Pasadena also has a great deal of art to explore, thanks, indirectly, to the climate: many millionaires used to hibernate in the town, and they ultimately left their collections to local institutions. The **Huntington Complex**, consisting of the Library, Museum and Botanical Gardens, has even achieved international renown. Its collections were once the pride and joy of railroad and real estate magnate Henry E. Huntington.

A more recent millionaire – Norton Simon – has also turned over his art collection to Pasadena. His museum is filled with a remarkable array of masterpieces including works by Rembrandt, Rafael, Goya, Monet, Renoir, Degas, van Gogh, Cezanne, Picasso, Braque, Kandinsky and Klee. Complementing the western art is an outstanding sculpture collection from the Indian sub-continent and Southeast Asia.

One of the hobbies of millionaires is horses. Keeping thoroughbreds in the stable for riding or breeding purposes has certain tax advantages, in addition to helping one tap into the kind of aristocratic image usually associated with the British Isles. Furthermore, horse-racing is a fun way of risking one's fortune for owner/breeder and common bettor alike. The wealthy families who came to Pasadena in the past brought their equestrian interest with them. Horse-racing began at the end of the 19th century, when one Lucky Baldwin, a colorful pioneer to California, built a racecourse

Right: At the foot of the Giant Sequoias in Sequoia National Park.

in Santa Anita, near Pasadena. It has been functioning without interruption ever since. The current track, far more luxurious in its appointments, was opened on Christmas Day, 1934.

Exploring the High Sierra

I-5 on the way to the **Sierra Nevada** is not without its own special sights. **Bakersfield**, the largest town in famous **Kern County** in the south of the San Joaquin Valley, provides a comprehensive look at the toils and troubles of Californian history. Great derricks, their pumps serenely swinging, stand out in the landscape of expansive wheat and cotton fields. The oil boom, which still governs the regional economy, replaced the gold boom at the end of the 19th century. Bakersfield was founded as a gold-digger's town in 1885. The history of its rise to prominence is exposed in the **Kern County Museum**, the **Pioneer Village**, as well as in the **West Kern Oil Museum**. A trip along the Kern River on Rte. 178 east is probably the best way to experience the region's idyllic landscape. It should include a visit to the nearby **Tule Elk State Reserve**, home to a herd of elk of a species only to be found in California.

To prepare for a trip through the Sierra Nevada, spend some time exploring the **California Living Museum**. In this combination of a zoo and botanical garden, you can see all the plants and animals you might come across later in their natural habitats.

SEQUOIA AND KING'S CANYON NATIONAL PARK

After leaving Bakersfield, the drive northward on Rte. CA 99 heads towards the Californian equivalent of the Alps, through one of America's most bountiful farming areas.

At the junction with CA Rte. 198, head east along the latter, passing through **Vi-**

salia and into **Sequoia National Park** through its **Ash Mountain Entrance.** Be sure to pick up the most recent issue of *The Sequoia Park* at the entrance gate; this is a free newspaper which lists all local activities by day, week and month. The possibilities for recreation and relaxation are endless, from self-guided nature walks to ranger-directed hikes, bus excursions and even exploring the park on horseback.

Although they're technically two separate National Parks, Sequoia and King's Canyon are really one contiguous mountain area covering more than 1,300 square miles of gorgeous California countryside, crowned by Mount Whitney, at 14,494 feet the highest peak in the 48 contiguous U.S. states. Both National Parks are part of the Sierra Nevada, a plateau that was created by tectonic shifts in the earth's crust about 150 million years ago. About two million years ago, i.e. relatively recently, glaciers planed down these piled-up layers and exposed the great granite formations that one can see today.

The Sierra Nevada is, without doubt or exaggeration, a unique natural paradise. In addition to alpine lakes, virtually untouched forests and wildlife ranging from mule deer to coyotes, this area also boasts the fantastic sequoias – giant evergreens which are older than any other living thing on this planet. Though not quite as tall as their sister trees, the redwoods, which grow further north, the sequoias are hardier than anything else alive. They are so strong indeed, that they never die. At some point they topple over, uprooting themselves, and it's the fall which kills them. Around the world, there are just 75 remaining groves of these monster trees, and 30 of these are in the Sequoia/King's Canyon National Parks.

In and out of these groves, and the Park's almost 864,000 acres, there are some 800 miles of mountain walking and hiking trails, but not a single paved road crosses the parks east to west.

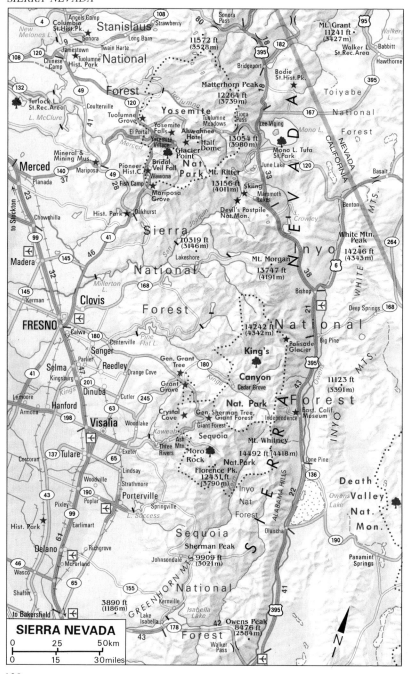

SIERRA NEVADA

| 0 | 25 | 50km |
| 0 | 15 | 30miles |

Not far from the main gate is a perfect stopping point to grasp the grandeur all around. It's called **Moro Rock**, a high point more than 6,500 feet above sea level overlooking the **Giant Forest**. During the Great Depression, the Civilian Conservation Corps (CCC) built a 400-step staircase to the top of the rock, and the view from the crowning platform is one of the most spectacular in all of California. Below are briskly flowing, white-flecked rivers, like the **Kaweah**, and to the east is the Great Western Divide.

Just a short ride away is **Tharp's Log**, a giant, fallen sequoia which was hollowed out into a rustic cabin in the late 19th-century by one Hale Tharp, a plucky cattleman.

Connecting the Sequoia and **King's Canyon** parks is the **General's Highway**, running from the Ash Mountain gate through **Giant Forest** and **Grant Grove** – passing **General Grant Tree** (265 ft.) – and into Kings Canyon, where it ends at **Cedar Grove**. It's a wonderfully scenic road, and links all four of the major visitor areas by a single ribbon of asphalt. Almost everywhere else in these parks visitors have to make their way on foot, on horseback, or in tour busses.

General Sherman of American Civil War fame is very prominent in these National Parks because the highest tree in Sequoia was named after him. It is estimated to be over 2,500 years old, is close to 276 feet high and weighs about 1,400 tons. With its base girth well over 100 ft, the General Sherman tree is frustrating to photograph because it's impossible to encompass it all in a single frame.

All around are other giant sequoias: one is the **Otto Log**, a fallen tree wide enough for your car to drive across. Another is the **Tunnel Log** which has been hollowed out at its base so a car can drive through it. These are indeed remarkable trees, when you think about it. Trees that were alive when Egypt's pyramids were

being built; trees as high as the dome of the U.S. Capitol Building in Washington, D.C.

These trees haven't always been worshipped. Nearby is the **Big Stump Area**, the sad remains of a massive logging effort which took place in these forests during the 1880s. The sea of stumps remaining from these once-beautiful forests are a powerful indictment of those timber interests which, to this day, would like to continue clearing forests away on an unregulated basis.

Not all the greatness of these National Parks is above ground. You can also take a look under the surface in **Crystal Cave**, which has been closed in recent years due to road construction, but which opened again in the summer of 1994. A twisting path leads down to the cave's entrance from the main road, and while the half-mile descent is easy, the 30-minute hike back up can be a little tiring for the unfit. There are close to 80 caves within the Parks, but Crystal Cave is the only one open to the public.

After a couple of days of looking at God's handiwork, many visitors either leave the Park via Rte. 180 and head back to Fresno, or go north for yet another natural wonderland, Yosemite National Park.

YOSEMITE NATIONAL PARK

The road to **Yosemite** begins in **Fresno**, and, following Rte. 41 northward, leads to the southern entrance of Yosemite, the most magnificent National Park in California. It's approximately a six-hour drive from Los Angeles, and more than three million visitors make the pilgrimage annually. So, expect it to be cramped and crowded during the busiest summer months.

Among the first white men to visit Yosemite was a member of the California militia, and his awe-struck comment sums up the feelings that many visitors have when they behold the beauty of the Yosemite wilderness for the first time: "As

I looked, a peculiar sensation seemed to fill my whole being, and I found my eyes in tears of emotion." John Muir, the famed California naturalist, also had words of reverence for Yosemite, which made a profound impression on him, as the following comment suggests: "As long as I live, I will hear waterfalls, birds and winds sing."

Native Americans were here first, however, specifically a tribe called the Ahwahneechees. The areas which they called Ahwahnee (meaning "deep, grassy valley"), was for a long time their home until Major James Savage and his Mariposa Battalion moved in on them in 1851. Even though the white man cut timber from the forests and mined in the hills, some had foresight enough to see that Yosemite's virgin beauty simply had to be preserved, and in 1864, while the Civil War was raging, President Ab-

Above: Family excursion in Yosemite National Park. Right: The Jeffrey Pine in Yosemite National Park.

raham Lincoln decreed that the area was to become the first state park in the entire country.

Yosemite consists of 1,170 square miles of mountain peaks, deep valleys, soaring granite spires, rushing waterfalls and thick, richly foliated forests. It takes its name from the Indian ward for grizzly bear – "u-zu-ma-te," which the white men eventually corrupted into "Yosemite."

Most visitors circle the main valley on a convenient sightseeing tram. Hikers take to the many trails winding their way down the valleys and up the hills. There are rental bikes available, as well as horses to mount. Rock climbers can tackle the many granite faces, accompanied by experienced guides. The Yosemite Mountaineering School offers courses. At **Fish Camp**, just south of the Park, there's even an old, narrow-gauge railroad that chugs its way along a four-mile track into the piney woods.

Entering the Park from the south, via Rte. 41, the first major stop is the **Mariposa Grove of Big Trees**. King of this forest of huge trees is the **Grizzly Giant**, estimated to be almost 3,000 years old. It has a base diameter of about 31 feet, a circumference of almost 100 feet, and it reaches over 210 feet into the California skies. The Grizzly Giant and many of the 500 or so magnificent trees in this forest, were all growing as long ago as 800 BC. It would take almost two dozen people linking hands to encircle the trunk of the largest of these trees.

Alongside the Wawona, at **Yosemite Village**, is Yosemite's **Pioneer History Center** and the Park's visitors' center, a collection of transplanted and recreated buildings designed to take visitors back to the late 1800s.

The "Ahwahnee"

Queen of the valley is the legendary **Ahwahnee** Hotel. Like virtually every hotel in the area, rooms must be booked

at least a year in advance. The Ahwahnee is one mile east of Yosemite Village on Rte. 140, and was built after a titled English woman once visited Yosemite and was inconvenienced by the primitive appointments of the few lodgings in the area. She complained loudly to the Director of the U.S. National Park Service that local accommodation was a disgrace, and largely because of her complaints plans were drawn up for a luxury hotel.

It was built of stone and timber, with beams of sugar pine logs, and has handcrafted ballustrades. Its huge fireplace usually holds a blazing fire and the restaurant is truly magnificent. Its doors opened in 1927, and since then a number of VIPs, including Queen Elizabeth, Emperor Haile Selassie and several U.S. Presidents, have enjoyed its warm and elegant hospitality.

Even if you're not actually staying at the Ahwahnee, try to eat there. The emphasis is on elegance: jackets and ties for gentlemen, dresses for the ladies. The Ahwahnee even boasts a ghost: in August of 1962, President John F. Kennedy stayed at the hotel, and the management thoughtfully constructed a special rocking chair for him because rocking soothed his war-injured back. Guests today swear they can sometimes hear the rocker creaking in the night.

Water, water everywhere

There's water rushing, surging, falling around almost every turn in the path in Yosemite. The Valley's highest single fall is **Ribbon Fall** where water cascades down 1,612 feet in a blur of spray and mist.

The highest waterfall in all of North America is **Yosemite Falls**, but it comes in three parts. This is the fifth-highest water drop in the world with the **Upper Falls** tumbling 1,430 feet, **Middle Spill** 675 feet, and Lower Cascade 320 feet. It's a quarter-mile walk from the always-crowded parking lot to see the water as it hits bottom. Alternatively, you can climb a posted three-and-a-half-mile path, ris-

141

ing almost a half a mile, to see the magnificent spill from the top. Another favorite is **Bridal Veil Falls**, which is fed by melting snows from the Sierra Range.

The most famous rock in Yosemite is **El Capitan** (7569 ft.), which rises about 3000 feet above the valley floor. Visitors examining it through their binoculars can usually discern the tiny figures of climbers who come from around the world to ascend its face. Photographer Ansel Adams shot this sheet of stone time and time again, finding a different angle and a brand-new image on almost every occasion. It's quite a peak – almost twice as high as the Rock of Gibraltar.

Another memorable hunk of stone is **Half Dome**, which stands almost 4600 feet over the valley floor at an altitude of 8,842 feet above sea level.

Tectonic forces allegedly split Half Dome away from **North Dome**, an adjacent peak, but the Native Americans

tell a more romantic tale; they have a legend about a lovers' quarrel which ended when the two sweethearts were turned into two peaks facing each other.

For the most spectacular panorama of Yosemite Valley, travel the 32 miles up to **Glacier Point** at the top of a 3,200-foot cliff. From here, you can see all the way to Nevada over the entire Sierra Nevada Range.

Rte. 120, which ends in the east at **Tioga Pass**, is the only road that crosses Yosemite from end to end. The main reason to follow it is to reach **Tuolumne**, an expansive alpine meadow ideal for picnics and gentle hikes. Farther east, outside the park proper, is the photogenic **Mono Lake** (6,200 feet) with chalk formations on the southern bank that seem literally to grow out of the water.

To get to San Francisco take the western exit of the Park. Rte. 140 east leads to I-5 north. Catch the turn-off for Rte. 580 which feeds into Rte. 80. You will cross the Bay Bridge to get into the city.

Above: Bizarre chalk towers on the South Bank of Mono Lake.

GREATER PASADENA AREA
All phonen numbers have area code 818.
Accommodation
LUXURY: **The Ritz-Carlton Huntington**, 1401 Oak Knoll Ave., Pasadena, CA 91106, Tel: 568-3900. Restored, elegant hotel dating from the turn of the century. *MODERATE:* **Holiday Inn**, 303 E. Cordova St., Pasadena, CA 91101, Tel: 449-4000.
Attractions, Museums and Parks
Fenyes Estate, 470 W Walnut, Tel: 577-1660. 1905 mansion showcasing the Pasadena millionaires' wealth. **Huntington Library, Art Collections and Botanical Gardens**, 1151 Oxford Rd., San Marino, Tel: 405-2141. **Los Angeles State and County Arboretum**, 301 North Balwin Ave., Arcadia, Tel: 821-3222. Man-made plant paradise with species from all over the world. **Mission San Gabriel**, 537 W Mission Dr., San Gabriel, Tel: 282-5191. One of the most beautiful examples of early Spanish mission style (chapel and museum dating from the early 18th century). **Norton Simon Museum of Art**, 411 W Colorado Blvd., Tel: 449-6840. **Rose Bowl**, Rose Bowl Dr. (off Arroyo Blvd.) Tel: 577-3106. **Santa Anita Park**, 285 W Huntingdon Dr., Arcadia, Tel: 574-6400. Historical racecourse. **The Gamble House**, 4 Westmoreland Pl., Pasadena, Tel: 7903-3334. One of the most beautiful American villas with complete wooden interior and impressive woodcarvings (1908). **Tournament House and Wrigley Gardens**, 391 S Orange Grove Blvd., Tel. 449-4100.
Tourist Information
Pasadena C & V Bureau, 171 S. Los Robles Ave., Pasadena, CA 91101, Tel: 795-9311.

SIERRA NEVADA, SEQUOIA AND KING'S CANYON
Accommodation
MODERATE: **Cedar Grove Lodge**, Box 789, Three Rivers, CA 93271 (at the end of CA 180, 30 miles east of General Grant Grove), Tel: 209/561-3314. Hotel in Sequoia/King's Canyon National Park. **Giant Forest Lodge**, Box 789, Three Rivers, CA 93271 (17 miles north of park entrance on CA 198), Tel: 209/561-3314. Nature resort with cottages and cabins in Sequoia/King's Canyon National Park. **Quarter Circle U Rankin Ranch**, Box 36, Caliente, CA 93518, three miles east of Caliente, near Bakersfield, Tel: 867-2511. Huge working ranch in Tehachapi Mountains. **Rio Bravo Resort**, 11200 Lake Ming Rd., Bakersfield, CA 93306, Tel: 805/872-5000. **Spalding House**, 631 N Encina, Visalia, CA 93291, Tel: 209/739-7877. Colonial-revival house, fully restored.
BUDGET: **Rio Mirada**, 4500 Pierce Rd., Bakersfield, CA 93308, Tel: 805/324-5555.

Campgrounds
For information on camping sites in Sequoia and King's Canyon National Parks contact Park Headquarters (see below).
Attractions, Museums and Parks
California Living Museum, 14000 Alfred Harrell Hwy., Bakersfield, Tel: 805/872-2256. **Kern County Museum**, 3801 Chester Ave., Bakersfield, Tel: 805/861-2345. **Sequoia and King's Canyon National Parks**, Information Tel: 209/565-3314. With **Foothills** (Tel: 209/565-3134), **Lodgepole** (Tel: 209/565-3782) and **Grant Grove Visitor Centers** (Tel: 209/335-2856). **Tule Elk State Reserve**, Rte. 1, Buttonwillow, Tel: 805/765-5004. **West Kern Oil Museum**, 184 Wood St./Hwy. 33, Taft (near Bakersfield), no phone.
Tourist Information
Bakersfield C & V Bureau, 1033 Truxturn Ave., Bakersfield, CA 93301, Tel: 805/325-5051. **Sequoia and King's Canyon National Parks**, Three Rivers, CA 93271, Tel: 209/565-3134.

YOSEMITE NATIONAL PARK
All phone numbers have area code 209.
Accommodation
LUXURY: **Ahwahnee**, Yosemite Village, CA 95389 (14 miles east of entrance on CA 140), Tel: 252-4848. **Marriott's Tenaya Lodge at Yosemite**, Box 159, Fish Camp, CA 93623 (near south gate, on CA 41), Tel: 683-6555.
MODERATE: **Pines Resorts**, Box 329, Bass Lake, CA 98604 (five miles off CA 41, on North Shore Rd.), Tel: 642-3121. Cottage colony.
BUDGET: **Mariposa Lodge**, Box 733, 5052 CA 140, Mariposa, CA 95338 (at junction CA 140/49), Tel: 966-3607.
Campgrounds
For reservations and information, Tel: 1-800/452-1111.
Attractions and Museums
Mono Lake, east of Lee Vining, at Mono Lake Basin National Forest, Tel: 619/647-6572. One of the oldest (salt) lakes in the world with famous tufa and stratified limestone rock formations. **Pioneer Yosemite History Center**, a few miles from Mariposa Grove, at Wawona. Living history museum. **Yosemite National Park Visitor Center**, at Park Headquarters in Yosemite Valley, Tel: 372-0299. **Yosemite Moutain-Sugar Pine Railroad**, four miles south of southern park gate, on CA 41, Tel: 683-7273. Narrow-gauge steam train excursion.
Tourist Information
Yosemite National Park, Yosemite Park & Carry Co. Yosemite National Park, CA 95389, Tel: 372-0264.

FROM SAN FRANCISCO TO SALT LAKE CITY

**SAN FRANCISCO
SACRAMENTO
LAKE TAHOE
NEVADA DESERT
SALT LAKE CITY**

San Francisco, it has been said, is the most European city in the United States. Salt Lake City, 735 miles to the east (1,176 km), is probably the most mainstream of American communities, a town originally founded and developed by a ragged group of religious break-aways, the Mormons. Parts of the route are known as "the loneliest road in America." While there may not be towns and crowds aplenty to amuse the traveler, there is still magnificent scenery to enjoy: huge woods of ancient trees, craggy mountains topped with snow and striated with ski lifts, broad blue mountain lakes and shimmering desert wastes. Done at a leisurely pace, this 850-mile trip (1,360 km) should take at least nine days.

SAN FRANCISCO – THE CITY BY THE BAY

San Francisco is a community with a gaudy and bawdy past and a bright future. The city was founded in 1776 when Juan Bautista de Anza established a Spanish stronghold on the bay now bearing the city's name. Several years later,

Previous pages: Heavy traffic at 220 feet altitude on the 8,981 feet long Golden Gate Bridge. Left: Christopher Street Day here honored with artful hair creation.

Father Junipero Serra founded the Mission Dolores. It was a backwater of Spanish colonialism until the year 1848 when one James Marshall, while building a mill for one John Sutter on the Indian River about 100 miles northeast of the city, found some nuggets of gold. Once news of his find leaked out, San Francisco's fortune grew. In just four years, the city grew to a community of close to a quarter million miners, victuallers, barkeepers, saloon girls, day laborers and desperadoes, many culled from the fresh waves of immigrants disembarking in the east.

The town needed that rousing spirit to recover from the 1906 earthquake and subsequent fire that destroyed 464 city blocks, in other words nearly half of the city's dwellings. San Francisco, now covering 46.6 square miles on a peninsula jutting into the Pacific, was built on shaky ground, namely the **San Andreas Fault**. In 1989 the city rocked again, killing nearly 100 people and leaving a trail of destruction. It has once again recovered from the trauma, but each time Mother Earth shivers, all America wonders "Is it the Big One that will heave San Francisco into the ocean?"

The best way to get an overview of town before honing in on some of its special sights, is to take the 49-mile scenic drive that is plainly signposted by blue-

and-white signs. What strikes everyone first are the hills. If you get tired of climbing one, so a local quip, just lean up against it. Some of these hills have achieved high ranking in the city's social structure. **Nob Hill**, for instance, soaring over Union Square, was where four wealthy San Francisco families built their mansions; even today, it is capped by the homes of many prominent San Franciscans and some luxury hotels.

Telegraph Hill is where the harbormaster used to signal incoming ships to request information on their provenance and cargos. Today, it is topped by **Coit Tower**, a conical construction built as a tribute to the city's firemen by a wealthy dowager who had been an enthusiastic fire buff since she was a teenager. A platform at the top, accessible by elevator, provides one of the most breathtaking views of the city, its two great bridges, the sea of houses, the glittering bay with sinister Alcatraz Island. The inner walls of the 210-foot tower are covered in murals painted in the 1930s by 25 artists sponsored by a New Deal job program.

Another of the city's 42 hills that should be ascended is **Russian Hill**, not so much for its summit, but rather to experience the nine hairpin turns of **Lombard Street**, the most crooked street of San Francisco (no offense meant).

The city's hills caused the deaths of many a horse in the era before gasoline engines. In 1873 Andrew Hallidie saw a horse-drawn carriage roll back down a San Francisco hill, dragging its horses behind it, and decided that the town needed the *cable cars* to get passengers up and over the peaks without killing animals in the process. Today, his system comprises 39 cars on three lines in a network covering 12 miles. They weigh six tons, travel at 9.5 mph and can overcome the 21 percent gradient of some streets. The cars, many of which still date from the Victorian Age, seat 30 with plenty more standing or straphanging.

Exploring the City's Neighborhoods

San Francisco boasts many distinct neighborhoods, and each differs from the other: Italian North Beach, Latino Mission, toney Pacific Heights, stoned-out Haight and gay Castro. The **Italian section** spreads out from **Washington Square** – which isn't a square at all because it has five sides. In its middle stands a statue of Benjamin Franklin, not George Washington. **Haight-Ashbury** used to be home to Janis Joplin, Jefferson Airplane and the Grateful Dead. Most of the druggies have long since moved on, and this is a yuppified neighborhood now with trendy clothing stores, busy restaurants and lively entertainment.

The heart of San Francisco's downtown is **Union Square**. The name goes back to the pre-Civil-War days, when anti-Secessionists successfully demonstrated to convince the state's government to stand by the Union. The square itself consists of pleasant greenery. Unfortunately, on some days, it has become the haven for a rather aggressive community of panhandlers, and can not be recommended as a place to stroll or take a lunch break. In typical American contrast, the immediate area boasts more than 40 hotels and a long list of America's finest department stores.

The heavily Latino **Mission District** has grown up around **Mission Dolores**, the Franciscan church built by Indian labor in 1791. Its elaborate altar is a beautiful example of Mexican naive artistry. The adjacent museum has a range of exhibits. The simple pioneer cemetery was the last resting ground for many of San Francisco's earliest residents.

Chinatown – Gateway to Asia

Chinatown is a remarkable area which was born in 1847 when Chinese laborers began arriving in San Francisco. They originally came to work in the mines, but

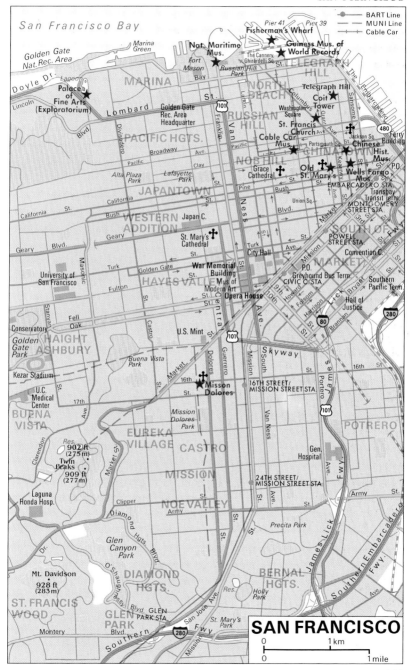

San Francisco Bay

Golden Gate
Nat. Rec. Area

Marina
Green

Pier 41 Pier 39
Fisherman's Wharf

Nat. Maritime
Mus.

Guiness Mus. of
World Records

BART Line
MUNI Line
Cable Car

Doyle Dr.

Lagoon

Palace
of
Fine Arts
(Exploratorium)

Lincoln

Lombard

Fort
Mason

Bay

The Cannery,
Ghirardelli Sq.

Russian
Park

TELEGRAPH
HILL

The
Embarcadero

MARINA

St.

NORTH
BEACH

Columbus

Telegraph Hill
Coit
Tower

Golden Gate
Rec. Area
Headquarter

RUSSIAN
HILL

Washington
Square

St. Francis
Church

Sansome

480

Ferry
Building

Broadway

Ave.

Pacific

Cable Car
Mus.

Portsmouth Sq.

Grant

Jackson Sq.

Chinese
Hist.
Mus.

Pacific

Clay

NOB HILL

Kearny

P.O.

Alta Plaza
Park

Lafayette
Park

Grace
Cathedral

Old
St. Mary's

Wells Fargo
Mus.

EMBARCADERO STA.

Pine

Bush

Transbay
Transit Term.

JAPANTOWN

California

Union Sq.

MONTGOMERY
STREET STA.

California

Bush

WESTERN
ADDITION

Japan C.

Blvd.

SOUTH OF

Geary

Geary

Blvd.

St. Mary's
Cathedral

Turk
City Hall

Ave.

POWELL
STREET STA.

Market

Convention C.

MARKET

Masonic

Turk

Golden Gate

War Memorial
Building
Mus. of
Modern Art
Opera House

P.O.

Southern
Pacific Term.

University of
San Francisco

Fulton

HAYES VALLEY

Greyhound Bus Term.

CIVIC C. STA.

Stanyan

Fell

Oak

St.

Central

Ave.

9th

10th

Howard

Folsom

Harrison

Bryant

Brannan

Hall of
Justice

80

280

Conservatory

Golden
Gate
Park

HAIGHT
ASHBURY

U.S. Mint

101

Skyway

Lick

Kezar Stadium

Buena Vista
Park

Market

16th

Guerrero

Mission

South

St.

Van Ness

16TH STREET/
MISSION STREET STA.

Portrero

16th

101

U.C.
Medical
Center

17th

St.

Misson
Dolores

Ave.

POTRERO

BUENA
VISTA

EUREKA
VILLAGE

Castro

Mission
Dolores
Park

CASTRO

Clarendon

Res.
902 ft
(275 m)

Twin
Peaks
909 ft
(277 m)

MISSION

Gen.
Hospital

Army

St.

Laguna
Honda Hosp.

Clipper

NOE VALLEY

Diamond

Army

St.

24TH STREET/
MISSION STREET STA.

Ave.

James Lick

Army

St.

Hgts.

Blvd.

Precita Park

Mt. Davidson
928 ft
(283 m)

O'Shaughnessy

Glen
Canyon
Park

DIAMOND
HGTS.

Res.

Holly
Park

BERNAL
HGTS.

Southern Embarcadero Fwy.

ST. FRANCIS
WOOD

GLEN
PARK

Blvd. GLEN
PARK STA.

San Jose Ave.

St. Mary's
Park

Ave.

Monterey

Blvd.

280

Mission

Fwy.

Southern

SAN FRANCISCO

0 — 1 km

0 — 1 mile

were soon heavily involved in building the transcontinental railway. It is thought to be the largest single Chinese community outside Asia and is expected to swell even further when Hong Kong reverts to Chinese rule in 1997. Walking through the green-tiled dragon-topped Chinatown gate at **Bush Street** and **Grant Avenue**, you enter another world. Men in loose-fitting clothes do slow *tai chi* exercises in the early morning mists to the steady clicking of mah-jongg tiles. **Grant Avenue** is the main street to visit. It leads through brightly-colored ethnic markets with displays of orange-painted ducks, paper-thin dried fish and bright, green and white *bok choi.*

Strolling along Fisherman's Wharf

The fish may have gone, but **Fisherman's Wharf** today attracts large schools

Above: Cable car climbs steep Hyde Street (Alcatraz Island in the background). Right: Wall painting in Chinatown.

of tourists with its shops, galleries and seafood restaurants. Many have spilled over from nearby **Ghirardelli Square** where an erstwhile chocolate factory has become a profitable complex of trendy tourist shops. From nearby **Pier 41**, curious visitors can sail off on the two-and-a-half hour cruise around **Alcatraz** and hear the stories of America's Public Enemies once incarcerated there. The most unusual residents of **Pier 39**, a two-storey, bayfront tourist attraction, are more than 600 sea lions who have completely taken over certain areas of the marina. They lie around on the docks all day, barking at the tourists or merely staring down on them.

Golden Gate Park and Bridge

There are two dramatic avenues out of San Francisco. The **Golden Gate Bridge**, 8,981 feet long and rising 220 feet above the bay, carries about three million vehicles a month to and from **Marin County**. To date, some 1,100

people have jumped from this striking construction to commit suicide. The Bayside villages of **Sausalito** and **Tiburon** offer spectacular views back across the Bay to San Francisco. Both are artists' colonies, harboring exquisite restaurants with balconies overlooking the bay.

17 miles northwest of San Francisco is the 580-acre **Muir Woods National Monument**, a majestic grove of redwoods, some close to 1,000 years old, and almost 250 feet high.

The other famous span is the eight-and-one-quarter-mile **Bay Bridge**, the longest suspension bridge in the world, four miles of which are over water. It leads travelers to **Oakland**, a cosmopolitan metropolitan area and seaport where more than 80 languages are spoken. **Preservation Park**, a complex of 16 restored Victorian houses, and the **Jack London waterfront area** with its old saloons and homes, including the author's Yukon cabin which was transplanted south, are among the major tourist attractions here.

Berkeley houses the famous **University of California**. The visitor should walk down bazaar-like Telegraph Ave. to the campus. Worth a visit are the **Museum of Anthropology** and the **University Art Museum**.

SACRAMENTO

Four major freeways intersect at **Sacramento**, the capital of California, and one of its oldest, most famous communities. I-580 is probably the most modern road leading from San Francisco into the broad San Joaquin valley. Mile after mile of agricultural landscape unfolds as you move northwest on I-5 towards the signature **Capitol Dome** which stands out in Sacramento skyline. This area began to boom as early as 1839, when Swiss immigrant John Augustus Sutter arrived on the banks of the American River and build a fort and trading post he called New Helvetia.

By 1848, Sutter's community was prosperous enough so that he could start

151

a mill in the nearby foothills. When John Marshall commenced the construction of Sutter's mill, he chanced upon a gold nugget in the river. This discovery changed the face of western America forever. Within months, most of Sutter's employees and neighbors were chasing lodes of gold up in the hills, and the population of nearby Sacramento and its adjoining areas multiplied exponentially as gold fever spread nationwide.

Downtown Sacramento today is very much a replica of the city as it prospered in the era from 1850 until the turn of the century. **Sutter's Fort** has been completely reconstructed, and there are self-guided tours with explanations of the exhibits, which include a smithy, a prison, a bakery, living quarters and a corral.

Sacramento was so important as a communications hub in its early days that the famous Pony Express had its Western

Above: What came in the mail? (Mailboxes in Sausalito).

terminus here. Just before the telegraph came West, California was linked to St Joseph, Missouri and the rest of the East, by a network of 80 riders who galloped swift ponies over the 1,966-mile route in under ten days. This epic era in American history is marked by a monument at Second and J Streets.

Sacramento's major business, besides tourism, is government. The **State Capitol** is a massive, domed, marble-encrusted affair, where the business of leading America's most populous state is concentrated. The building boasts seven historic rooms, plus a theater and some exhibits. Visitors can join tours through the State Capitol twice a day. Not far away is the **Governor's Mansion**, a 30-room Victorian residence which Ronald Reagan refused to live in during his tenure as Governor; it has been empty ever since.

After the Pony Express, the railroad became the essential link between Sacramento and the East. The heyday of rail travel is lavishly documented at the

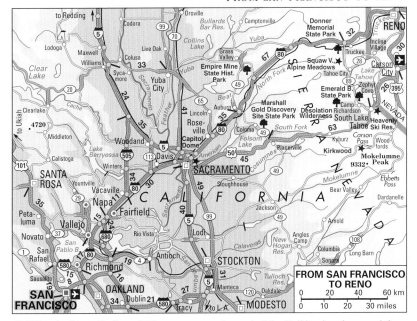

California State Railroad Museum, a huge enclosure housing 46 separate exhibits and 21 restored locomotives and cars.

With Sacramento bounded by two rivers, the American and the Sacramento, water recreation tops the list of outdoor activities. There are plenty of fishing boats eager to take interested parties out after salmon and steelhead trout. River rafting along some of the upland streams is very popular. Houseboating is a favorite pastime in the area as well. With over 1,000 miles of navigable waterways, there's plenty of room to find solitude on the rivers.

Gold Country

Just about everyone who originally came to Sacramento was after gold, so you should plan to visit the coast **Mother Lode** as well. It stretches over 120 miles along Hwy. 49. North on 49 is the **Empire Mine State Historic Park** in Grass Valley. This was the largest, richest and deepest of the California mines, and there continue to be visible traces of the digging and dredging that went on frantically in the area.

South on 49 is **James Marshall State Historic Monument** and **Gold Discovery Site State Park**. Here's where it all began: on a hilltop stands a statue of Marshall pointing dramatically to the spot where he allegedly made his historic discovery of gold.

Further south on 49 is **Columbia**, a fully-restored Gold Rush town, where visitors can actually pan for gold themselves, climb aboard stagecoaches, drink and dine in Wild West-style saloons, and relive the past in a compact, historical museum.

Like most of the Forty-Niners, few today leave the Sacramento and Gold Country area with a gold nugget in their pocket. They do depart, however, with golden memories of what California used to be in the bad old days. Heading East on US 50, they are bound for Lake Tahoe and Reno.

153

LAKE TAHOE

Mark Twain said it all when he described **Lake Tahoe**, which sits high in the Sierras astride the California-Nevada border: "The fairest picture the whole earth affords..."

Its brilliant blue surface reflects the green forest and snow-capped Sierras around it. This spectacular oasis of color, 22 miles long and 8 miles wide, has been attracting vacationers and settlers since the 1800s. The lake is both deep and clear. In some areas it's almost 1,700 feet to the bottom. The water is so transparent that the locals say you can spot a dinner plate on the bottom from 75 feet up.

The 72-mile drive around the lake on Rtes. 28, 50 and 88 is a tour through some of the best skiing in North America, and through some of its gaudiest gambling palaces. 105 miles from Sacramento, 191 miles from San Francisco, Lake Tahoe has become Northern California's principal recreational center.

Steamships were the preferred mode of transportation around the lake in earlier days, and two paddlewheelers still chug tourists along the shoreline. The newest is the 151-foot *MS Dixie II*, which takes passengers over to **Emerald Bay**, a gash cut into the lake eons ago by a glacier. For those who prefer to get closer to the water, there are kayaks available for rent at the **Camp Richardson Resort** on the south shore. The kayaks are virtually tip-proof, and a course of instruction is given before paddlers set out on their journey.

Captain Kirk's Beach Club at **Zephyr Cove** has an enormous fleet of jet-skis, ski boats, pedal boats and fishing boats for rent. Those who prefer a more elevated view of the lake can hang in the air from a parasail.

Right: Reno, by day not nearly so glittery as by night.

Fishing has no special season on the lake. Anglers will find Mackinaw trout biting 12 months out of the year. Hikers are everywhere around Tahoe, walking through the pink thistle and red columbine, the yellow buttercup and mule ears, the purple astors and lupine. With a little luck they'll spot an occasional coyote, a couple of mule deer and perhaps even a black bear or two.

Biking has become a major Tahoe activity; rental agencies offer everything from standard models for casual bike rides along the lake, to rock-hopping, mud-squishing mountain bikes. The adventurous strap on their helmets and chance the exhilarating ride down the breathtaking **Flume Trail**, tracing the original system which was built for log-ging during the heyday of the Comstock Lode.

Another place to take chances is at Tahoe's gambling tables. Lady Luck arrived at the lake and unpacked her bags in 1944 when **Harvey's Wagonwheel** opened the area's first gaming establishment. This occurred just across the California line in Nevada (where gambling has been legal since 1931). **South Lake Tahoe**, within Nevada, now boasts six 24-hour casinos, with over 7,000 slot machines and more than 500 gaming tables. Most of the huge casinos offer massive buffets at bargain prices, designed to lure customers in to where they might become inspired by the jingling sound of jackpots being won.

The best overall views of the Tahoe region are from the basket of one or another of the various hot-air balloons which take passengers aloft at dawn and at dusk when the weather's good. Or, there's the option of going to the **Heavenly Ski Resort** with its 50-passenger tram which carries its human load 2,000 feet up the slopes, where they enjoy a breathtaking view of the countryside.

Some of the attractions to be seen in this region include the **Vikingsholm**, a

38-room mansion finished in 1929, a replica of an 8th-century Viking castle. In springtime flowers bloom on its sod roof. East of **Incline Village** on Rte. 28, is the **Ponderosa Ranch**, instantly recognizable to anyone who's seen episodes of the beloved TV series *Bonanza*, which was shot here. On display are the Cartwrights' ranch, a complete Western town, and, of course, a cowboy saloon.

In winter, Tahoe is difficult to drive to and through, because, at over 6,000 feet, there's plenty of snow on the ground. On the other hand, it is an ideal area for skiing, with 19 resorts located within a 45-minute drive of the lake. The most famous resort is **Squaw Valley**, primarily because it was the site of the 1960 Winter Olympics. What is a golf course in summer becomes a cross-country skiing area in winter.

Alpine Meadows is usually the first of Tahoe's ski resorts to open in the fall because of an extensive network of snow-making machines. Insiders report that the runs leading into Nevada are usually less crowded than those on the California side of the hill. **Kirkwood**, at 7,800 feet, is the highest of the Tahoe resorts, making for more light, dry powder than the heavier snows which local skiers describe as "Sierra cement." The resort takes its name from a pioneer, Zachary Kirkwood, who established his inn in 1874 to service silver miners.

A few miles north of Tahoe, off I-80, is the most historic monument in the area, a tribute to the Donner party, a group of 89 pioneers who headed West in late 1846 and early 1847, and got trapped in Sierras by snows 22 feet high. The 47 who survived admitted that they had eaten the remains of some of their fellow travelers. A 22-foot-high marker commemorates the tragedy. Also worth visiting is **Desolation Wilderness**, 64,000 acres at the southwest corner of the lake, which consists of a jungle of granite peaks, heavy forests, glacier-carved valleys and more than 50 smaller lakes ideal for fishing in and hiking around.

155

NEVADA DESERT

Reno, which bills itself as the "biggest little city in the world," is just a few miles to the east of Tahoe along I-80. This neon-lit town has recently invested in an enjoyable **River Walk** along the banks of the **Truckee River**, and it stages a year-long calendar of events ranging from rodeos and logger jamborees to wine-tastings and ethnic events in an effort to attract clients to its gaudy gambling casinos and five-minute wedding chapels.

Reno is the last populous stop for a while on the way east. South of it is Nevada's capital **Carson City**, which bathes in the tourism of Lake Tahoe. But the eastward drive ending in Salt Lake City is through the **Great Basin** of the Nevada Desert.

There are two major east-west arteries across this wasteland. Travelers heading for Salt Lake City usually take I-80, which shares with its parallel highway, I-50, the nickname of "the loneliest road in America." In earlier days the route was called the *Humboldt Trail*, and was trod by tens of thousands of Forty-Niners headed for the gold fields around Sacramento.

It crosses a land virtually without water, a barren waste of alkaline sand. The saying here is that the topography is so harsh, it takes 40 acres to feed a cow, several square miles to support a human, and a ton of stone to get an ounce of gold. One goes for dozens of miles without seeing much more than sagebrush or creosote bushes, with the only sign of civilization an occasional ranch house amidst a cooling cluster of cottonwood trees. Here and there are isolated houses without cattle, often surrounded by sleek limousines from Vegas or Reno. It's another of Nevada's legal brothels which do a lively business, often hosting busloads full of visiting Japanese tourists

Right: Too much salt can also be profitable – salt production on Great Salt Lake.

or delegates escaping a boring trade show. Stopping in for just a drink is not discouraged for those interested in watching the action for a little while.

Few towns have even the barest of tourist facilities, but **Winnemucca** is worth a stop-over, perhaps the logical place to spend a night. In 1850 it was known as Frenchman's Ford and had a toll booth that charged crossing the Humboldt River on their way to California. The town takes its name from the Indian chief who used to hold sway in the area.

The most famous (apocryphal) event in Winnamucca's history is the bank robbery staged by Butch Cassidy and the Sundance Kid. They allegedly rode off with almost $33,000. Winnamucca still runs its annual **Butch Cassidy Days Fiesta**, and hopes in vain that Paul Newman or Robert Redford will show up. To ward off boredom in the evening, the town has four casinos designed to separate travelers from their funds in an entertaining fashion.

Closer to the Utah border is **Elko**, the hub of northeastern Nevada, and with 13,000 residents, the largest town between Reno and Salt Lake City. Chances of getting authentic French/Spanish food in town are quite good because of the large numbers of Basque shepherds who once settled nearby to tend their flocks of sheep.

SALT LAKE CITY
The Mormon Capital

Salt Lake City is unique, perhaps the only theocratically run city in the US. Clean, honest, forthright, it tries also to be cosmopolitan, with modern high-rise commercial centers, some interesting sightseeing and a lot of history.

The city is sandwiched between two dramatic ranges of the Rockies: the **Wasatch** and the **Oquirra**. The first white settlers to arrive in large numbers were pioneers of a brand new sect, the Church

of Jesus Christ of Latter-Day Saints – more commonly known as **Mormons.** They were led into the valley in 1847 by Brigham Young, a church patriarch who was looking for a locale where they could practice their religion – which included polygamy – without persecution. Young uttered the immortal and prosaic phrase when he saw the valley: "This is the right place!" And the Mormons have been ensconced here ever since.

Their pioneer town was planted alongside the huge **Salt Lake**, 48 miles wide and 90 miles long. It's the largest lake in the U.S. west of the Mississippi, a left-over of Lake Bonneville, which evaporated over thousands of years, and its salt content is up to 27 percent. Floating in the lake water is easy; tasting it is unpleasant.

The best place from which to view the lake is the **Saltair Resort**, less than 15 minutes from downtown. It's a fun park with a bit of bad luck behind it; it has burned down three times and was flooded once. When it opened in 1893, it boasted the world's largest dance pavilion.

Following the Gospel

A tour of Salt Lake City probably should begin at the **State Capitol** with its granite walls and unique copper dome, perched majestically on a hillside high over the city, one of the first buildings to be sighted by new arrivals. It was too expensive for the state to put up until a local millionaire railway baron passed away, and the tax collectors used the revenue from his estate to erect it.

The **Mormon Tabernacle Headquarters** on historic **Temple Square** should be visited to learn more about Mormon theology. There are docents on hand throughout the day who will explain Mormonism and trace its history through the past 150 years. Each Thursday evening, from 8:00 pm to 9:30 pm, the famous Mormon Tabernacle Choir, a choral group of some 320 voices, practices, and visitors are invited to listen. Early risers on Sunday who can be in their seats by 9:15 am can catch the choir's weekly national radio and TV concert.

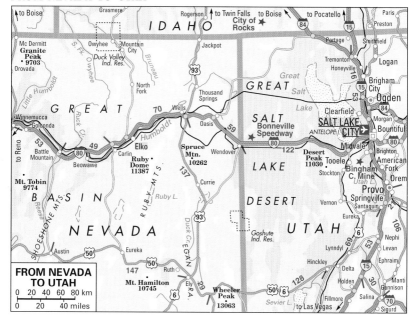

Next to the King's College Choir in Cambridge, this is probably the best-known religious choral group in the world. They have performed at four Presidential inaugurations, with a number of famous symphony orchestras, and have produced more than 150 recordings, several of which have gone gold. Singing is a family tradition with the 20 husbands and wives performing, and a number of families have more than one generation in the choir.

Also on Temple Square is the **Family History Library** which is a collection of genealogical information totaling 1.9 million rolls of microfilm plus 250,000 books. Given a little time, its staff can trace just about any name genealogically during the period from the mid-1500s up until today.

Salt Lake City has long been a transportation hub. The golden spike celebrating the first completed railway link be-

tween the East and West coasts in the mid 1800s was driven in approximately 90 miles north of the city. Trolley cars were once the major form of local transportation, and today **Trolley Square**, located just a few blocks from downtown, is a remodelled complex housing specialty shops, several theaters, art galleries and restaurants.

Salt Lake City is very much an outdoors-minded community. Less than 20 minutes from downtown, a driver can step out of his car amidst secluded mountain paths of exquisite beauty, flanked by multicolored wildflower meadows and clear streams, with the distinct possibility that with a bit of patience there will be deer and elk in view.

The **Brighton Resort** at the top of **Big Cottonwood Canyon** is the start of a two-and-a-half-mile trail to Lakes **Mary**, **Martha** and **Catherine**, all fed by a melting mountain glacier. For those who want to go up the hills without too much strain, there's the tram at Little Cottonwood Canyon which drops off hikers and

Right: The Mormon Tabernacle Choir is one of the most well-known church choirs in America.

bikers 11,000 feet up, where they can see five states.

One of the most remarkable annual events in America takes place on **Antelope Island** in Salt Lake each November. It's a ten-day affair, as cowboys and helicopters combine to corral one of the largest and oldest buffalo herds in the country. The cowboys move the herd into holding pens for their annual autumn physicals, and to sort out the weak animals.

Since mining has contributed to much of Salt Lake City's more recent wealth, people are interested in seeing where the ore comes from. This makes the **Bingham Canyon Mine** a major tourist attraction. It used to be a mountain; now it is a huge bowl covering 1,900 acres, twice as deep as the world's tallest building. From the rim, the trucks and steam shovels below look like toys, as they move their loads to the ore crusher. A ton of ore yields just 11 pounds of copper.

The Visitors' Center, which is off State Rd. U-48 and I-15, has shown exhibits and a video presentation of mining operations. Not far away are the ghost towns of **Leadmine** and **Bingham**, with their **House of Copper Museum** and gift shop, and the rustic **Leadmine Bar** which still boasts the traditional swinging doors and vintage bullet holes.

The continued growth of skiing as a winter sport has been kind to Salt Lake City. There are several ski resorts within an hour of downtown, 75 chair lifts, and uncrowded slopes making for an enjoyable trip down. The **Wasatch Mountains** receive an average of 460 inches of light, fluffy snowfall a year, all of which has prompted the community to bid for the Winter Olympic Games in 2002. The U.S. Ski Team headquarters is in Utah, meaning there's a lot of top-flight talent on the slopes.

Not far away is **Sundance**, where Robert Redford purchased some land 20 years ago. It now boasts 47 trails spread out over 450 acres. When the snow disappears in summer, the town gears up for its annual film festival which is known for its alternative air.

SAN FRANCISCO BAY AREA

All phone numbers have area code 415.

Accommodation

LUXURY: **Four Seasons Clift**, 495 Geary St., San Francisco, CA 94102, Tel: 775-4700.

MODERATE: **Alamo Square**, 719 Scott St., San Francisco, CA 94117, Tel: 922-2055. Nicely restored inn. **Sausalito Hotel**, 16 El Portal, Sausalito, CA 94965, Tel: 332-4155. **Washington Inn**, 465 10th St., Oakland, CA 94607, Tel: 510/452-1776. Historic hotel from the turn of the century.

BUDGET: **Grant Plaza**, 465 Grant St., San Francisco, CA 94108, Tel: 434-3883. Small hotel in Chinatown. **Sheehan**, 620 Sutter St., San Francisco, CA 94102, Tel: 775-6500. Close to Union Square.

Cafés and Restaurants

EXPENSIVE: **Victor's**, Westin St. Francis, Union Sq., San Francisco, Tel: 956-7777. Fine Californian cuisine.

MODERATE: **Chic's Place**, Pier 39, Fisherman's Wharf, San Francisco, Tel: 421-2442. Wonderful sight of Alcatraz and Golden Gate Bridge. Serving seafood. **Ghirardelli Square**, 900 N. Point St., San Francisco, Tel: 775-5500. Old chocolate manufactury now housing shops and the famous café Ghirardelli.

Attractions and Museums

Alcatraz Island, San Francisco, Tel: 456-BOAT (info), Tel: 546-2882 (tickets for ferry). **The Cannery**, 2801 Leavenworth St., San Francisco, Tel. 771-3112. Old Del Monte cannery restored as upscale shopping center. **Chinese Historical Museum**, 650 Commercial St., San Francisco, Tel: 391-1188. Chinese-American artifacts. **Coit Tower** (on Telegraph Hill), 1 Telegraph Hill Blvd., San Francisco, Tel: 362-0808. **Fort Point National Historic Site**, Presidio of San Francisco, Tel: 556-1693. **Golden Gate National Recreation Area**, Park Headquarters, Fort Mason, San Francisco, Tel: 556-0560. **Golden Gate Park**, McLaren Lodge (Fell/Stanyan Sts.), San Francisco, Tel: 666-7200. **Guiness Museum of World Records**, 235 Jefferson St., San Francisco, Tel: 771-9890. **Jack London Square**, 30 Jack London Square, Oakland, Tel: 893-7956. **Mission Dolores**, 3321 16th St., San Francisco, Tel: 621-8203. **Muir Woods National Monument**, Mill Valley, 12 miles north on Hwy. 101, Tel: 388-2595. **Pier 39**, San Francisco, Tel: 705-5500. **Ripley's "Believe it or Not" Museum**, 175 Jefferson St., Fisherman's Wharf, San Francisco, Tel: 771-6188. Displays of the odd and unbelievable. **San Francisco Museum of Modern Art**, Van Ness Ave., San Francisco, Tel: 252-4000. **San Francisco War Memorial and Performing Arts Center**, 401 Van Ness Ave., San Francisco, Tel: 621-6600. **San Francisco Zoo**, 1 Zoo Rd., San Francisco, Tel: 753-7080. **Union Square**, 323 Geary St., San Francisco, Tel: 781-7880 (information). **Wells Fargo Bank History Museum**, 420 Montgomery St., San Francisco, Tel: 396-2619. Stagecoach, gold coins and nuggets on exhibition.

Tourist Information

Oakland C & V Bureau, 1000 Broadway, Suite 200, Oakland, CA 94607, Tel: 510/839-9000.

San Francisco V & C Bureau, 201 Third Street, Ste. 900, San Francisco, CA 94103, Tel: 974-6900.

San Francisco Visitor Information Center, Hallidie Plaza, Lower Level, 900 Market St., San Francisco, Tel: 391-2000.

Sausalito Chamber of Commerce, 333 Caledonia St., PO Box 566, Sausalito, CA 94965, Tel: 332-0505.

SACRAMENTO AND GOLD COUNTRY

All phone numbers have area code 916.

Accommodation

MODERATE: **Amber House**, 1315 22nd St., Sacramento, CA 95816, Tel: 444-8085. Historic inn. **Best Western Placerville Inn**, 6850 Greenleaf Dr., south of US 50 at Missouri Flat Rd., Placerville, CA 95667, Tel: 622-9100. **Vizcaya**, 2019 21st St., Sacramento, CA 95818, Tel: 455-5243. *BUDGET:* **Holiday Lodge**, 1221 E Main St., Grass Valley, CA 95945, Tel: 273-4406. **La Quinta**, 4604 Madison Ave., Sacramento, CA 95841, Tel: 348-0900.

Attractions, Museums and Parks

California State Railroad Museum, 125 I St., Sacramento, Tel: 552-5252, ext. 7245. **Columbia State Historic Park**, 4 miles north via CA 49 and Parrotts Ferry Rd., near Sonora, Tel: 209/532-4301. **Empire Mine State Historic Park**, 10791 E. Empire St., Grass Valley, Tel: 273-8522. **Governor's Mansion State Historic Park**, 1526 H St., Oakland, Tel: 323-3047. **Marshall Gold Discovery Site State Historic Park**, 310 Back St. (8 miles northwest on CA 49), Coloma, Tel: 622-3470. **Old Sacramento**, 1104 Front St., Old Sacramento, Tel: 264-7777. Historic city district. **Sacramento History Museum**, 101 I St., Sacramento, Tel: 264-7057. Exhibition on the Gold Rush. **State Capitol Museum**, State Capitol, Room B-27, Sacramento, Tel: 324-0333. **Sutter's Fort State Historic Park**, 2701 L Street, Sacramento, Tel: 445-4422. Open-air museum. **State Indian Museum**, 2618 K Street, Tel: 324-0971. Exhibition; Indian canoes, weapons, weaving, pottery. **Towe Ford Museum**, 2200 Front St., Sacramento, Tel: 442-8602, Exhibition of 180 Oldtimer-Fords.

Tourist Information

Grass Valley / Nevada County Chamber of Commerce, 248 Mill St., Grass Valley, CA 95945,

Tel: 273-4667. **Sacramento Visitor Information Center**, 1104 Front St., Sacramento, Tel: 442-7644.

RENO, LAKE TAHOE AND NEVADA DESERT
Accommodation
MODERATE: **Best Western Station House Inn**, 901 Park Ave., South Lake Tahoe, CA 98150, Tel: 916/542-1101. **Cal-Neva Lodge Hotel Spa Casino**, 2 Stateline Rd. PO Box 368, Crystal Bay, NV 89402, Tel: 702/832-4000. **Circus Circus**, PO Box 5880, 500 N Sierra St., Reno, NV 89513, Tel: 702/329-0711. Hotel with casino. **Inn at Incline**, PO Box 4545, 1003 Tahoe Blvd. (NV 28), Incline Village, NV 89451, Tel: 702/831-1052. **Zephyr Cove Resort**, Box 830, 760 Hwy. 50, Zephyr Cove, NV 89448, Tel: 702/588-6644.
BUDGET: **South Shore Inn**, Box 6470, 3900 Pioneer Trail, South Lake Tahoe, CA 96157, Tel: 916/544-1000.

Campgrounds
Tahoe Valley Campground, Box 9026, 1175 Melba St., South Lake Tahoe, CA 96158, Tel: 916/541-2222. Campgrounds and RV parks are also open at Camp Richardson Resort and Zephyr Cove Resort.

Attractions, Museums and Parks
Emerald Bay State Park, 22 miles south of Tahoe City on CA 89, Tel: 916/541-3030. **Lake Tahoe Nevada State Park**, Incline Village, Tel: 702/831-0494. **Lake Tahoe Historical Society Museum**, 3058 US 50, Tel. 916/541-5458. Displays history of local Native Americans. **Ponderosa Ranch**, 100 Ponderosa Ranch Rd., Incline Village, Tel: 702/831-0691. **Tahoe Rim Trail**, 3170 Hwy. 50, Myers, Information Tel: 916/577-0676. **Toiyabe National Forest**, 10 miles west on I-80, then west on the NV 27, Tel: 702/331-6444. Extensive forest area; horseriding, hunting, fishing and camping. **Vikingsholm**, Emerald Bay, one mile off Hwy. 89, Tel: 916/525-7232. **William F. Harrah Foundation National Automobile Museum**, 10 S Lake St., Reno, Tel: 702/333-9300. Exhibition showing more than 200 oldtimers, with motor shows.

Sport, Boat Trips, Cruises and Outdoor Activities
Alpine Meadows, 6 miles northwest of Tahoe City off CA 89, Tel: 916/538-4232. **Camp Richardson Corral**, Hwy. 89 So., PO Box 8335, South Lake Tahoe, CA 96158, Tel: 916/541-1801. **Captain Kirk's Beach**, at Zephyr Cove Resort, see above. **Club Kirkwood**, 30 miles south off CA 88, Tel: 209/258-6000. **Squaw Valley USA**, five miles northwest of Tahoe City off CA 89, Tel: 916/583-6955. **Heavenly Ski Resort**, one mile east of US

50, South Lake Tahoe, Tel: 702/541-7544. **Mountain High Balloons**, Tahoe City & Truckee, Tel: 916/587-6922. Offers balloon rides over the Sierra. **MS Dixie Cruiseship**, 760 Hwy. 50, Zephyr Cove, Tel: 702/588-3508. Cruises depart daily from Zephyr Cove Resort. **Northstar-at-Tahoe**, Hwy. 267 at Northstar Dr., Tel: 916/587-0248. Offers mountain biking tours.

Tourist Information
Humboldt County Chamber of Commerce (Winnemucca), 30 W Winnemucca, NV 89445, Tel: 702/623-2225.
North Lake Tahoe Chamber of Commerce, PO Box 884, Tahoe City, CA 96145, Tel: 916/581-6900.
Lake Tahoe Visitors Authority, PO Box 16299, South Lake Tahoe, CA 96151, Tel: 1-800/AT-TAHOE.
Reno-Tahoe Visitors Center, 275 N Virginia St., Reno and **Reno Chamber of Commerce**, PO Box 3499, Reno, NV 89505, Tel: 702/329-3558.

SALT LAKE CITY
All phone numbers have area code 801.
Accommodation
MODERATE: **Brigham Street Inn**, 1135 E South Temple St., Salt Lake City, UT 84102, Tel: 364-4461. Historic Victorian mansion. **Brighton Lodge**, 15 miles west via UT 190, in Big Cottonwood Canyon, Brighton, UT 84121, Tel: 532-4731.
BUDGET: **Super 8**, 616 S 200 West St., Salt Lake City, UT 84101, Tel: 534-0808. Convenient downtown location.

Attractions, Museums and Parks
Bingham Canyon Mine, 25 miles southwest on UT 48, Tel: 322-7300. **Family History Library**, 35 N West Temple, Tel: 240-2331. **State Capitol**, Head of State St., Tel: 538-3000. **Lion House/Beehive House**, 63 & 67 E South Temple, Tel: 240-2977/2672. Family mansions for Brigham Young and his family. **Pioneer Memorial Museum with Carriage House**, 300 N Main St., Tel: 538-1050. Exhibits on the pioneer heritage and the Pony Express. **Temple Square with Temple, Tabernacle, Assembly Hall**, Temple/Main Sts., Tel: 240-2534. **Trolley Square**, 500-600 South St./600-700 East St., Tel: 521-9877.

Sports and Outdoor Activities
Brighton Resort, 25 miles southeast via I-215, exit 6, Big Cottonwood Canyon, Tel: 1-800-873-5512. **Moki Mac River Expeditions**, Tel: 268-6667. Offers whitewater trips on the Green and Colorado Rivers.

Tourist Information
Salt Lake C & V Bureau, 180 S West Temple, Salt Lake City, UT 84101-1493, Tel: 521-2822.

FROM SALT LAKE CITY INTO YELLOWSTONE NATIONAL PARK

POCATELLO AND IDAHO FALLS
GRAND TETON NATIONAL PARK
YELLOWSTONE NATIONAL PARK

The road winding its path through **Idaho** is long and lonely. Huge areas of the state are still almost uninhabited. Population density averages about ten humans per square mile. It's spectacularly beautiful country: drivers are seldom out of sight of snow-capped mountains, and almost always within earshot of frothy, white rivers plunging their way through steep, walled canyons. Idaho calls itself the *Gem State*, and nearly all of the souvenir shops feature counters selling attractively polished and displayed semi-precious stones.

The drive north from Salt Lake City out of Utah and on into Idaho and Wyoming, to Grand Teton and Yellowstone National Parks, begins on Interstate 15. This is a drive of well over 500 miles (800 km), including side trips, and depending on fishing, hiking and camping diversions, could last a week or more.

POCATELLO AND IDAHO FALLS

Pocatello is the largest industrial city on the road, but not much of a tourist attraction. **Bannock County Historical Museum** and the **Museum of Idaho State University** display objects from

Left: There are about 200 geysers in Yellowstone National Park.

Shoshone Indian culture. The reconstructed **Fort Hall Trading Post**, on the indian reservation of the same name, tells the history of the Buffalo Soldiers, a unique unit of African-American soldiers who, liberated after the Civil War, were sent West by the government to quell Indian rebellions. The large **American Falls Reservoir** nearby is a center for boating and fishing activities.

Idaho Falls, to the northeast, is as prosperous and bucolic as Pocatello is industrial and rundown. The east bank of the river is the old downtown where a large number of shops still do business. The Idaho Falls skyline is dominated by a seven-storey **Mormon Temple** which some have described as a wedding cake.

The river no longer falls at Idaho Falls; it has been tamed by a dam near the town center. Green belts along the banks near the dam lend a peaceful air to the downtown area. **Lindsay Boulevard** is one of the town's most important streets, and along it travelers will discover the new **Visitors Center** (don't miss the relief, scale model of the entire valley which is on display). An excursion 90 miles westward on US 20 leads to the Craters of the Moon. Halfway, there's an unassuming red brick building with a remarkable history; it's the world's first **nuclear power station**, and it's open for inspection. Be-

163

hind it lies 800 square miles of wilderness which serve as a national nuclear waste dump.

The **Craters of the Moon National Monument** is composed of 83 square miles of black hell. Mid-summer, the surface temperatures here can reach 200°F. This lunar landscape of volcanic basalt was created as molten lava oozed to the surface and crusted over every thousand years or so. A seven-mile loop road leads through the cones, lava tunnels, craters and caves, all of which have been sandblasted into eerie shapes by winds whipping across the wasteland.

GRAND TETON
NATIONAL PARK

From Idaho Falls, many travelers follow Rte. 26, a hilly, winding road, east to Wyoming. Near the entrance to **Grand Teton National Park** is the city of Jackson, at the southern edge of the valley **Jackson Hole**.

The area has been inhabited for over 12,000 years, according to archaeologists. Blackfoot, Crow, Shoshone and many other Native American tribes used to come down into this valley during the winter periods. The first white man to arrive here was John Colter, a pioneer and trapper who hit the jackpot in the area in 1807/08. When word got out of his discovery, hordes of fellow trappers followed, eager for beaver pelts to sell at great profit to the fashionable hatters on the U.S. East Coast and in Europe. When the fashion for beaver petered out in the 1840s, things went quiet in Jackson Hole until the mid-1880s when cattle and sheep ranchers began moving their herds in. "Hole" is what these pioneers called any valley in a mountain range.

As 20th-century tourism began to take hold, some alert ranchers began to realize that tourists would even pay to visit Jackson Hole in the winter. As these ranchers put it, "dudes winter better than cows."

And so farming and grazing areas began to be converted into dude ranches and ski slopes. Since then, big money has flowed into Jackson Hole. Some years ago, billionaire **John D. Rockefeller, Jr**. purchased a huge chunk of the area and gave it, as a gift, to the U.S. government, demanding, as any good businessman would, that the Park concession company which he owned would control all future concession activities in the area.

The **Grand Teton National Park** was established in 1929. Its landscape is dominated by the Teton Range, jagged, glacially carved peaks from the Ice Age that jut sharply into the skies.

Exploring Grand Teton

The park totals about 310,000 acres and is flanked on its west side by some 40 miles of mountains, the "youngest" in the Rockies, some of them mere babies, less than 10 million years old. The highest of these Grand Tetons ascend 13,770 feet into the heavens. Earthquakes which have occurred over the past 1,000 years or so have shaken the valley mightily, and ensuing glaciers have carved and gouged deep valleys between the peaks. These were named by sex-starved French trappers in the pioneer era, who thought the mountain peaks looked like the attractive snow-white breasts of the women they left behind (*teton* is French for "breast").

At the feet of these mountains glitter seven sparkling lakes, flanked by banks of silvery and green sagebrush and acres of colorful wildflowers. Bisecting the valley is the **Snake River**, its banks lined with tall cottonwoods and spruce trees. A fascinating array of wild animals and birds come down to the lakeside to drink.

Jackson itself is a real Wild West town, with wooden boardwalks and old-fashioned saloons complete with swinging doors and elk heads on the walls. You enter the town's central square through

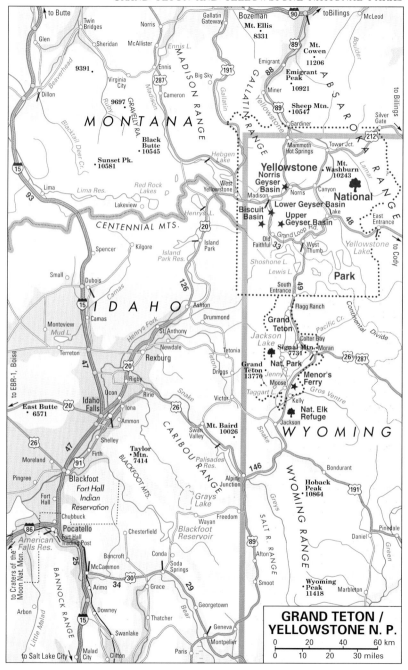

GRAND TETON / YELLOWSTONE N. P.

| 0 | 20 | 40 | 60 km |
| 0 | 10 | 20 | 30 miles |

165

arches fashioned of countless antlers; and Wild West shows are held throughout the summer on the square itself. Yet the atmosphere here also reflects the jet set; almost every other shop is a chic art gallery, designer boutique, or café selling many exotic types of coffee.

The **Wildlife of the American West Museum** displays North American landscape and wildlife painting; the **Teton County Historical Center** documents the development of the fur trade and the history of the local Indians, and the **Jackson Hole Museum** is devoted to the history of the valley's settlement. In winter, the area becomes a luxury ski resort with some of the longest runs in the U.S. It usually has 100 inches of snow before other resorts get their first winter's dusting.

On the northern edge of town is the impressive **National Elk Refuge** where at the beginning of winter you can see more

Above: The National Elk Refuge. Right: The 13,000 feet peaks of Grand Teton National Park are mirrored here in Jackson Lake.

than 10,000 of these massive animals fleeing the bitter cold of the mountain peaks for the relative warmth of the valley. From mid-December to March, park rangers give talks, hikes, and horse-drawn sled tours to observe the wildlife.

Trails, Lakes and the Pioneer Heritage

There are more than 200 miles of hiking trails within the park, ranging in degrees of difficulty from easy walks along the valley slopes to difficult climbs up the steep mountain sides. Two of the tougher trails are the **Teton Crest**, which takes hikers to 11,000 feet above sea level, and **Indian Paintbrush Trail**, so named because of its beautiful wildflowers. There are easier, less taxing trails, as well: the **Lunch Tree Hill Trail** is only a one-half mile walk, starting not far from the **Jackson Lake Lodge**, which is entirely self-interpreting; at intervals along the way are small signs explaining the flora and fauna that can be seen. **Cunningham Cabin Trail** is an interesting three-quar-

ter-mile walk that gives visitors some vivid insights into the early ranching days in the Grand Tetons area.

At the **Taggart Lake** parking area begins the 3.2-mile **Taggart Lake Trail** which leads past many of the area's major historical sites, including the blackened ruins of the 1,028-acre **Beaver Creek Fire**. Fire is a favorite subject in the Grand Teton Park and at the **Cottonwood Creek Picnic** area, the **Jackson Lake Overlook**, and the **Flagg Ranch**, there are signs which explain the various aspects of forest fire ecology and give some history of major forest fires in the region in days past.

Solo climbing of the local mountains is not encouraged. All climbers are required to sign on and sign off at the **Jenny Lake Ranger Station**, where you can also pick uphiking and climbing information.

A number of raft operators organize tours on the Snake River, where they frequently get to see herds of moose strolling along the banks, and bald eagles gliding lazily in air currents overhead.

Anglers have to get a special Wyoming license to toss a line into one of the Teton streams. These can be purchased at the stores found in the various camp areas around the park. At **Colter Bay** and Jackson Lake Lodge, there are wranglers who, given prior warning, will hire out horses for leisurely tours.

Driving north from Jackson on Rte 191, an early stop is **Menor's Ferry** and the **Chapel of the Transfiguration**. This step into the Grand Tetons of yesteryear is enhanced by a visit to the cabin of pioneer Bill Menor to inspect the replica of the ferry that used to cross the Snake River almost 100 years ago. The adjacent chapel has an altar window which artfully frames the tallest of the Tetons' peaks. The chapel is still used for worship today.

Heading north once again, the Teton Park Road wiggles along the east bank of Jenny Lake. At the **Cathedral Group Turnout**, there's a parking area that commands a spectacular view of **Mount Owen, Tweewinot** and **Grand Teton**, three dramati-

167

cally prominent peaks. There's a six-mile walking trail around Jenny Lake, and shuttle boats that take visitors to the west side of the lake in summer.

A little higher up is a fork onto a five-mile road leading to the top of **Signal Mountain**, some 8,000 feet above the valley. The vista here is breathtaking with a panoramic view of the entire Teton Range, Jackson Lake and most of Jackson Hole. Get there early, or plan to arrive late, because parking at the overlook is severely restricted; trailers and large motor homes are discouraged from trying to make it up the road.

Further north on the banks of Jackson Lake are the **Colter Bay Visitor Center** and the **Indian Arts Museum**. The museum contains an impressive collection of the art and craft of the Shoshone, Blackfoot and Crow tribes to whom this whole area once belonged.

Above: Ground squirrel. Right: Morning Glory Pool in Yellowstone National Park, a breathtaking play of color.

Grand Teton Wildlife

Grand Teton is to America what the *veldt* is to South Africa – an area where an enormous amount of wildlife roams about in its natural habitat. South of Jenny Lake, for instance, small bands of prong-horns, America's fastest land animal, forage on the sweet sagebrush. Elk leave the shade of the forest at dusk to feed on other native grasses that grow along the Teton's slopes. Out in **Cascade Canyon**, west of Jenny Lake, there are golden-pelt ground squirrels that dash about at **Inspiration Point**, and yellow-bellied marmots living in the boulder fields. Occasionally, mule deer and moose can be spotted munching contentedly on shrubs growing at the mouth of the canyon.

Jackson Lake was formed from an enormous glacier. Its cool waters provide a habitat for trout and suckers which in turn become food for river otters, ospreys, bald eagles, American white pelicans and ducks, all of which can be observed fish-

ing during the day. At dawn and dusk beavers emerge to swim the lake.

Hiking along the trails gives one ample opportunity to examine the park's flora. June in Jackson Hole park is particularly colorful, with clusters of yellow arrowleaf and balsam root, a daisy-like flower with arrow-shaped leaves. As the month progresses, spikes of blue-purple lupines appear, as well as yellow mountain sunflowers, pink hollyhock, pink sticky geraniums and purple upland larkspur.

In the canyons between the Teton peaks, hikers can stroll through meadows with a rainbow mix of colors: bluebells, yellow columbine, lavender asters, red paintbrush and pink daisies. And the official flower of Grand Teton is the blue alpine forget-me-not found on the slopes.

Surprisingly, forest fires increase the wildflower population in subsequent years, because the unexpected sunlight reaching the forest floor enhances the fertilizer effect of the nitrogen-rich ash. Magenta firewood and yellow heartleaf arnica, pink spreading dogbane and snow-brushed ceanothus are all flourishing along the **Taggart Lake Trail**, which goes through an area that suffered a major forest fire in 1985.

After taking in the Tetons' majesty over several days, the pioneering urge to see what's over the next ridge will take hold. To most visitors, this means heading north to **Yellowstone**.

YELLOWSTONE NATIONAL PARK

There are five entrances to **Yellowstone National Park**, but most summer guests who have visited Grand Teton National Park go to Yellowstone's southern end via the **John D. Rockefeller Jr. Memorial Parkway**. Of the five entrances, only the northern one is open to vehicles year round. Snow and ice very often block the other four entrances during the winter months.

Yellowstone is America's oldest National Park and the largest in the lower 48 states. Covering 3,472 square miles, it sits in the northwest corner of Wyoming,

169

also touching on the states of Montana and Idaho. It is also one of America's most popular parks, so do not expect to see it in solitude. There are crowds everywhere, and only the bravest visitor who cuts through winter's snow and ice can hope to see Yellowstone in its natural, crowd-free state.

But even in summer, Yellowstone is a remarkable experience. Its volcanic origins are still visible in the form of geysers, pools of bubbling mud and steamy thermal springs. The rich soil, another gift from the volcanoes, is a fertile bed for myriad wildflowers. Majestic snow-capped peaks rise dramatically along valleys where herds of buffalo and elk graze away, sometimes oblivious to tourists. With luck you might even spot a bald eagle soaring high overhead.

This is not land which has been reclaimed from farmers and herders; Yellowstone is the only large area (2.2-million acres) in the 48 contiguous states that has never been farmed, fenced in or developed. It was in 1807 that John Colter wandered across this wilderness and discovered, to his amazement, acres of scalding hot springs, bubbling pools and plumy geysers that squirted boiling water and steam hundreds of feet into the air. A veteran of the Lewis and Clark Expedition, Colter was ridiculed when he returned to the east with his stories of what became laughed at as "Colter's Hell." But others soon confirmed his stories and, in 1870, the U.S. government dispatched survey teams to the area. Their reports urged that the landscape not be exploited by hunters, lumbermen or miners. In 1872, President Ulysses S. Grant signed the documents which made Yellowstone the first National Park in America, in the words of the document, "...reserved and withdrawn from settlement and dedicated and set apart as a public park or pleasuring ground for the benefit and enjoyment of the people."

Above: Lime terraces in Yellowstone Park.
Right: Old Faithful, the largest geyser, attracts many tourists.

In its earliest days there was little funding to protect the park from its visitors – and vice-versa. Jokers were fond of sticking soap down the geyser holes so that bubbles would come up with the steam. Outlaws hid along the first paths and stripped tourists of their wallets and valuables as they came by. The Nez Percé Indians even scalped some of the early visitors. Things got so bad that in 1886 the U.S. Cavalry was put in charge of policing the park. **Mammoth Hot Springs**, now Yellowstone's headquarters, is constructed on the site of Fort Yellowstone, built during the era when the army ran things. The **Albright Visitor Center** on the site of the former Army Bachelor Officers' Quarters has slide shows and exhibits exploring the history, fauna and flora of the Park.

There are other visitors' centers approximately every 20 miles along the figure-eight-shaped **Grand Loop Road** which links most of the major tourist attractions.

Geyser Country

The Grand Loop Road, including all the roads linking it to the park's entrance, totals about 200 miles. What sets Yellowstone apart from all other National Parks are its approximately 200 active geysers – a world record for density. Most of these geysers are found on the park's west side, along a 50-mile stretch of road between Mammoth Hot Springs in the northwest and the geyser of Old Faithful in the southwest. The thermal **Mammoth Hot Springs** are a tremendous natural spectacle; the hot water runs down through ten terrace-like natural pools, one over the other, into the depths. Farther south is the **Norris Geyser Basin**; here, the Echinus Geyser shoots aloft every hour; the Steamboat Geyser, the largest in the world, spouts 425-foot jets of water; and the Norris Museum communicates detailed information about

geysers. Southwest of here is the **Lower Geyser Basin**; here, you can see the Fountain Paint Pot, filled with red mud, and the Great Fountain Geyser, which sends its fountains aloft once a day.

In the **Upper Geyser Basin**, legion geysers show their stuff. One highlight is the **Morning Glory Pool**, shaped like a huge blossom, blue within and gold without. The magma which drives this steam and water to the surface is between two and three miles below the surface. Ground water seeps into the red-hot rocks, which are at around 1,000°F; the water then shoots up to the surface.

Supreme among the geysers is **Old Faithful**, discovered by explorers in the 1880s. About every 70 minutes, it fires steam and 8,400 gallons of water almost 200 feet into the air, the jet sometimes continuing for as long as five minutes.

Don't, however, let spectacle distract you from more ordinary, yet no less beautiful, forms of water. Take **Yellowstone Lake**, North America's largest alpine lake with 110 miles of shoreline, and

They are not the most dangerous. Much more dangerous are the grizzlies, weighing up to 700 pounds, and varying in color from black to blond, depending on the time of year. Standing on their hind legs, they can be as tall as six feet.

The most important advice about bears is: try not to meet one. They dislike noise, so conversation on the trail, whistling, singing, will usually drive the bear away from visitors. Bears, like bison, are fast-moving, running at speeds of around 30 mph, faster than the fastest Olympic sprinter. Faced by a bear, therefore, don't try to run; running can move it to attack, and it will be faster to you anyway. Sometimes, a bear bluffs a charge and will pull up at the last minute. Standing still and facing down the bear seems to be the best advice. If it does attack, drop into the fetal position, cover up your head and hope for the best.

Bears have an acute sense of smell, so it's important not to leave food or garbage out under any circumstances. If you want to sleep under the stars, never do so close to food; stash both food and garbage, well covered and weighted-down, at least 100 yards or so away from your campsite.

a favorite with fishermen. At **Roosevelt Lodge**, you can embark on a real stagecoach ride. For more air-conditioned comfort, climb into a luxury bus for a sightseeing tour of the park; the bus stops at the most scenic spots.

Yellowstone boasts the greatest concentration of mammals in the lower 48 states: everything from white pelicans to bison, elk, moose, wapiti and mule deer, black bears and grizzlies. The early-morning and early-evening hours are the best times to see the animals when they flock to the watering holes. Beware of bison: they look big and slow, but they have bad tempers and move very swiftly indeed when provoked. A 2,000-pound bison can charge at speeds of up to 30 mph, three times faster than the average human can run.

Bear attacks are not infrequent. Black bears weigh about 300 pounds and are about three feet high when on all fours.

If you wish to sleep under a roof rather than in a tent, there are a number of hotels within Yellowstone. Two stand out because of their long and colorful history. **Old Faithful Inn** is a National Historic Landmark, a huge log hotel constructed in 1904. Its rooms are rustic but comfortable, and its lobby is unique, seven stories high, and constructed around a 40-foot-high fireplace and an 80-foot chimney built of hand-quarried lava blocks. Guests are constantly flocking in and out of the building every 75 minutes or so to watch the steamy explosions of nearby Old Faithful. The ghost of the hotel's designer, Robert Reamer, is reportedly sometimes seen worriedly pacing the halls of his old abode, which is the largest log cabin ever built.

Above: Careful! Don't disturb! Bisons are easily excitable.

IDAHO FALLS AND POCATELLO
All phone numbers have area code 208.

Accommodation
MODERATE: **Best Western Cottontree Inn**, 1415 Bench Rd., Pocatello, ID 83201, Tel: 237-7650. **Quality Inn Convention Center**, 1555 Pocatello Creek, Pocatello, ID 83201, Tel: 233-2200, at junction I-15 and I-86. **Shilo Inn**, 780 Lindsay Blvd., Idaho Falls, ID 83402, Tel: 523-0088.
BUDGET: **Comfort Inn**, 1333 Bench Rd., Pocatello, ID 83201, Tel: 237-8155. **Day's Inn**, 133 W Burnside Ave., Pocatello, ID 83202, Tel: 237-0020. **Comfort Inn**, 1333 Bench Rd., Pocatello, ID 83201, Tel: 237-8155. **Super 8**, 705 Lindsay Blvd., Idaho Falls, ID 83402, Tel: 522-8880.

Attractions, Museums and Parks
American Falls Dam, I-86, exit 40, Tel: 226-2688. **Bannock County Hist. Museum**, Ross Park, S 2nd Ave., Pocatello, Tel: 233-0434. **Craters of the Moon Nat. Monument**, Information Tel: 527-3257. **Experimental Breeder Reactor Number One** (First nuclear power plant), 18 miles southeast via US 20/26 off Arco, Tel: 526-0050. **Idaho Museum of Nat. History**, on the campus of Idaho State University, 741 S 7th Avenue, Pocatello, Tel: 236-3168, includes exhibits of Native American Art.

Tourist Information
Greater Pocatello Chamber of Commerce, 427 N Main St., PO Box 626, Pocatello, ID 83204, Tel: 233-1525.
Idaho Falls Chamber of Commerce, 505 Lindsay Blvd., Idaho Falls, ID 83405, Tel: 523-1010.

GRAND TETON NATIONAL PARK JACKSON HOLE
All phone numbers have area code 307.

Accommodation
LUXURY: **Jackson Lake Lodge**, Box 240, Moran, WY 83013, Tel: 543-2855. **Rusty Parrot**, Box 1657, 175 n Jackson, Jackson, WY 83001, Tel: 773-2000. *MODERATE:* **Colter Bay Village**, Box 240, Grand Teton National Park, WY 83013, Tel: 543-2855. Trapper, Box 1712, 235 N Cache St., Jackson, WY 83001, Tel: 733-2648.
BUDGET: **Pioneer**, Box 604, 325 N Cache St. (US Hwy. 89), Jackson, WY 83001, Tel: 733-3673.

Guest Ranches
Flagg Ranch, Box 187, Moran, WY 83013 (on US Hwy. 89), Tel: 543-2861. **Heart Six**, Box 70, Moran, WY 83013 (5 miles east of Moran, on Buffalo Valley Rd.), Tel: 543-2477. **Jenny Lake Lodge**, Box 240, Moran, WY 83013 (14 miles southwest of Moran, on Jenny Lake Rd.), Tel: 733-4647. Restored 100-year-old homesteader cabins in the national park. **R Lazy S**, Box 308, Teton Village, Jackson, WY 83025, Tel: 733-2655, west of town at Teton Village Rd.

Camping
There are five campgrounds maintained at Grand Teton National Park: Colter Bay, Signal Mountain, Jenny Lake, Lizard Creek and Gros Ventre. For information and reservation, contact the Park Superintendent (see below), Tel: 733-2880.

Attractions, Museums and Parks
Grand Teton National Forest, Information Tel: 733-2880. Taped information on weather conditions: Tel: 733-2220. **Jackson Hole Museum**, 105 N Glenwood, Jackson, Tel: 733-2414, local and geological history. **National Elk Refuge**, Jackson Hole, Tel: 733-9212. **Teton County Historical Center**, 105 Mercill Ave., Jackson, Tel: 733-9605, exhibits on fur trade and local Indians. **Wildlife of the American West**, 110 N Center, Jackson, Tel: 733-5771, typical Western paintings.

Outdoor Activities
River Rafting at Grand Teton, Information Tel: 543-2855.
Teton Country Prairie Schooner Holiday, Tel: 733-5386, offers guided covered wagon trips between Grand Teton and Yellowstone Parks (mid-June to late August only).
Triangle X Float Trips, Triangle X Ranch, Moose, (26 miles northeast of Jackson, one mile off US Hwys 89-189-26), Tel: 733-5500. Daily (wildlife) floats on the Snake River.
Wagon Treks, Jackson, Tel: 886-9693. Covered wagon treks through the foothills of Grand Teton. Departs from several area hotels.

Tourist Information
Grand Teton and Yellowstone National Park, Superintendent, PO Drawer 170, Moose, WY 83012, Tel: 733-2880.
Jackson Hole Area Chamber of Commerce, 532 N Cache, PO Box E, Jackson Hole, WY 83001, Tel: 733-3316.

YELLOWSTONE NATIONAL PARK
All phone numbers have area code 307.

Accommodation
MODERATE: **Old Faithful Inn**, on Loop Road, Yellowstone National Park, WY 82190, Tel: 344-7311. *BUDGET:* **Grant Village**, 18 miles southeast of Old Faithful, two miles south of Loop Road, Yellowstone National Park, WY 82190, Tel: 344-7311. All accommodations in Yellowstone National Park can be reached by calling **TW Recreational Services Inc.**, Tel: 344-7311.

Camping
There are 13 campgrounds and RV sites in the National Park which are open without reservations.

Tourist Information
Yellowstone National Park Headquarters Information, Tel: 344-7381.

FROM
SAN FRANCISCO
TO SEATTLE

NORTHERN CALIFORNIA
OREGON
COLUMBIA RIVER / MT. HOOD
WASHINGTON STATE
MT. ST. HELENS / MT. RAINIER

Hardly any other coastal region in the world offers such an unbelievable wealth of rugged natural beauty as the coast of northern California, Oregon, and Washington State. The drive begins north of San Francisco on the legendary State Hwy. 1, which runs along the Pacific Ocean, passing through remote bays and beaches in Oregon, and ends in the Pacific Northwest just before Seattle at the foot of two extinct volcanoes. It's a long road, almost 1,400 miles (2,240 km), and you should allow at least two weeks to cover the distance, especially considering the possibility of several side trips inland.

NORTHERN CALIFORNIA:
FOG BANKS AND GIANT TREES

The old **Pacific Route (Hwy. 1)** slithers northward from San Francisco. It hugs the coast for a long while, bypassing steep, rocky cliffs and small, protected inlets. The combination of sand dunes and cliffs so typical for the region is perfectly documented at the **Point Reyes National Seashore** that lies just a few miles north of the city. In winter and in early spring, **Point Reyes Lighthouse** is

Previous pages: Mount Rainier. Left: The Chandelier Tree in Redwoods State Park near Leggett is over 2000 years old.

a good spot to observe pods of whales making their way up toward Alaska. In fact they can be spotted all along the coast.

The wildly romantic coast, dotted with diminutive fishing villages, stretches all the way to **Mendocino**, a small but very fine artists' colony that has unfortunately been overrun by tourists in the past years. Looking over the ocean are well-preserved Victorian houses, some built of wood.

Route 1 crosses **Westport** and **Rockport** before turning into Hwy. 101 near the town of **Legett**. The most significant and impressive attraction on the way to Oregon begins just a few miles to the north of this: the gigantic trees of the three **Redwoods State Parks**. The first of these, **Humboldt Redwoods State Park**, can best be explored beginning in **Garberville**. The so-called **Avenue of the Giants**, an approximately 30-mile-long stretch of road running parallel to 101, is lined with these huge, centuries-old redwoods. But the oldest and largest specimens are to be found some way to the north in the **Redwood National Park**.

On the way there is the old farming village of **Ferndale**, a very pretty place which wears its 19th-century origins on its sleeve. Hwy. 101 then leads to **Orick**

and from there to the Redwoods National Park where one can hike around for days and completely forget the passage of time. Redwoods, which can grow up to 280 feet high with a diameter of up to 25 feet, are thought to be the oldest trees growing on earth. Some of them began their lives over 2,000 years ago. Hiking paths have been laid out throughout the park to guide visitors to the most special groves, such as **Lady Bird Johnson Grove** (named after the wife of President Johnson). The tallest trees in the world stand near **Redwood Creek**, whose king is the laconically-named **Tall Tree**, 367.8 feet high and 44 feet in diameter. The trees are so dense at this point that their branches mingle to form a kind of roof worthy of a cathedral.

Yet in spite of it all, there is another side to the redwood forests. In the past centuries about 95 percent of the forests have been cut down. The redwoods pro-

vide one of the most resistant woods with excellent insulating qualities. The logging industry, which still owns the rights to the timber, is still hard at work cutting down these gigantic trees.

The primordial feeling of the landscape here, barring modern man's hiking paths of course, has been preserved, especially along the coast of the National Park. The trail between **Gold Bluffs Beach** and **Klamath** explores some particularly natural scenery.

OREGON

The state line between California and **Oregon** is just a few miles north of the Redwood State Parks. Officially, the Pacific Northwest begins here, where nature is at its most untamed along the entire West Coast. Oregon and Washington State were only admitted to the Union in 1859 and 1889 respectively, and both states have maintained much of their "virginity" to this day, with deep and dense forests that seem to sprawl end-

Above: Evening atmosphere in Mendocino, an artists' colony on State Highway 1.

lessly, extinct volcanoes, and mountain ranges that have never been conquered. Settlement by the white man is of more recent date, and one suspects sometimes – and hopes, too – that it is not yet complete.

The whole story began when a handful of fur dealers and daring trappers wandered over the Rockies and encountered Shuswap and Nez Percé Indian tribes with whom they went into business. The Gold Rush later brought more people into the region, mostly of the adventurer class.

A side trip over **Grants Pass** and **Medford** takes you to an unusual natural phenomenon in eastern Oregon: **Crater Lake National Park**, which is accessible over Rte. 62. The main sight here is the 10,800-foot-high **Mt. Mazama**, an extinct volcano whose crater has become a lake of dark and mysterious waters. The deep blue color of **Crater Lake** comes from its great depth of 1,932 feet, making it the deepest lake in the United States. **Rim Drive**, a 33-mile road that circles the lake, allows you to go once around the crater without leaving the car. Hiking paths begin at **Rim Village**. The most beautiful of these is **Cleetwood Trail**, which is at the northeastern edge of the crater. It leads down to the lake shore, where there are boats to take you out to **Wizard Island**, which stands out in the middle of the lake, a volcanic island in the middle of a crater.

The Coast of Oregon

The 30-mile stretch between **Brookings** and **Gold Beach**, one of the most beautiful along the Oregon coast, may make one forget the past entirely. The little community of Gold Beach, however, which lies on the banks of the Rogue River, is a reminder of the days when gold fever struck the nation. White intruders looked for gold here over 150 years ago, and no sooner had they started

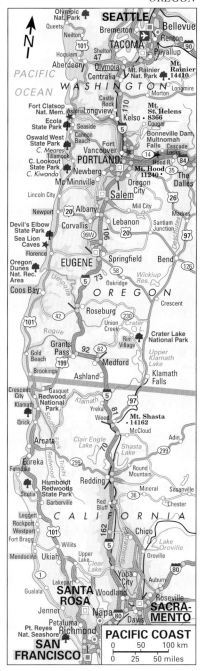

than they ran into trouble with the Indians, for whom the salmon in the river was far more important.

At **Coos Bay**, Hwy. 101 begins making its way through the **Oregon Dunes National Recreation Area**, a 47-mile tableau of dunes shaped by wind and water that have been placed under nature protection order. These great sand masses, some of which are in excess of 500 feet, represent the largest area of dunes on the West Coast. Paths through them lead to observation points, but many visitors prefer exploring the dunes by undertaking wild drives in motorized beach buggies or ATV cars. The softness of the sand is deceptive, by the way. The dunes are a considerable force of nature. The coastal winds blow them inland, and since the time of their creation, thought to be about 7,000 years ago, they have buried large

Above. Pacific Coast Highway 1 is one of the most impressive roads of the U.S.A. Right: RV-riding in the Oregon Dunes.

180

tracts of land. When the dunes moved on, they left behind oases of tree stumps and little lakes.

This dunescape continues as far as **Florence**, site of another worthwhile stop at the **Sea Lion Caves**, where hundreds of sea lions lie about or play in the water, their roars echoing from the cliffs. A little further along is **Devil's Elbow State Park**, followed by **Newport**, actually an old port which derived its main revenue from the transportation of wood. The **Hatfield Marine Science Center** has an aquarium with a wide selection of wildlife from the local waters. Another way to get a closer look at the fauna of the Pacific Ocean is to climb down to the **Undersea Gardens**. An ingenious construction here allows one to see the underwater world "live."

The entire Newport area is dotted with interesting State Parks where one can spend a few pleasant hours gazing at nature. Many consist of cozy bays with simple lighthouses that peer out over the sea (such as **Yaquina Bay**). Others are known for their fascinating rock formations, like the **Devil's Punch Bowl**.

The next stop on the way is **Tillamook**, a town of about 22,000. A detour to the 22-mile-long **Three Capes Scenic Drive** is well worth the time. The three capes referred to are **Meares**, **Lookout**, and **Kiwanda**, and their claim to fame is the particular combination of sand and rock, that is dunes and cliffs. This is another good spot to do some land-based whale watching in late fall and early spring.

Two classic seaside resorts lie to the north of Tillamook, **Cannon Beach** and **Seaside**, though it should be mentioned that the cold waters of the Pacific Ocean are hardly conducive to long, relaxing swims. Cannon Beach, named after the cannon of a ship that sank in 1846 which washed up on the shore here, has miles of beach and cliffs. The most prominent

sight of the coast is the 235-foot **Hay-stack Rock**, a giant stone monolith that rears out of the water. For a while, Cannon Beach was something of an artists' colony, but those days are long gone, and little of them remains to be seen. Far more interesting for the visitor are the neighboring parks: **Ecola State Park** and **Oswald West State Park**. Both are nature conservation areas with extensive dune formations. They have lookouts that give a broad view of the bays in the region.

The remoteness and solitude of the parks is a far cry from the old resort of Seaside, which has been the place where Portlanders have enjoyed some rest and recreation since the turn of the century. The town has two distinct faces. On the one hand, it is a dreamy community along the coast, with romantic old beach houses. On the other hand, it is a modern and overcrowded resort with cheap hotels, a two-mile boardwalk, and all the gaudy amenities one would expect of such a place.

The Lewis and Clark Expedition

In the summer of 1792, Captain Robert Gray discovered the **Columbia River** at the spot where it spills into the Pacific near **Astoria** today. He, like many of his foreruners and followers, was searching for the elusive Northwest Passage. This little town, nowadays a sleepy port, has had quite a history since its birth as a fort and trading post for local fur traders. One of America's wealthiest families began its financial rise here. John Jacob Astor started out as nothing more than a hard-bargaining fur trader, but he laid the cornerstone of the Astor family fortune here. His modest beginnings are well documented in **Fort Astoria**, the family's former warehouse.

Astoria also has the largest Victorian Old Town in Oregon. Among its fine old houses is **Flavel House**, which once belonged to a seafarer named Flavel. As for the history of the port itself, its rise to prominence, its business, its trials and tribulations, can be found at the **River**

Maritime Museum. It has exhibitions on specialized subjects such as fishing, the advent of steamboats, and navigation.

Five miles southwest of Astoria is the **Fort Clatsop National Memorial**, which is associated with two of America's greatest explorers, **Lewis & Clark**, who spent the winter of 1805/1806 here. These two officers were commissioned by President Thomas Jefferson to leave St. Louis and explore the West.

Back in those days, the young nation had just acquired the entire area from the Mississippi River to the Rockies in the **Louisiana Purchase** from the French. The country's surface area was suddenly more than twice what it had been. Lewis and Clark's task was to find out more about this bit of real estate and see if there was a possible shipping passage between the East and West Coasts.

Above: The lumber industry is an important industrial branch of the area around Portland. Right: Wine-tasting in Willamette Valley.

In May 1804, with a company of 30 men, Meriwether Lewis and William Clark left St. Louis heading west. They spent one winter in South Dakota, and then continued slogging their way through the western wilderness, over the Rocky Mountains, all the way to Oregon and Washington State. They explored the Columbia River, established friendly contacts with local Indian tribes, and finally returned east in 1806. Lewis and Clark went down in the annals of American history as a pair of heros and great (American) discoverers of the frontier era.

A Visit to Portland

Portland, which lies at the confluence of the Columbia and Willamette Rivers, is not generally praised as much for its urban architecture as for its splendid parks and gardens. The city began modestly in the middle of the last century as a stopover on the way from San Francisco to Seattle, but rose to prominence thanks

to its protected harbor and to the fishing and logging industries in its immediate vicinity. Its origins are outlined in **Fort Vancouver** to the northwest of town. At the beginning of the 19th century, this fort belonged to the famous Hudson Bay Company, and served as a warehouse for trappers and fur dealers.

Portland calls itself the City of Roses. This is hardly an idle boast: in springtime, much of the town seems covered in a bed of colorful roses, and in June, Portlanders celebrate their **Rose Festival**. It's the best time perhaps to stroll through the city's parks, especially **Washington Park**, with the **International Rose Test Garden** and the **Japanese Garden**. Besides all the roses, the park boasts a large number of different trees and shrubs. In contrast, the Japanese Garden is the epitome of the cultivation and breeding of flowers, and it has a little tea pavilion.

Portland is one of the West Coast's up-and-coming cities, and is in the process of rebuilding itself, adding a new transportation network and giving downtown a new face. Still, the most interesting quarter is **Old Town**, which extends to both sides of Burnside Street from SW Front Street to 5th Street. The old warehouses and shops here successfully resisted the attempts of real estate speculators to turn the area into a modern nightmare. Of interest to visitors is the unique **American Advertising Museum**, which is entirely devoted to the history of advertising in the United States. The **Portland Art Museum** has a very special collection of Indian art.

South of Portland is one of Oregon's most fertile wine-growing regions, the **Willamette Valley**. Should time allow, you should make an excursion into this area, which is reminiscent of the Rhine Valley. Rte. 99W south passes by about two dozen wineries, each of which offers wine tastings of Pinot Noir, Riesling, or even a local champagne. Just watch how much you drink, as the Highway Patrol might be out and about just as you are heading to the Columbia River.

COLUMBIA RIVER
AND MT. HOOD

The **Mt. Hood-Columbia Gorge Loop Scenic Drive**, a 163-mile road, begins just east of Portland. Some parts of it follow the river closely, other parts climb high up into the mountains. The Columbia is the longest river in the United States after the Mississippi. It springs somewhere in the mountains of Canada, and over the past 50 million years has eaten its way into the mountains of the North Cascades. It flows into the Pacific near the town of Astoria. The river landscape along the Columbia is still very much as it has always been. After all, the region was just being settled a century ago.

The journey eastward on the **Historic Columbia River Highway** (drive east of Portland on I-84 and take the signposted exit) provides spectacular views of the pristine, mountainous world on the Oregon side of the river. Every now and then a huge, gushing waterfall provides for a special side show. The most famous is **Multnomah Falls**, which crashes down a cliff 620 feet high, making it the highest in all Oregon and one of the highest in the United States. Multnomah is a favorite along the way because of the little bridge built opposite the falls; standing on it, you almost feel you're under the tormented water.

Shortly after the falls, near **Bonneville Lock and Dam**, the Highway leads back to I-84. The 192-foot Bonneville Dam, which was completed in 1938, is one of ten that have been built on the Columbia River in order to produce electricity. This artificial interference with the natural flow of the river had its consequences on the local ecology. The Columbia River serves as a breeding ground for about half a million salmon every year, before they swim downstream to the Pacific Ocean. The fish have no problem swimming the rapids in either direction,

or even hoping over smaller obstacles such as rocks or snags, but the great walls of the dam blocked their path eastward, and was lethal on the way west. Ecologists were already raising Cain by the late 1930s because the salmon were jumping to their death. After the war, the authorities built fish ladders on the dams, allowing the salmon to get through without damage. Bonneville offers an excellent opportunity to observe closely how the salmon swim upstream and gradually jump up through the fish ladder.

To the south of the dam is a short hiking path called **Eagle Creek Trail**. It gives some intimate insight into the local greenery, passes by more waterfalls, and has some restful picnic grounds.

Cascades Locks recalls a bit of genuine Wild West history. In the 19th century, the pioneers making their way down the river from the Oregon Trail had to interrupt their journey owing to the very dangerous rapids that suddenly developed at this point. They were forced to unload, take their boats over land to a point farther west, and then re-embark. The **Cascade Locks Historical Museum** brings those difficult times to life again. Nowadays the rapids have been conquered by human hand, and can even be visited on an old paddlewheel steamer, the *Columbia Gorge*.

Today, adventurous spirits take voluntarily to the white waters of the Columbia near **Hood River**. This section of the Columbia is also a boon for windsurfers, because the cold winds of the Pacific meet with the warm air of eastern Oregon and produce a great deal of fast winds. Surfers from all over the world come here to test their skills on the river.

The Dalles, which lies a little to the west, is a town of no significance nowadays, but it did have its historic moments. It was the final stop of the **Oregon Trail**, a path trampled by thousands of pioneers between 1843 and 1848, after news spread from missionaries and trappers

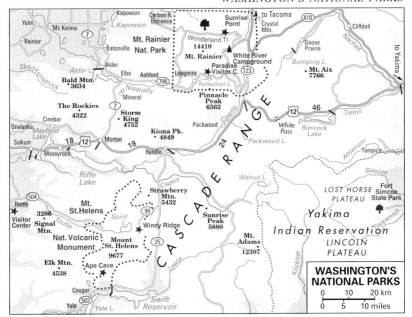

that the new territories in the northwest were a "paradise for pioneers." In Dalles the prairie schooners were unloaded, and the journey westward continued on the Columbia River. Statistically speaking, the process of settling Oregon was modest at best, but the convoys of pioneers that came here represented the last great thrust into the west, and signalled the demise of the Pacific Indian tribes.

Before crossing over to Washington State on a bridge farther to the west, try to make the side trip up to **Mt. Hood**. Rte. 35 leads south to this extinct volcano which is also Oregon's highest mountain, with an altitude of 11,235 feet. The entire area around Mt. Hood is known for its winter sports, in particular downhill skiing. **Mt. Hood Meadows** and **Mt. Hood Ski Bowl** have a wide range of slopes for any degree of expertise. The **Timberline Ski Area** even offers skiing all year round. Movie buffs might recognize **Timberline Lodge** as one of the locations for the grisly film *The Shining* with Jack Nicholson.

Heading back on Rte. 35, one crosses the Columbia to Washington State on the so-called **Bridge of the Gods**. An old Indian legend tells of a massive stone bridge built by the gods that spanned the river at this point. Hwy. 14 then heads back west, with a breathtaking view of the north side of the river and the mountain ranges around Mt. Hood. A special stopover should be made at **Beacon Rock**, an 800-foot crag, a veritable stone monolith. I-5, however, takes you northwards to another monolith of sorts, but one that is not so peaceful.

MT. ST. HELENS NATIONAL VOLCANIC MONUMENT

In 1987, **Mt. St. Helens** was still a barren landscape that seemed dead to the world. For miles and miles trees lay about like matchsticks broken by an absent-minded hand. An entire forest had been flattened. Not a blade of grass sprang from the soil, not a single flower; no birds chirped, no insects buzzed about on warm

summer days. The ground was either grey or black, and the breeze kicked up a film of volcanic ash into the air.

In the past few years, **Mt. St. Helens National Volcanic Monument** has been reforested to a great extent, and nature has recovered in many parts, especially on the lava beds. Still, the overall gloomy atmosphere (dramatic as well) vividly recalls Helens' violent erruption over a decade ago. On May 18, 1980, Mt. St. Helens, considered until then to be inactive, suddenly errupted with an incredible force, annihilating 250 square miles of the surrounding National Park. The great masses of lava and a steady rain of ash buried entire villages. 60 people died during the three-day eruption.

The explosions tore a 1,300-foot chunk out of the northern side of the volcano, lowering the mountain's altitude to 8,364 feet. The climatic effect of all the ash

Above: Traces of the volcanic explosion of Mt. St. Helens are still to be seen. Right: Eunice Lake in Mount Rainier National Park.

thrown up into the atmosphere was felt all the way to the East Coast, reflected in a notably cool summer. The volcano has piped down in the meantime, and scientists are not expecting another eruption in the near future. As for the National Park, it was deemed a National Monument in the year 1982.

Mt. St. Helens Visitor Center, between **Castle Rock** and **Toutle**, east on I-5, provides a full documentation of this natural catastrophe. This is also the starting point for a side trip on Rte. 504 that will take you right up to the northwestern slope of the volcano. The journey back south on I-5 (forking on 504) goes through **Cougar** and **Ape Cave**. The latter, a cavern hollowed out in a lava flow, was produced by an eruption over 2,000 years ago. As the lava cooled it formed a hard crust in which hot lava continued to flow. It is a full two miles long, making it the longest lava cave on the American continent. The observation terraces along the road south of Mt. St. Helens are the starting point for hikes through the park, where one can get first-hand knowledge of the destruction wrought by the volcano.

Route 25 makes its way across mountain crests all the way to **Strawberry Mountain**, which provides the best view of the collapsed crater and **Spirit Lake** that lies before it. The best view of Mt. St. Helens as a whole is from **Windy Ridge**, which can be reached along Rte. 99. This is the closest one can get to the mountain using a car. Toward the end of the traveling season, when few tourists are roaming around the park, the uncanny peace and quiet up here can be overwhelming. Steep trails lead from Windy Ridge up to spots where the volcano seems so near one can almost touch it.

The way away from Mt. St. Helens back to I-5 is over **Randle** and **Morton**, neither of which are of particular interest, especially considering the dramatic scenery one has just left behind. A short distance away, however, is **Mt. Rainier**,

which, ironically, looks exactly like Mt. St. Helens *before* its 1980 eruption.

MT. RAINIER NATIONAL PARK

Incontestibly the greatest attraction in the state of Washington is this giant of stone, fire and ice. Mt. Rainier (14,411 feet), a cool and distant beauty, dominates the stage between southern Washington and Seattle. The inhabitants of the capital on Puget Sound are often granted a colorful spectacle, especially during clear weather when Rainier shows off 60 miles away. In the morning the mountain slowly sheds its mists, gradually revealing its shape; at midday the snow-covered summit flashes in the distance; and when the sun goes down, it bathes the mountain in a deep red light.

Mt. Rainier is at this point an inactive volcano permanently covered by ice and snow and surrounded by about 80 glaciers. The mountains here form the largest glacier region outside Alaska. The last eruption occurred about 150 years ago; still there are little wisps of smoke coming from the top of Rainier. An eruption would be a disaster for the city of Seattle, but no one is counting on one for at least the next 500 years. Mt. Rainier is part of a chain of volcanoes connected underground to Mt. St. Helens, Mt. Adams, Mt. Baker in the North Cascades and Mt. Hood in Oregon.

A few thousand years ago, Rainier was a perfectly normal mountain, a little higher than it is today. Volcanic activity and gradual glacial erosion gave it a different shape, however. It was in fact glaciers that carved away at the rocks in the region, even building separate mountains, and their melting ices created numerous small rivers. This slow but consistent game of nature continues to be played in **Mt. Rainier National Park**, where three great glaciers still do their job of eroding the landscape.

The landscape of the park explains immediately why it was chosen as one of the first five National Parks in the USA.

Its picture-book nature was recognized as early as 1899. Rte. 706 makes access very comfortable, but unfortunately this means that during the summer months Mt. Rainier is completely overrun by Seattlites in surch of some relief.

The best way to get there is by driving to the southwest entrance, through **Long-mire** to the **Jackson Visitor Center** on the southern slope of Mt. Rainier. A number of trails begin next to the **Paradise Hotel**, and lead quite close to the glaciers (**Skyline Trail** and **Nisqually Vista Trail**, for example). Mother Nature has her way of showing strength in this region, especially in winter. In early 1972, at Paradise Point, 93 feet of fresh snow was recorded, a record for the United States.

Route 706 proceeds farther to the southwest, bypassing **Reflection Lake**, whose clear, quiet waters reflect the towering mountain above it and the blue skies striated with white clouds: a picture-post-

Above: Mt. Rainier National Park is an ideal area for mountain hikers.

card view if you've ever seen one! Take Route 123 which hugs the mountain closely, and then take the fork to the north to **Sunset Point**, which is the best spot to gaze at Mt. Rainier. At 6,600 feet, this is the closest one can get to the mountain by car.

In the distance, yet appearing close enough to grasp, are the **Cascades Range**, **Mt. Adams** and **Mt. Baker**. The most popular trail, **Wonderland Trail** (30 miles), begins its tour of the mountain here. It's by no means an easy hike, taking at least two days to complete, and only fit hikers should attempt it. The **White River Campground** offers space for an overnight stay, but you will need to get the permission of a park ranger. If you want to avoid well-trodden paths and crowded picnic places, you should enter the park from the northwestern side by the **Carbon River**.

The thickly settled coast of Puget Sound is not very far. In under two hours I-5 takes you into Seattle, the much praised "Pearl of the Northwest."

NORTHERN CALIFORNIA
Accommodation
MODERATE: **Blackberry**, 44951 Larkin Rd., Mendocino, CA 95460, Tel: 937-5281. **Mendocino**, 45080 Main St., Box 587, Mendocino, CA 95460, Tel: 707/937-0511. *BUDGET:* **Garberville**, 948 Redwood Dr., Garberville, CA 95440, Tel: 707/923-2422.

Attractions, Museums and Parks
Humboldt Redwoods State Park, Park Headquarters, PO Box 100, Weott, CA 95571, Tel: 707/946-2409. **Pacific Lumber Company Museum**, 125 Main St., Scotia, CA 95565, Tel: 707/764-2222. Exhibition with old lumber tools. **Point Reyes National Seashore**, Point Reyes, Tel: 415/663-1092. **Redwood National Park Information Center**, PO Box 7, Orick, CA 95555, Tel: 707/488-3461.

Tourist Information
Crescent City Chamber of Commerce, Visitor Information Center, 1001 Front St., Crescent City, CA 95531, Tel: 707/464- 3174. **Fort Bragg-Mendocino Coast Chamber of Commerce**, 332 N Main St., PO Box 1141, Fort Bragg, CA 95437, Tel: 707/961-6300. **Redwood Empire Association**, 785 Market St., San Francisco, CA 94103, Tel: 415/543-8334.

OREGON
All phone numbers have area code 503.
Accommodation
LUXURY: **The Benson**, 309 SW Broadway, Portland, OR 07205, Tel: 228-2000. Elegant and old hotel downtown. *MODERATE:* **Ebb Tide**, 300 N Promenade/3rd Ave, Seaside, OR 97138, Tel: 738-8371. **Heron Haus**, 2524 NW Westover Rd., Portland, OR 97210, Tel: 274- 1846. Classic inn on historic Nob Hill. **Shore Cliff Inn**, 1100 S Hwy. US 101, Gold Beach, OR 97444, Tel: 247-7091. *BUDGET:* **Riverhouse**, 1202 Bay St., Florence, OR 97439, Tel: 997- 3933. Motel on the Siuslaw River.

Attractions, Museums and Parks
American Advertising Museum, 9 NW 2nd Ave., Portland, Tel: 226-0000. **Cape Lookout State Park**, 12 miles southwest off Hwy. US 101, near Tillamook, Tel: 368-5943. **Cascade Locks Historical Museum**, Marine Park, Cascade Locks, Tel: 374-8535. **Columbia River Maritime Museum**, 17th St./Marine Dr., Astoria, Tel: 325-2323. **Crater Lake National Park**, PO Box 7, Crater Lake, OR 97604, Tel: 594-2211. **Ecola State Park**, 2 miles north off US 101. **Flavel House**, 441 8th St., Astoria, Tel: 325 2203. **End of the Oregon Trail Interpretive Center**, 500 Washington St., Oregon City, Tel: 657-9336. **Fort Clatsop National Memorial**, 6 miles southwest off US 101A, Astoria, Tel: 861-2471. **Fort Dalles Museum**,

15th/Garrison Sts., The Dalles, Tel: 296-4547. **Fort Vancouver Historic Site**, 1501 E. Evergreen Blvd., Portland, Tel: 206/696 7655. **Hatfield Marine Science Center**, Marine Science Dr., Newport, Tel: 867-0100. **Japanese Garden**, Portland, Tel: 223-4070. **Mount Hood National Forest**, Forest Supervisor's Office, 2955 NW Division St., Information Section, Gresham, OR 97030, Tel: 666-0700. **Oswald West State Park**, 10 miles south on US 101, Tel: 842-3182. **Portland Art Museum**, 1219 SW Park Ave./Jefferson St., Portland, Tel: 226-2811. **Sea Lion Caves**, 12 miles north on US 101, Tel: 547-3111. **The Dalles Dam and Reservoir**, 3 miles east off I-84, The Dalles, Tel: 296-1181. **Timberline Ski Area/Lodge**, Mt. Hood National Forest, Tel. 272- 3311. **Undersea Gardens**, 250 SW Bay Blvd., off US Hwy. 101, Newport, Tel: 265-2206. **Washington Park**, Portland, Tel: 796-5193.

Sports and Outdoor Activities
Columbia River Cruises, Cascade Locks, Tel: 223-3928. River cruises on a historic stern-wheeler. **Jerry's Rogue River Jet Boat Trips**, Gold Beach Boat Basin (southern end of Rogue River Bridge), Tel: 247-4571. **Sand Dunes Frontier**, 3.5 miles south on US 101, Tel: 997-3391. Tours through dunes.

Tourist Information
Columbia Gorge National Scenic Area, 902 Wasco Ave., Suite 200, Hood River, OR 97031, Tel: 386-2333. **Portland/Oregon Visitors Association**, 26 SW Salmon, Portland, OR 97204, Tel: 222-2223. **The Dalles Chamber of Commerce**, 404 W 2nd St., The Dalles, OR 97058, Tel: 296-2231. **Tillamook Chamber of Commerce**, 3705 US 101 N, Tillamook, OR 97141, Tel: 842-7525.

MT. ST. HELENS AND MT. RAINIER
All phone numbers have area code 206.
Accommodation
MODERATE: **Paradise Inn**, PO Box 108, Ashford, WA 98304, Tel: 569-2275.
CAMPING: Information on camping near Mt. Rainier, Tel: 569-2211, ext. 3301.

Attractions, Visitor Centers and Parks
Mount Rainier National Park, Tahoma Woods, State Rte., Ashford, WA 98304, Tel. 569-2211. **Mount St. Helens National Volcanic Monument**, 42218 NE Yale Bridge Rd., Amboy, WA 98601, Tel: 247-5473. **Mt. St. Helens Visitor Center** at Silver Lake, 3029 Spirit Lake Hwy., Tel: 274-6644.

Sports and Outdoor Activities
Information on mountain climbing in the Mt. Rainer area, Tel: 569-2227 (summer) or 627-6242 (winter). For climbing information in the Mt. St. Helens region, Tel: 247-5800.

THE PACIFIC NORTHWEST

SEATTLE
OLYMPIC PENINSULA
PUGET SOUND
NORTH CASCADES
AND MT. BAKER
VANCOUVER

Few European tourists make tracks out to this part of the U.S. and Canada. This is all to the good for those who do: the Pacific coast of the Northwest has successfully maintained its unspoilt quality, revealing a world of mountains, great glaciers, and the ice-cold waters of the Pacific Ocean.

This itinerary begins in Seattle, or the "Pearl of the Northwest," as it is called by its admirers; steers a course through the islands of the Puget Sound; and ends in Vancouver, British Columbia. The two cities are only three hours apart by car, but one should allow for at least a week in order to cover all the side trips (which include a number of ferry rides). All in all, you will be driving around 400 miles (640 km).

SEATTLE: OUT OF THE CLOSET

For quite some time Seattle was touted as the secret tip for contemporary Americans on the lookout for new frontiers and willing to move. The city, which lies at the northwestern tip of the U.S.A., well beyond the reach of the great American metropolises with their excruciating

Previous pages: Seattle skyline with the Space Needle and Mt. Rainier. Left: Indian mask from the Burke Museum, Seattle.

rents, high crime rates and violence, offered a quiet life, the amenities of any city and a natural wilderness beyond town limits. Shortly after their move, newcomers quickly became Seattlites, which essentially meant that they would spread the news that the town was unpleasant to live in. This was a neat ruse designed to discourage the next wave of huddled masses seeking refuge. One of the most used and abused complaints about the town was that it rained all year in Seattle. Now who in earth would ever want to move to such a place?

Budding Seattlites were always insisting on how their move to the Northwest had been involuntary, a quirk of fate, done under economic duress, to find a job with, say, Boeing, which has settled in town. The truth, however, has been revealed in the meantime. Seattle has even less rain than Boston and Washington, and its cultural array is just as important and of high quality.

Indeed, Seattle has become so popular in the last decade that real estate prices have soared, the local government has ordered an end to the settling of certain parts of the city, and the first drug deaths have been reported in one of the suburbs. While Seattle is becoming the financial and economic hub of the Northwest, the city maintains its own atmosphere, a dis-

193

tinctive blend of American casualness, Asian friendliness and European style.

A City of Lumberjacks and Gold-Diggers

Seattle's popularity rests squarely on its natural setting. It is entirely surrounded by water, which determines its generally mild climate. In the west are the Pacific waters of **Puget Sound**, while in the east one finds the gigantic surface of **Lake Washington**. And wherever one looks, there seems to be a snow-topped mountain catching the rays of the sun.

Seattle and its inhabitants both seem very natural and casual, perhaps reflecting the youth of the town and its pioneer past. It was born in the middle of the 19th century as a small port where the **Yesler Sawmill** made lumber from the local forests and shipped it down to California

Above: Shopping bustle in Pike Place Market. Right: Inside the Seattle Market Hall.

or off to Asia. At the time it was nothing more than a small agglomeration of log cabins standing at the frontier of civilization inhabited by lumberjacks and visited by the odd trapper seeking his fortune in the wilds of the Northwest. This changed rapidly in 1897 when the cry of "Gold!" spread throughout the country. Within a few months, Seattle grew to a middle-sized town, as over 20,000 hopefuls flocked here to ship off to the Yukon Territories in Canada in order to profit from the so-called **Klondike Goldrush**. For Seattle it meant a brief, profitable economic boom.

A Meeting Point for Asia and America

Until fairly recently, the Seattle harbor was still the embarcation point for ships to Alaska. Nowadays its main business is loading and unloading container ships headed for Singapore and Hong Kong and other points in Asia.

The **Waterfront**, a promenade-like street running along the dock wall, can be

best investigated using the **Waterfront Trolley**, an old trolley car that has been refurbished for the comforts of modern tourists. To the north, near historic **Pier 57**, is **Waterfront Park**. Pier 57 is the place where the *Portland* docked nearly 100 years ago, carrying over one ton of Klondike gold. Waterfront Park, besides being a relaxing place for a stroll, focusses attention on the underwater world, with the **Omnidome Theater** showing 3-D films made in the depths of the Pacific, and with the **Seattle Aquarium**.

To the south, set a little way from the waterfront, is the famous **Pike Place Market**, an old market hall built around the turn of the 20th century to serve the growing Seattle population. In those heady days, Seattle housewives complained loudly of high prices in the stores. The city financed the market so that fishermen and farmers could offer their wares directly to the consumer. Nothing has changed since, except for the goods: farmers have bountiful stalls, and the fishermen sell mountains of fresh sal-

mon, mussels and king crabs from Alaska. A natural economic by-product of this trading activity are the many fish restaurants that have sprung up around the market.

Back on the waterfront, the path continues southward by **Ye Olde Curiosity Shop**, which is located in an architecturally fascinating building. Its specialty, as the name indicates, are oddities, including allegedly the smallest shrunken heads in the world and a perfectly-preserved corpse discovered in the Arizona Desert. The old Yesler Sawmill, whose industry paved the way for Seattle's rise to prominence, once stood to the left of the building; **Yesler Way** is named after the industrious businessman who founded it. The street, appropriately enough, leads east to the real center of town, **Pioneer Square**. The foundation stone of Seattle was laid in the middle of this plaza on the spot where the **Totem Pole** stands today. The staid 19th-century houses with artless façades that line the sides of the square now house fancy restaurants,

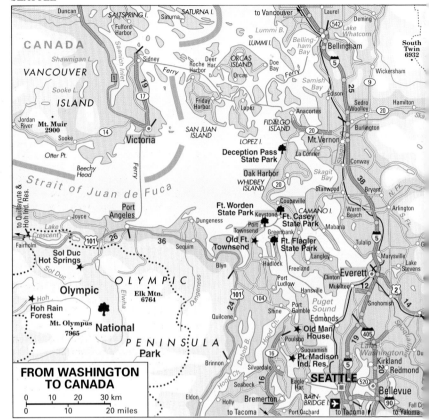

FROM WASHINGTON TO CANADA

| 0 | 10 | 20 | 30 km |
| 0 | | 10 | 20 miles |

cafés, shops and galleries. One of the tragic ironies is that much Native American craft and art is traded here, while the descendants of the original inhabitants hang around Pioneer Square either sleeping, or begging for a quarter.

Pioneer Square also has another side to it, which was for a while equally important for the homeless: after a city-wide fire in 1889, some parts of the town were rebuilt a little higher, namely on the ground floor of the first buildings in the city. **Underground Seattle** is a fascinating place to visit nowadays, a series of interconnected streets running under the town itself, a veritable city within a city. During the mean days of Prohibition it served as a hideout for bootleggers and smug-glers, and in more recent times, before it became a tourist attraction, as a home to the homeless.

To find out more about what made Seattle famous, you must make your way to the **Klondike Goldrush Museum** at 117 South Main Street. The history of that 1897 rush, its social and economic statistics, are thoroughly investigated in the rooms of the museum.

To the southeast of Pioneer Square is the **International District**, the destination mainly for Korean and Chinese immigrants. Continue on through **Downtown Seattle** to the **Seattle Art Museum,** whose daring modern architecture succeeded in arousing the tempers of even the rather liberal Seattlites when it

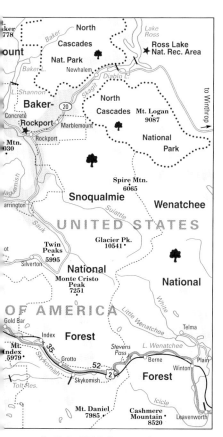

The **Monorail**, a hover train, begins its journey through the highrises to the **Seattle Center** at the corner of Pine and 4th Avenue. The device looks somewhat on the old side, but consider that when it was built back in 1962 as part of the preparations for the World's Fair, it was considered extremely modern. What is left of that fair is the Seattle center, a collection of museums and restaurants, the **Opera House** (known especially for its production of Wagner's complete *Ring* cycle), and of course the famous **Space Needle**, which has become a hallmark of the city. This nearly 600-foot television tower, carrying a platform with a spectacular view, still seems futuristic with its filigree architecture. It also gives the Seattle skyline its special touch. The view from the top stretches all the way over to the necklace of islands in Puget Sound, over to the mountain range of the Cascades, to Lake Washington and **Lake Union. Washington Park** (adjacent to the lake) boasts a diverse **Arboretum** and a very special **Japanese Tea Garden**.

Mountlake Blvd. leads to the campus of the **University of Washington**, where the **Burke Museum** offers a large collection of artifacts and crafts culled from the Northwest's Native American heritage. Interlaken Blvd. takes you to Lake Union, where a colorful collection of houseboats line the shore.

was built in 1992. Its most important exhibitions are the collections of Indian art from the Northwest and the modern art created in the region.

To the north of the downtown area one comes across **Broadway** (Broad St.), which cuts a diagonal swath through the city grid. This is the entertainment strip of Seattle, with numerous restaurants, bistros, bars and cafés all lying cheek by jowl. Young bands beginning what might be a reasonable career often try out their skills on the public in one of Broadway's rock cafés. If you tend to hear a great deal of *grunge rock*, that amusing, playful version of regular rock, do not be surprised: Seattle was the birthplace of grunge, and proud of it.

OLYMPIC PENINSULA

Unfortunately, it is not possible to explore the beauties of Puget Sound in a houseboat. The next-best alternative is to catch a car ferry from Pier 52 in Seattle harbor that takes you, for instance, to **Bainbridge Island** which is off the **Olympic Peninsula**.

After a short crossing the ferry docks at **Eagle Harbor**, a village with a host of souvenir shops, restaurants and wine bars. Hwy. 305 bears to the north, passing through remote (and expensive)

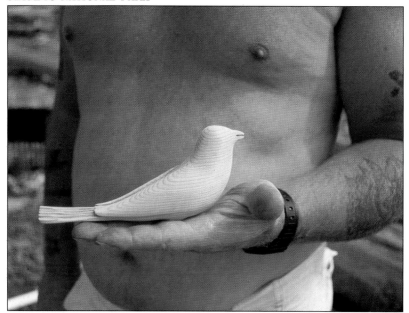

residential quarters. The roads forking off to the shore offer spectacular views of Seattle with Mt. Rainier in the background. At one point one reaches the **Port Madison Indian Reservation** with the **Suquamish Museum** that gives a vivid portrayal of Native American life in the area, with live demonstrations of ancient Indian handcrafts (such as the building of canoes).

Another interesting sight is the so-called **Old Man House**, the largest longhouse in America. The grave of **Chief Seattle** lies nearby, the Indian chief who gave his name to the city. In recent years, this Indian chieftain has achieved considerable prominence, particularly among nature conservationists, for a speech he is supposed to have held nearly a century ago accusing the white man of destroying nature and painting a bleak picture of an ecologically dead world.

Above: Driftwood from the Olympic Peninsula is good carving material. Right: The rainforests of Olympic National Park.

Further on is **Poulsbo**, a community founded by a group of Scandinavians, on to Olympic Peninsula. Here the road turns into Hwy. 101 which takes you into **Port Angeles**. As it did a hundred years ago, this little port town still lives from fishing and the lumber industry.

The fauna and flora of the **Olympic National Park** is unique and paradoxical. Absolutely opposite climatic zones lie cheek by jowl here, from dense, damp forests watered by nearly 10 feet of rain a year, to dry, barren slopes populated with elks, brown bears and other wild animals, and seals along the coast. A visit to this huge park (1,478 sq. miles) should only be undertaken in good weather, as a steady rainfall with dense fog would make any hike unpleasant, even useless. It's advisable to check the weather report before coming.

In order to investigate the entire park, in particular the road along the coast, you might have to count on several days. But even a few short trips out from Port Angeles will give you an idea of the wild,

pristine nature in the area. The route along **Hurricane Ridge** leads through a jagged mountainous region; a number of lookout spots have been arranged along the road with excellent views of Puget Sound. To penetrate untouched nature, however, you'll have to walk along any of the numerous hiking paths that crisscross the park.

The mountain ranges of the Olympic Peninsula, whose altitude ranges from 4,800 feet to 6,700 feet, were created about 10,000 years ago by glaciers, a process that can still be observed to this day. Almost 60 glaciers are active today, most of them moving down **Mt. Olympus**, which at 7,965 feet is the highest peak on the peninsula. Since the discovery of the Olympic Peninsula in 1592, the Salish Indians, who lived in the region, have almost completely disappeared. Their descendants now live in the **Quillayute and Hoh Indian Reservations**.

Back on Hwy. 101, the journey heads westward past **Lake Crescent**, whose dark blue waters may appear ice-cold, but

are in fact warm enough to swim in – in summer, at least. Campers will find some very pleasant recreational opportunities at **Sold Duc Hot Springs**, a natural thermal water source which is particularly good for people with back problems.

A final, crowning sampling trip of a visit to the park should be to the **Hoh Rain Forest Visitor Center** (over **Hoh River Road**). A hiking path begins here that takes one through a virtual rain forest, with incredibly damp air and green, mossy vegetation.

CRUISING THE ISLANDS OF PUGET SOUND

Hwy. 101 leads back in easterly direction to **Port Townsend** at the extreme tip of the Olympic Peninsula. Its obvious strategic location made it ideal for fortifying, and in fact a total of three forts were built here.

Old Fort Townsend and **Fort Worden** (about a mile and a half north of town) have been turned into parks, with a

series of recreational facilities. Fort Worden has a number of Victorian buildings on display.

, A car ferry links Port Townsend to **Keystone** on **Whidbey Island**, the actual beginning of the island world of Puget Sound. The area was first explored by George Vancouver in the 1790s. It consists of a virtually countless chain of islands, many uninhabited, that stretches all the way up the coast to Canada. The mainstay of the local population used to be salmon and timber felling. Nowadays the little villages have become mostly vacation spots for stressed Seattlites who maintain secluded weekend houses on the islands. Being relatively protected, these skerry-like islands are also a paradise for anyone who enjoys water sports, be it sailing or canoeing.

There are two ways to reach the mainland from Keystone in the middle of

Above. Fishermen gut their salmon. Right: The Boeing factories in Everett are the most important employers in the region.

Whidbey Island. The northern route leads over Coupeville to **Deception Pass**, Washington's most popular state park. The southern route is somewhat longer, but it passes through a number of quaint fishing villages that dot the southern coast of Whidbey. The way back to the mainland is by ferry.

Coupeville, just a few minutes drive north of Keystone on Rte. 20, is one of the prettiest and oldest of the fishing villages in the state of Washington. Its narrow streets are lined with carefully restored Victorian houses. Visitors are made to feel welcome in the bed-and-breakfast inns and the excellent restaurants. For nature lovers there is the neighboring **Rhododendron State Park**, which every June turns into a veritable sea of red, pink and white blossoms. The rhododendron, in fact, is Washington's state flower.

Deception Pass State Park, mentioned above, is reached by way of **Oak Harbor**, originally founded by Dutch colonists. The park itself is beloved for its untamed nature, its forests and crystalline lakes, its jagged coastline providing long and dramatic walks; but what every visitor unanimously admires is actually manmade.

At **Deception Point** is a bridge connecting Whidbey and Fidalgo Islands. Below it, the dark Pacific waters flow into the peaceful **Skagit Bay**, an unbelievable sight to behold. Rte. 20 then continues on to the mainland. After a short detour over **La Conner**, a remote and picturesque fishing village, one finally arrives at **Burlington**.

The aforementioned southern route first makes a stop at **Langley**, which appears more commercial than Coupeville or La Conner. Nevertheless, it is the right place to shop for genuine antiques or local art and artifacts. The ferry to the mainland departs from **Clinton** and arrives after a short trip in **Mukilteo** to the south of Everett.

Everett's main attraction, the **Boeing Works**, already makes its presence felt from afar. Great green jumbo jets without any telltale markings on the fuselage circle the skies as they are taken through their final tests before being sold. The world's largest hangar is adjacent to the factory's own runway, a building that can easily accomodate a dozen or so jumbo jets. A tour of this gigantic hall should not be missed.

With a payroll of over 100,000, the Boeing works is the single largest employer in the Northwest. The first Boeing aircraft took off from the waters of Lake Washington near Seattle in 1916. Nowadays all the company's planes and parts are built in Everett and neighboring **Reston**.

The danger of having all one's economic eggs in one basket was made clear at the end of the 1960s when Boeing cut 50,000 jobs after a number of important military contracts had fallen through. Seattle was virtually at the edge of ruin, as people flocked away from the city to look for work elsewhere in the country. Now, nearly 30 years later, the development of the airplane Boeing 777 and new space-related contracts provide the company with a solid economic foundation in spite of competition from various Airbus Industries.

San Juan Islands

The **San Juan Islands**, an archipelago numbering 170 little islands, invite one to a bout of island-hopping. But the ferries leaving from Anacortes (Northern Whidbey Island) often have to do battle with heavy seas and strong winds.

Two islands of special note are **Orcas Island** and **San Juan Island**. A **Whale Museum** in **Friday Harbor** (once upon a time a whaling station) gives a rundown of the history of whaling in the region. Nowadays the fishing boats docked in the harbor are used for salmon fishing, while in the distance, with a little luck, you might spot the fin of a passing killer whale.

NORTH CASCADES AND MT. BAKER NATIONAL PARKS

The drive north on I-5 leads northward to Canada through the town of Burlington. On the way is **North Cascades National Park**, an elongated mid-sized mountain range that crosses the border from Washington State to Canada. The jagged summits of this world of rocks and glaciers can be seen all the way from Seattle, provided the air is clear. Just as it has been doing for thousands of years, Mother Nature is hard at work here still, with glaciers carving away the mountains forming new peaks, creating great waterfalls and leaving crystal-clear lakes in their wake. Hwy. 20 turns into the **North Cascades Scenic Highway**, which is only open from April to November. Some of the nation's heaviest snowfalls are registered here each winter.

Above: Bald eagles can be observed in North Cascades National Park. Right: View of Canada Place and Burrard Inlet, Vancouver.

The landscape along the highway is among the most beautiful in America. Even if you lack the time to attempt a thorough exploration, go at least as far as **Winthrop** in the eastern part of the state before turning around. The highway has plenty of parking spots with great lookout platforms. Among the best panoramas are those at **Lake Ross** and **Diabolo Lake**. Near **Rockport,** a side road leads through a state park known for its 300-year old pine trees. The **Visitors' Center** in **Marblemount** provides maps, brochures and other bits of important information about the park. In the south of the town, both banks of the **Skagit River** are home to the white-headed eagle, especially during the winter months.

Take the fork heading north near the town of Concrete (which was indeed named because of its concrete factory), and you will end up in the **Mt. Baker-Snoqualmie National Forest**, whose main sight is the 10,778-foot-high **Mt. Baker**. This extinct volcano is not as breathtaking as Mt. Rainier or Mt. St. Helens, but it does have the advantage of generally attracting less tourists and hikers than its two colleagues to the south.

To get to Canada one must take Rte. 9. Shortly before the border comes Rte. 42, which also leads to Mt. Baker. This side of the mountain has been well developed for skiing and is a favorite spot for all snow sports.

VANCOUVER: THE CITY IN THE MISTS

The trip up I-5 from the south and then Hwy. 99 to Vancouver gives one of the most beautiful views of any city in the world. The skyline, with its tall white, shiny skyscrapers of glass and steel seems virtually to spring from the deep blue waters of a bay, and behind them rise the dramatic slopes of an entire mountain range. The city was founded in 1886, almost a century after the English

captain George Vancouver discovered **Burrard Inlet** on his search for the Northwest Passage. Vancouver was built up on the northern end of this inlet, on a natural peninsula stretching out into its waters. Like Seattle, Vancouver was a gathering point for adventurers, gold-diggers and trappers, who set off from here to explore new frontiers in Alaska.

Before turning on to Hwy. 99, which takes you right into the city, make a stop at **Granville Island**, where restaurants and shops and an arts college have nested in the restored industrial and shipyard buildings. Some of the finest salmon can be eaten in the restaurants here, mainly Alaskan salmon, which is somewhat tastier (and a good deal cheaper) than European salmon.

To get to **Downtown Vancouver**, you will have to drive by the old **Coal Harbor**, which has undergone a complete transformation ever since the 1986 Expo festivities. The famous **Canada Place** rises up before the elegant buildings of the city, at the embarcation pier for fer-

ries to Alaska. This undeclared hallmark of Vancouver is remarkable for its harmonious design, that makes it look like a sailing ship. The white wings of the convention center do indeed remind one of wind-filled sails, and make the building look as if it were about to cast off any minute.

Farther to the east is **Gastown**, the official old town of Vancouver, which has some special curiosities: a steam-run clock, and the narrowest house of the city. The name of this quarter, which has numerous office buildings and shops, dates back to the year 1867, when "Gassy Jack" Deighton opened a popular saloon here. South of **Hastings Street**, between Gore and Carall Streets, lies Vancouver's **Chinatown,** whose restaurants and market spread exotic and indefinable smells through the neighborhood. It's the second largest Chinatown on the continent after San Francisco's.

Stanley Park occupies the western section of the city; this is a forested area covering almost 1,000 acres, with hiking

paths and innumerable totem poles left by the Native Americans.

The fauna of the local waters is exhibited live in the **Vancouver Aquarium** in the park, which offers special shows with killer and beluga whales. In late summer in particular, the great fins of these giant mammals plough their way quite visibly through the waters by Seattle, Vancouver and around the myriad islands in the region.

Vancouver Island

The largest island along the Canadian Pacific coast is **Vancouver Island**, which is about 300 miles long and can be accessed by car ferry. It is a great stage for nature's own performances: sea lions sun themselves along the beaches, before a backdrop of high and rugged cliffs with, behind them, vast, dark forests and snow-capped peaks. You get the finest pan-

Above: Whales are plentiful in the area (Whale Museum in Friday Harbor).

oramas from along **Malahat Drive** (Hwy. 1) or along Hwy. 14 west.

Victoria, the capital of the Canadian province of British Columbia, lies to the south of Vancouver Island. The city started out as a modest trading post and fort built in 1843 by the Hudson Bay Company. Canadians frozen stiff in their harsh winters enjoy Victoria for its generally mild climate, which also supports the blossoming flowers in the town's many parks and gardens. Among the prettiest of these are **Butchart Gardens** outside town, and **Crystal Gardens** which has tropical gardens, a monkey house and a waterfall.

Due to its large number of Tudor-style houses, Victoria has a very British flair. Particularly worth a visit are the pompous **Parliament Building** (501 Belleville St.) and the restored **Empress Hotel** (721 Government St.). Ferries connect Victoria with Seattle (summer only) and Port Angeles; from nearby Sidney ferries leave for the San Juan Islands and the U.S. mainland.

SEATTLE

All phone numbers have area code 206.

Accommodation

LUXURY: **The Edgewater**, Pier 67, 2411 Alaskan Way, Seattle, WA 98121-1398, Tel: 728-7000. Fine first-class hotel on the waterfront.

MODERATE: **Pacific Plaza Hotel**, 400 Spring St., Seattle, WA 98104, Tel: 623-3900. Historically restored hotel downtown. **Tugboat Challenger Bunk & Breakfast**, 1001 Fairview Ave. N., Seattle, WA 98109, Tel: 340-1201. B & B in an old and nicely restored tugboat in Seattle Harbor.

BUDGET: **Nendel's Valu Inn**, 2100 Fifth Ave., Seattle, WA 98121, Tel: 441-8833.

Attractions, Museums and Parks

Burke Museum, 17th Ave. NE/NE 45th St., Tel: 543-5590. **Japanese Garden with Arboretum**, Washington Park, Tel: 684-4725. **Klondike Rush National Historic Park**, 117 S Main St., Tel: 553-7220. **Pacific Science Center** (with **Omnidome Theatre**), 200 2nd Ave. N., Tel: 443-2001. **Pike Place Market**, Information: Tel: 682-7453. **Seattle Aquarium**, Pier 59, Tel: 386-4320. **Seattle Art Museum**, 100 University St., Tel: 654-3100. **Seattle Center and Space Needle**, 305 Harrison St., Tel: 684 7200 and 1-800/937-9582 (Space Needle). **Underground Tour**, 610 1st Ave., Tel: 682-4646.

Ferries to Victoria and other Canada destinations

Washington State Ferries, Pier 52, Tel: 464-6400 or Tel: 1-800/843-3779.

Tourist Information

Seattle-King County C & V Bureau, Washington State Convention & Trade Center, 520 Pike St., Suite 1300, Galleria Level, Seattle, WA 98101, Tel: 461-5800.

OLYMPIC PENINSULA, PUGET SOUND, NORTH CASCADES

All phone numbers have area code 206.

Accommodation

MODERATE: **Katty's**, PO Box 869, 503 S 3rd St., La Conner, Wa 98257, Tel: 466-3366. **Lake Crescent Lodge**, HC 62, Box 11, Port Angeles, WA 98362-9798, Tel: 928-3211. **Sol Duc Hot Spring Resort**, PO Box 2169, Sol Duc Rd., Hwy. 101, Port Angeles, WA 98362, Tel: 327-3583.

BUDGET: **Winthrop Inn**, Box 265, on Hwy. WA 20, Winthrop, WA 98862, Tel: 509/996-2217. **Island Lodge at Friday Harbor**, 1016 Guard St., Friday Harbor, San Juan Island, WA 98250, Tel: 206/378-2000.

Attractions, Museums and Parks

Deception Pass State Park, Tel: 675-2417. **Everett Industrial Tour at Boeing**, off I-5, exit 189, on Hwy. WA 526, Tel: 342-4801. **Fort Casey State Park**, near Coupeville, Tel: 678-4519. **Fort Worden State Park**, Tel: 385-0854. **Hoh River Visitor Center**, Tel: 374-6925. **Mt. Baker-Snoqualmie National Forest**, Tel: 856-5700. **North Cascades Scenic Highway**, Sedro Woolley, Tel: 856-5700. **Olympic Park Visitor Center**, 600 E Park Ave., Port Angeles, Tel: 452-0330. **Suquamish Museum** (on Bainbridge Island, Sandy Hook Rd.), Sedro Woolley, Tel: 598-3311. **Whale Museum**, 62 1st St. N, Friday Harbor, San Juan Island, Tel: 206/378-5240.

Sports and Outdoor Activities

Olympic Raft & Guide Service, Port Angeles, Tel: 457-7011. River rafting in Olympic National Park. **Olympic Van Tours**, Coho Ferry Terminal at Port Angeles, Tel: 452-3858. Sightseeing tours exploring Olympic National Park.

Viking Cruises, Lime Dock Building, 109 N. First St., Coupeville, Tel: 466-2639. Jet boat excursions in Deception Pass waters.

Tourist Information

Washington State Tourism Office, Tel: 1-800/544-1800. **San Juan Islands Chamber of Commerce**, PO Box 98, Friday Harbor, WA 98250, Tel: 206/378-5240.

VANCOUVER AND VANCOUVER ISLAND

All phone numbers have area code 604.

Accommodation

LUXURY: **Meridien**, 845 Burrard St., Vancouver V6Z 2K6, downtown, Tel: 682-5511, res.: 1-800/543-4300. **Empress**, 721 Government St., V8W 1B2, Victoria, Vancouver Island, Tel: 384-8111.

MODERATE: **Best Western Château Granville**, 1100 Granville St., V6Z 2B6, Vancouver, Tel: 669-7070. **Biltmore**, 395 Kingsway (Hwy. 1A/99A), Vancouver V5T 3J7, Tel: 872-5252, res.: 1-800/663-5713, south of downtown. **West End Guest House**, 1362 Haro St., V6E 1G2, Vancouver, Tel: 681-2889.

Attractions, Museums and Parks

Butchart Gardens, Benvenuto Ave., Victoria, Tel: 652-4422. **Crystal Garden**, 713 Douglas St., Victoria, 381-1277. **Parliament Buildings**, 501 Bellevue St., Tel: 387-3046. **Royal British Columbia Museum**, 675 Bellevue St., Tel: 387-3701. Exhibitions on natural history. **Stanley Park and Vancouver Aquarium**, Vancouver, Tel: 681-1141 and 682-1118 (Aquarium).

Tourist Information

Tourism Vancouver InfoCentre, Plaza Level, Waterfront Centre, 200 Burrard St., Tel: 683-2000. **Tourism Victoria**, 1175 Douglas St., Suite 710, V8W 2E1, Victoria, Tel: 382-2127.

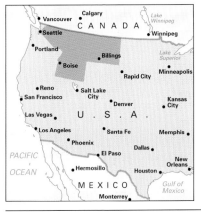

FROM SEATTLE
TO YELLOWSTONE
NATIONAL PARK

YAKIMA
WENATCHEE AND COULEE
SPOKANE
IDAHO
MONTANA

The vast, boundless prairie crouches beneath the azure sky, the snow-capped Rocky Mountains glitter off in the distance, and the highway snakes along apparently without an end. This 780-mile (1,248 km) stretch from Seattle to Yellowstone Park is an encounter with pure nature, of a kind one can hardly ever get enough of. The road leads from Seattle through eastern Washington State, across the northern part of Idaho, through Montana, the land of cowboys and gold-diggers, on to the northern entrance of Yellowstone. This itinerary, which covers the northern section of the Rocky Mountains, is not as spectacular as a drive through Colorado. On the other hand, you'll hardly encounter any fellow tourists (least of all Europeans).

YAKIMA

The drive begins in **Seattle**, on I-90 to be precise, heading eastward out of the city. **Snoqualmie Falls** is worth a brief stop in order to gawk at the grand waterfall which supplies one of the oldest hydroelectric plants in the U.S. The plant itself can barely be seen, as it is tucked

Left: Portrait of a young Indian boy (at a "Pow Wow", a tribal meeting with ritualistic dancing in Seattle).

away at the bottom of the nearby cliffs behind the waterfall itself. **Snoqualmie Pass**, one of the few accessible mountain crossing points beyond Seattle, was once part of the path used by settlers heading for the Pacific coast.

The eastern part of Washington State is drastically different from the west of the state along the Pacific coast. While the residents of the latter, in and around Seattle, sometimes feel they are being subjected to a continuous deluge, the inhabitants of the eastern part could not survive without expensive and complex irrigation systems. Without the largess of the great Columbia River, whose waters keep fields and orchards from drying out, agricultural pursuits in eastern Washington would never be possible. The reason for this climatic imbalance is the presence of the North Cascades Range which form a barrier to the weather fronts from the Pacific. The rain stays on the western side, while the east gets no more than ten inches of precipitation a year.

Two side trips can be undertaken at the intersection of I-90 and I-82. One goes in southerly direction to **Yakima**. The other heads toward the north to Wenatchee, where you can switch to Rte. 2 heading east again. Both towns are known above all for the great orchards surrounding them. In fact they are in a sense the twin

capitals of Washington State apple growing. The most significant of the two is Yakima. The growing of fruit, and especially apples, began here in the 1870s, when farmers started irrigating this fertile, partially volcanic soil. The erstwhile "fruit exchange" has been turned into a large shopping center known as **Yesterday's Village**. The history of Yakima Valley is told at the **Yakima Valley Museum** (2105 Tieton Drive), which also has other exhibits, an interesting and curious collection of covered wagons.

If you have time and are not intending to drive a long stretch, stop in at some of the Yakima Valley cellars. In the past few years Washington State wines have become increasingly popular, and in fact nowadays it is the state with the second-largest wine production in the U.S. – behind California. What supports this industry are the 300 days of annual sun-

shine, which is so necessary for the cultivation of grapes. When tasting these strong and spicy wines, one is reminded of the wines of Greece or Turkey. All in all the flavor of the Washington grapes (even though they might bear the name Chardonnay or Riesling) are somewhat more extreme than the same grape in Europe. Most of the cellars with wine-tasting facilities are to be found in the villages around Yakima, including **Zillah**, **Sunnyside**, and **Grandview**.

Toppenish, too, offers several wine cellars, but it also boasts the **Yakima Indian Reservation**. The **Cultural Center** in the reservation provides a look into the history of the Native Americans in the area. In the 1850s, the Indians started rebelling against the increase in white settlement, which is why the army built nearby **Fort Simcoe**. The descendants of the original tribes now live on the reservation and have been degraded to tourist attractions, a sad fate, and one more blot on the romanticized settling of the frontier.

WENATCHEE AND COULEE

The northern side trip mentioned above takes you over Hwy. 97 to the town of **Wenatchee**, which is particularly beautiful in spring when the apple trees are all in bloom. The beginning of the blossoming season is celebrated each year between the last weekend in April and May 1st with the **Washington State Apple Blossom Festival**. To the north of the little town lie **Ohme Gardens**, an enchanting idyll with waterfalls and bright green fields covered in a colorful tapestry of mountain flowers.

Should time allow for a longer detour up north, **Leavenworth**, at the foot of the **North Cascades**, should be put on the list of sights to see. For Europeans, and Germans or Austrians in particular, this little town made up to look like an Alpine village in Bavaria, with all the trimmings including a May festival and oompah

Above: Ascent into the mountain chains of the North Cascades. Right: Farm in the Wenatchee Mountains.

bands, seems terribly out of place in the midst of an American environment. It's quite corny as well, one must admit. American tourists don't seem to mind, however, and it is, after all, a great deal cheaper than flying all the way to "good ole Bavaria."

Rte. 2 leads on to **Coulee City** and the so-called **Dry Falls State Park**, whose name can be taken quite literally: The 400-foot chasm that greets the visitor was once the receptacle of a huge waterfall that ran for nearly 3.5 miles. Once upon a time this waterfall was the largest in the world. At the end of the Ice Age, when the receding glaciers released their booty of water, this section of the Columbia River ultimately dried up.

Another superlative can be found a little farther east at the **Grand Coulee Dam**, which was considered the largest man-made construction when it was built in 1941. It is over 550 feet high, with a base length of 500 feet. Its upper roadway is 5,223 feet long, which still puts it in the world-class category of steel and concrete monuments. The engineers who designed it made ingenious use of the natural conditions of the area. The Columbia River was deviated into a gorge, which used to be the riverbed several million years ago, and then dammed.

Franklin D. Roosevelt Lake, which was formed from this procedure, irrigates the entire region. As for the power plant on the Grand Coulee Dam – it remains the world's largest hydroelectric plant to this day.

SPOKANE
The Little City on the River

The "little big city" of **Spokane** was long considered a provincial backwater lost somewhere out in the no man's land between the Pacific Ocean and Minneapolis. (City slickers from the sophisticated metropolises of the East Coast might point out that Minneapolis is not exactly what you'd call sophisticated, but this is open to debate.) Yet Spokane has a special charm of its own that even the

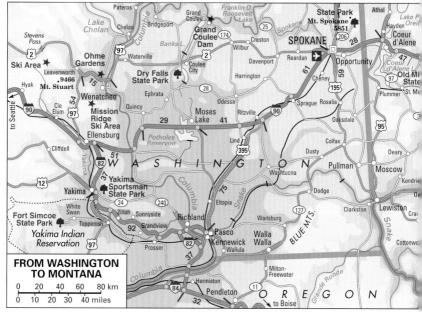

FROM WASHINGTON TO MONTANA

| 0 | 20 | 40 | 60 | 80 km |
| 0 | 10 | 20 | 30 | 40 miles |

twin cities of St. Paul and Minneapolis do not have. This old forward outpost for lumberjacks and trappers became one of the most important communities in the Inland Empire toward the end of the 19th century, when it was a stop on the transcontinental railroad. As it happened, Spokane was the only pass along hundreds of miles of Rocky Mountain territory where the rails could be laid down. It experienced another spurt of growth when gold was discovered in nearby Coeur d'Alene. Parallel to this development, the local Indian tribes (Spokane means "children of the sun" in the local language) were gradually pressured into reservations.

Thanks to its beautiful surroundings, Spokane is seen by many as one of America's finest places to live. Nevertheless, there are critics out there who in spite of it all still call Spokane a backwater.

The best place to get a taste of the old pioneer days is at the carefully restored **Riverfront**, with its office blocks and warehouses dating to the end of the 19th century. The revival of the inner city followed in the wake of Expo '74. One special project was the restoration of the **Riverfront Park**, a recreational area located on an island in the river. It has various paths with typical park furnishings (from benches to jungle gyms) and an IMAX projection house. Pedestrian bridges connect the island to both sides of the Spokane River. **Spokane Falls**, a modest waterfall on the river artificially illuminated at night, is visible from **Bridge Ave/Monroe St**.

Another aspect of local culture, one that is hardly visible any more in the area, can be inspected at the **Cheney Cowles Museum**, where artifacts from local Native American tribes are displayed.

But there are other parks and gardens in Spokane that are also worth visiting, such as **Manito Park**, and **Riverside State Park**, which has something for walkers, anglers and campers. **Mt. Spokane State Park**, which lies about 40 miles to the northeast of the town on Rte. 206 is another place worth seeing. It comprises among other things, two of the

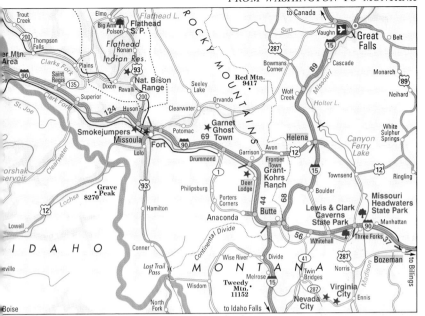

highest area mountains, Mt. Spokane (5,881 feet) and Mt. Kit Carson (5,306 feet), which both offer splendid views of the valley.

CROSSING IDAHO

I-90 cuts through northern Idaho, one of the most beautiful and diverse landscapes in the U.S.A. No other single region of continental America has so many different geographical and climatic zones, from high mountains and warm, damp forests, to spacious prairies that stretch as far as the eye can see. The earth here is rich, with precious metals such as silver, zinc and lead, especially in the region between **Boise** and **Coeur d'Alene**. The latter is the center of a recreational area that lies along the shores of **Coeur d'Alene Lake**. Hwy. 97, which steers southward, and Rte. 10 east are both particularly scenic. Furthermore, visitors should stop in at the **Museum of North Idaho** near the City Park, and at the **Silverwood Theme Park** in **Athol**, where

the history of the Wild West is enacted in particularly vivid fashion.

The Interstate heading east leads through the old mining areas of the state. **Kellogg**, a community of about 3,500 people 35 miles east of Coeur d'Alene, still boasts America's largest lead and silver mines. In the late 19th century it was the site of a violent miner's strike that paralized the entire region. The history of the back- and soul-breaking work underground is retold in the nearby **Wallace District Mining Museum** at. Silver mining is demonstrated live on tours of the now-defunct **Sierra Silver Mine** (also in Wallace, at 420 5th St.).

MONTANA

Just a few miles to the east is the border of **Montana**, where flat prairie meets the foothills of the Rocky Mountains. At one time the state was the most important gold-mining area in the entire country, and even today, though somewhat more modestly, gold mined in the eastern part of Montana still represents a major economic factor in the state's finances.

But what Montana is really known for is cattle: it has more cows than people. And then there are the cowboys, not actors or phonies for the tourists, but rather the real McCoy. The Wild West romance of tough guys riding the saddle day in, day out, herding cattle eastward, is still conjured up nowadays. Men, even managers and bureaucrats, come to Montana to recover from their daily urban stress in the local dude ranches and on dusty riding trails. If we look back at the meaning of the word dude, we find something not so flattering: a dandy, a fop, says Webster's; while for Westerners, a dude is always just a city slicker from the East.

On the dude ranch, people who feel limp-wristed from shifting paper from one side of the desk to the other can get a whiff of toughness, sweat, leather, courage. Dude ranches offer week-long programs consisting of riding, cattle herding and grilling steaks on the open fire. Many places along the Interstate offer this service, and adventures in the saddle can also be reserved from as far away as Europe.

The real life of the cowboys looked quite different than it does today, even when disregarding the vaudeville staged for the tourists. They were generally poverty-striken fellows, whose only skill was riding and herding. They seldom drew their Colts and shot about the place, because ammunition was expensive. As for the gallons of whiskey they are alleged to have drunk (if we are to believe Hollywood), it too was on the expensive list. By the turn of the 20th century, the cowboys had already become few and far between, thanks to technological improvements in husbandry and a very simple item, the invention of barbed wire.

Right: The smell of animals, sweat and leather banishes thoughts of the workaday world – on a dude ranch in Montana.

Near **St. Regis** you can divert on Rtes. 135 and 200 to the **National Bison Range**, where several hundred bisons roam and ruminate freely under the endless sky on about 19,000 acres of prime prairie land. A little farther north (for those with some time on their hands) is Flathead State Park, where the mountainous landscape is striated with deep gorges, and the eponymous lake offers secluded bays. Boats depart from **Big Arm** to **Wild Horse Island**, a wildlife sanctuary which the wild horses indicated by the island's name share with eagles and bighorn sheep.

To the south of Flathead State Park, right on I-90, lies the town of **Missoula**, a thoroughly unnoteworthy place with an interesting historical footnote. It was the first place in the U.S. to send a woman representative to Congress, namely Jeanette Rankin. This event took place in 1916, well before women even had the right to vote in America. And this in what was basically considered "men's country!"

Today, just as it was 150 years ago, Missoula is at the intersection of a number of important routes. The **Historical Museum** at **Fort Missoula** is housed in several of the fort's restored buildings. If you are interested in finding out more about the rough job of "smoke jumping," you should pass by the **Visitors' Center** seven miles westward on Hwy 10. This is where forest-fire fighters are trained to parachute into the fires that devastate large tracts all along the west coast. The risks they take have their reward in terms of money: some youths who enjoy hanging out on the slopes with their skis and snowboards throughout the winter and spring, or out surfing the Pacific, can earn enough money at this job to keep them going for the rest of the year.

South of Missoula is a 17-mile detour along a twisting and turning scenic road (Rte. 12) to **Lolo**. The Nez Percés Indians used this trail on their bison hunting ex-

peditions hundreds of years ago. Later it was explored by the Lewis and Clark Expedition, which left its traces all over Montana.

Rte. 12 joins I-90 again, which in turn leads to **Drummond**, an insignificant town. Not to be missed, however, is **Garnet Ghost Town** (10 miles west of the Drummond exit), one of the finest specimens of this kind of town left over from the Montana gold rush in the last century. Another side trip worth taking is to **Helena**, the state's capital (over Rte. 12), which also recalls the good old days of gold fever. The main drag is still appropriately named **Last Chance Gulch**: in 1864 a band of weary and discouraged diggers discovered a ravine here and considered it their last hope. They were luckier than they expected to be, for in subsequent years nuggets worth several million dollars were found in and around Helena.

The **Last Chance Tour Train** (at the museum at 225 N Roberts St.) offers trips through this memory lane. For a look at some real gold, however, you will have to go to the **Gold Collection** (350 N Last Chance Gulch). That Helena, a town of about 25,000 inhabitants, should be the capital of a state larger than Japan, might amuse some foreign visitors, but its government buildings are worthy of its status, especially the **State Capitol**, with its copper dome, and the 1888 **Governor's Mansion**.

15 miles to the west of town on Rte. 12, so-called **Frontier Town** offers some magnificient views of the surrounding valleys. As for the Interstate, it passes by **Deer Lodge**, the site of **Grant-Kohrs Ranch**, a 23-room mansion that gives an idea of what life was like for a ranching family owning over a million acres of land. The wealth of the mine operators, on the other hand, can be admired in nearby **Butte**, whose rise to prominence occurred thanks to copper and silver mining. **Copper King Mansion** was built in 1888 and testifies to the grandiloquent and opulent taste of these boom times. What brought about this wealth, the nitty-gritty of mining, is demonstrated at the

World Museum of Mining and **Hell Roarin' Gulch** (W Park St.). It includes displays relating to silver and gold mining, and a reconstructed gold miners' camp.

Two routes lead to **Yellowstone Park** (see p. 169 ff.) after leaving Butte. The one steers a northward course and is far more appealing in terms of landscape, the other (running in a southwesterly direction) takes you through a number of old gold mining locations.

The first stop on the northern road (I-90) is the **Lewis and Clark Caverns State Park** near the town of **Whitehall**. This extensive system of caves carved into the limestone rock is considered the largest in the Northwest. A short distance away, near **Three Forks**, Lewis and Clark left signs of their passage when they came across the "birthplace" of the Missouri River, at the confluence of three rivers. Then as now, it was a grandiose

Above: Service stations – a fixed point of human civilisation in the expanse of the country.

sight, and so they gave appropriate names to the three source rivers: Jefferson, Madison and Gallatin.

The road then heads to Yellowstone Park, passing through the town of **Bozeman**, named after a certain John M. Bozeman, who was the leader of one group of pioneers from Wyoming.

The southern route follows Hwys. 41 and 287, and is a paradise for ghost town buffs. **Virginia City** and **Nevada City** were both once upon a time wild and dangerous gold mining camps after gold was struck in 1863. Within a few weeks the hungry and the greedy were streaming into the region. The search for the great nugget was dangerous business: local authorities noted over 200 murders in the first half of the year. The survivors (and they were not few) could consider themselves lucky: the value of the gold discovered in the region has been estimated at nearly 300 million U.S. dollars. All that is left of these riches in the area today, however, are a few dusty and solitary ghost towns.

YAKIMA VALLEY AND SPOKANE
All phone numbers have area code 509.

Accommodation
MODERATE: **The Tudor Guest House**, 3111 Tieton Dr., Yakima, WA 98902, Tel: 452-8112. Spacious brick manor on the western outskirts of town.

BUDGET: **Coulee House**, 110 Roosevelt Way, Coulee Dam, WA 99116, Tel. 633-1101. **Shilo Inn**, 923 3rd Ave., Spokane, WA 99202, Tel: 535-9000.

Campgrounds
Yakima Sportsman State Park, three miles east on Hwy. WA 24, Keyes Rd., Tel. 575-2774.

Attractions, Museums and Parks
Central Washington Agricultural Museum, 4508 Main St., Yakima, Tel: 457-8735. Exhibition on historic farming. **Cheney Cowles Museum**, W 2316 1st Ave., Spokane, Tel: 456-3931. **Coulee Dam National Recreation Area** (with Franklin D. Roosevelt Lake), Tel: 633-9441. **Grand Coulee Dam**, near junction Hwys. WA 155/174, Tel: 633-9265. **Manito Park**, Grand Blvd./18th Ave., Spokane, Tel: 625-6622. **Mt. Spokane State Park**, 25 miles northeast on Hwy. WA 206, Tel: 456-4169. **Riverfront Park**, Spokane Falls Blvd./Howard St., Spokane, Tel: 625-6600. **Riverside State Park**, near Downriver Dr., Spokane, Tel: 456-3964. **Wenatchee National Forest**, Tel: 662-4335. **Yakima Indian Nation Cultural Center**, US Hwy. 97, Toppenish, Tel: 865-2800. **Yakima Valley Museum**, 2105 Tieton Dr., Franklin Park, Yakima, Tel: 248-0747.

Sports and Outdoor Activities
Mission Ridge Ski Area, near Wenatchee, SW on Squilchuck Rd., Tel: 663-7631.

Skiing Mt. Spokane, 30 miles northeast on Hwy. WA 206, Tel: 238-6281.

Steven Pass Ski Area, 36 miles northwest on Hwy. US 2, near Leavenworth, Tel: 206/973-2441.

Tourist Information
Spokane C & V Bureau, 926 W. Sprague Ave., Suite 180, Spokane, WA 98204, Tel: 624-1341.

Yakima Valley V & C Bureau, 10 North 8th St., Yakima, WA 98901-2515, Tel: 575-1300.

Yakima Valley Wine Growers Assn., PO Box 39, Grandview, WA 98930.

MONTANA AND IDAHO
Accommodation
LUXURY: **Coeur d'Alene Resort on the Lake**, 115 2nd St., Coeur d'Alene, ID 83814, Tel: 208/765-4000.

MODERATE: **Blackwell House**, 820 Sherman Ave., Coeur d'Alene, ID 83814, Tel: 208/664-0656. **Goldsmith's B & B**, 809 E Front St., Missoula, MT 59802 (I-90 exit Van Buren St.), Tel. 406/721-

6732. Nice Victorian manor. **Holiday Inn**, 200 S Pattee St., Missoula, MT 59802, Tel: 406/721-8550. **Red Lion Village Motor Inn**, 100 Madison St., Missoula, MT 59801, Tel: 406/728-3100, 1/4 mile SW of I-90 Van Buren exit. **Townhouse Inns**, 2777 Harrison Ave., Butte, MT 59701, Tel: 406/494-8850.

BUDGET: **Fairweather Inn & Nevada City Hotel**, Box 338, on US 287, Virginia City, MT 59755, Tel: 406/843-5377. Western-style motel. **Stardust**, 410 Pine St., Wallace, ID 83873, Tel: 208/752-1213. **Super 8**, 2929 Harrison Ave., Butte, MT 59701, Tel: 406/494-6000.

Attractions, Museums and Parks
Copper King Mansion, 219 W Granite St., Butte, Tel. 406/782-7580. **Flathead State Park**, US Hwys 2 and 93, near Kalispell, Tel: 406/755-5401. **Frontier Town**, 15 miles west on US 12, Tel. 406/442-4560. **Gold Collection**, Norwest Bank Helena, 350 N Last Chance Gulch, Helena, Tel: 406/447-2000. **Governor's Mansion**, 304 N Ewing St., Helena, Tel: 406/444-2694.

Grant-Kohrs Ranch National Historic Site, Deer Lodge, Tel: 406/846-2070. **Historical Museum at Fort Missoula**, five miles south from I-90, Tel: 406/728-3476. **Lewis and Clark Caverns State Park**, 19 miles west on MT 2, near Whitehall, Tel: 406/287-3541. **Missoula Aerial Fire Depot**, seven miles west on US 10, Tel: 406/329-4900.

Museum of North Idaho, 115 NW Blvd./near City Park, Coeur d'Alene, Tel: 208/664-3448.

Museum of the Rockies, S 7th Ave./Kagy Blvd. S, Bozeman, Tel: 406/994-2251. Exhibition on Native Americans and wildlife in the Rocky Mountains. **Old Mission State Park**, off I-90, exit 39, in Cataldo near Kellogg, Tel. 208/682-3814. Restored mission buildings. **Sierra Silver Mine Tour**, 420 5th St., Wallace, Tel: 208/752-5151.

Silverwood Theme Park, on I-95 in Athol, Tel: 208/772-0513. **State Capitol**, Helena, Tel: 406/444-4794. **Wallace District Mining Museum**, 509 Bank St., Wallace, no phone. **World Museum of Mining**, W Park St., Butte, Tel: 406/723-7211.

Sports and Outdoor Activities
Lake Coeur d'Alene Cruises, City Dock, east of City Park, Coeur d'Alene, Tel: 208/765-4000. **Lookout Pass Ski Area**, 13 miles east on I-90, near Wallace, Tel: 208/744-1392. **Silver Mountain Ski Area**, off I-90, exit 49, near Kellogg, Tel: 208/783-1111.

Tourist Information
Bovey Restoration, PO Box 338, Virginia City, MT 59755, Tel: 406/843-5377.

Greater Coeur d'Alene C & V Bureau, PO Box 1088, Coeur d'Alene, ID 83814, Tel: 208/664-0587.

NATIONAL PARKS

For the first European settlers, America appeared to be an immeasurably large, even endless land, with splendidly untamable nature. Nevertheless, as the lightening settlement of the western frontier began in the 19th century, a process that was brutal toward the Native Americans and their habitat as well, both settlers and politicians realized soon that in spite of its great size, the continent's ecosystem was by no means as rugged as it appeared to be.

It wasn't only the stream of pioneers, cowboys and other settlers pouring westward and experiencing the land's natural beauties which led to the promotion of nature conservation in the U.S.A. Such poets as Henry Wadsworth Longfellow and Walt Whitman, or the Transcendentalist philosopher Henry David Thoreau,

Previous pages: Antilope Island, Utah. White Sands, New Mexico. Above: Big Bend N. P. Right: Entrance to Glacier N. P., Montana.

romanticized the wilderness as the true Eden. American painters of the stamp of George Catlin and Thomas Moran captured the breathtaking beauty of the country in their oils. A German artist, Karl Blechen, immortalized the vast proportions of the country for Europeans to see. Even composers have been attracted to the wilderness, trying to reproduce its dimensions in their music (in this century, one thinks of Aaron Copland's delightful *Appalachian Spring*) Indirectly, it was from this enthusiasm that the first National Park came to be, in 1872; today, it is known as Yosemite National Park.

The most important nature conservation impulse came from none other than tough old Teddy Roosevelt, who has gone down in history as the first President to recognize the need and significance of protection measures. Under the heading of *Conservation,* he ordered a number of National Parks and Forests opened, and in 1916 the National Park Service was established. Even today, its rangers see to it that the parks are in

order, clean, and free of rowdiness. They currently supervise a total of 354 parks, forests, seashores and memorial sites comprising nearly 75 million acres of land. 270 million people visit these parks annually, making them also the most important tourist attraction in the nation.

Most of the national parks (which are the models for the state parks upkept by the individual states) lie in the western part of the country. Washington State, Arizona, Utah and California are endowed with the most beautiful natural splendors in the nation.

The second most important period in the history of the national parks was the era of another Roosevelt, FDR. In the wake of the New Deal, thousands of unemployed young men joined the Civilian Conservation Corps (CCC), and helped in building and improving roads, cleaning up forests and replanting new ones.

The latest threat to the parks, however, is not neglect or lack of concern, but rather acid rain, which is killing off the trees, and the pollution of ground waters.

Paradoxically, Americans are very proud of their parks, which have become an integral part of America-consciousness. They speak freely of their "national beauty" or "national heritage," and in general a great deal of effort and taxpayers' dollars go to keeping the national parks in order. Like the flag and the English language (as spoken in the U.S.), the parks are something patriotic. And there is something more: the magnificence of unspoiled nature or outstanding natural monuments, from Old Faithful to Mount Rainier, is for many a link to the national legend of the settling of the country, another symbol of the American Dream.

Americans behave accordingly in their national parks. People follow to the letter, uncomplainingly, the very strict rules and regulations governing behavior in the parks. In the parks, they suddenly become aware of their responsibility toward nature, even though when they are back home, they use up more water, energy and resources per capita than the people of any other nation on this earth.

AMERICAN CUISINE:
FAST FOOD AND ETHNO

America's most successful export is neither Hollywood films nor pop music, but rather fast food. Hamburgers, chicken wings, chili and pizza are sold all over the world today. Junk food is the great equivocator, enjoyed by Texans and Chinese alike. The huge fast food chains, with McDonalds in the lead, began by conquering American cities before moving into the country and then beyond the national borders. "Billions and billions served," is the proud proclamation under the golden arches of McDonalds's signs.

Fast food is a postwar phenomenon. Without cheap cars and well-developed highways, the hamburger could never have waged its victorious campaign on the American stomach. What more could the average weary driver ploughing

Above: A fast-food diet leads to overweight in a third of the population. Right: The motto is stay fit!

through the endless miles of his country want but a quick snack by the side of the road. At the beginning fast food was limited to sandwiches and hamburgers. The latter, a meat patty squeezed between the halves of a roll, were originally developed in New Haven, Connecticut, in 1900, and were served with tomatoes and onions optionally, not ketchup. Sandwiches, born with cheese and ham, developed an endless number of variations thanks in great part to the Jewish delicatessens.

Industrially prepared, the hamburger tends to taste like fried cardboard. Its influence on America quickly became visible around the national midriff. The current statistics suggest that a third of all Americans carry around an extra 30 pounds. This is not only a result of the intake of junk food, but of the general attitude toward nutrition in the country. Americans eat too much of the wrong stuff, and they tend to get too little exercise. Anyone eating in a restaurant for the first time in America will be aghast at the sheer quantities Americans eat in a brief space of time. Some places advertise "all you can eat," a genuinely American invention. Matching calory intake with hard-earned dollars leads to a virtual eating craze. Americans consume on average twice as much as their bodies need for subsistance, namely 3700 calories.

But America would not be America if it did not also spawn a counter-movement. Since the end of the 1970s a part of the nation has embraced a fitness craze. Since the Carter years, no American president has missed an opportunity to show his fighting spirit by going out for a jog every morning – even if the whole nation laughs at his wobbly thighs and thick calves, as in the case of Bill Clinton. Aerobics, bodybuilding, jazzercize and stretching are American inventions, developed and refined in the studios of New York and Los Angeles and on the beaches of California. Health foods are the boom product in the food industry: diet products, from Coke to sausages, turn over about 50 billion dollars a year!

Of course, the U.S. offers a lot more than fast food. Beyond the highways and commercial strips one finds dozens of delis and small ethnic-food establishments. The immigrants brought their cuisine with them and it slowly became an integral part of America's gastronomic landscape. The pizza, born in New Haven as well, and chop suey are two examples. Frankfurters or wieners (better known as hot dogs) and kaiser rolls hark back to the days of German immigration, even if these products no longer have much resemblance to their original models.

In the 1990s Latin-American and Mexican food rose to prominence. Tex-Mex food has appeared wherever Mexican immigrants have settled, and has made its way to Europe as well. Enchilladas, tortillas, tacos and quesadillas are part and parcel of American cuisine by now, and have even been incorporated into the fast food circuit.

Gourmets have a penchant for Californian cuisine, which is light and low in calories. It consists of a combination of American and European cooking, although Europeans might be a little surprised at the variations on their own themes: Fresh, dry salad with fish or chicken breast, without oil or vinegar, accompanied by lots of fruit or lightly steamed veggies. In California one sometimes is thankful for the nearest junk food station.

And finally a mention of what there is to drink: With junk food one drinks soda pops of all colors and flavors, some going into the purely artificial, or milk shakes served in industrial portions. America's large beer companies cannot hold a candle to the small European breweries, but the recent craze in micro-brewing is beginning to turn the tide. Only one has to know about these small establishments or at least inquire. And finally there is excellent wine from California or Washington State, always interesting to the taste buds.

IMMIGRATION

A father with Scottish and Sicilian ancestors, a mother from Hong Kong, an aunt with Russian Jewish background.... That is the kind of thing one can only find in the U.S. Americans are probably the people who have to spell their names most frequently for the benefit of their own countrymen. Read a telephone book in New York, for example, and you will find an anthology of the world's surnames. America is to this day the only veritable (and largest) immigration society in the world.

No other country, no other society, no other culture entertains and organizes immigration quite in the way America still does. Every year 530,000 people arrive in the country legally.

Some reasons for this are to be found in the history of the country itself.

Above: Barbed wire on the border to Mexico hardly hinders illegal immigrants. Right: Asians lead the immigration statistics.

America grew up on a social diet of colonists and immigrants. Until the middle of the last century most of these people came from Great Britain and Ireland. After the Civil War the immigration from Germany and Scandinavia got going. After 1890 Eastern and Southern Europeans from very poor backgrounds and with inadequate skills began arriving in droves. This second great wave of immigration reached its climax in 1907, when more than a million people arrived on the shores of the New World. It ended in 1924 with a law introducing far more stringent measures for the immigrants, a law specifically aimed at the huddled masses from Eastern and Southern Europe, who were suspected of bringing in the germs of political radicalism. A quota system was set up for each country based on the number of its nationals living in the U.S. in 1890. The last major change in the immigration laws took place in 1965 with the introduction of a preferred status system, by which relationship to U.S. citizens and job qualifications counted most.

Parallel to this comes the illegal immigration, especially from Mexico, which reached staggering proportions toward the end of the 1980s, when nearly 1.6 million Mexicans arrived in the country illegally per year.

A multicultural society

Today's immigration policies are relatively liberal, but the laws governing political asylum are only gradually changing. During the days of the Cold War, refugees from Communist countries were given preferential treatment, even if they were patently out for a buck like anyone else. Meanwhile, people fleeing right-wing dictatorships (notably from Latin America) were dismissed as "economic refugees."

About 6 percent of all Americans were born in another country. 47 percent of the

annual immigrants come from Asia, followed by 35 percent from Latin America. European immigrants number less than 10 percent. This shift in the makeup of new arrivals is definitely increasing the multicultural aspect of American society. America today consists of 77 percent Caucasian (or white), 12 percent African-American, 8 percent Hispanic and 2 percent Asian. The latter group is expected to reach the 5 percent mark by the year 2020; the Hispanics will number 11 percent of the population by the same year.

Having said all this, one must add that America was never a genuine melting pot. Most of the immigrant groups have by and large maintained their ethnic identity from generation to generation. Many Americans are still very proud of their ancestry. And the coexistence of various ethnic groups still functions rather well, considering the densely populated areas. One reason lies in the promise of equal opportunity; every new arrival has a chance to climb up the social and economic ladder. In addition, new immigrants find large communities of their own people in most of the larger towns in the country. Races only mix in the poorest or richest neighborhoods. Yet in spite of these clearly defined borders, society does put pressure on everyone to conform to culture and language, and these are still primarily dominated by white Americans. It can happen that a Chinese child suddenly Americanizes its name after a few years in the country. The same applies to children of Mexican, Indian or Korean parents.

But the free marketplace does not really give equal opportunity to the immigrants of today. State-run institutions apply the rules of affirmative action, whereby every public institution has to fill a quota of minorities proportional to the quota in society when hiring. This system is the subject of heated debates in the States. White Conservatives complain about reverse discrimination, the idea that members of a particular minority might be hired because of racial status rather than ability.

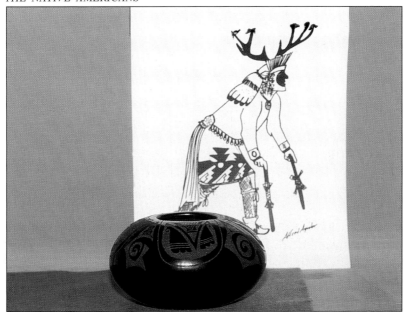

THE NATIVE AMERICANS

"Indians," Columbus called them, supposing he had succeeded in finding a sea route to India; and settlers lumped them together ever after. But the hundreds of thousands of tribespeople who inhabited North America before the Europeans ever got there were members of different distinct civilizations with their own tribes, languages and customs. To settle their constant disputes, Iroquois tribes drew up an alliance called the Five Nations in the 16th century. Their democratic, state-like system of government was similar to that of the United States, except that it predated it by a couple of hundred years.

The attempts of early settlers to take advantage of the Indians for their land solidified into law under the fledgling U.S. Government. The Indian Removal Act of

Above: Desirable artistic craft – ceramic art of the Pueblo Indians. Right: Pueblo Indian in Taos.

1830 "allowed" members of the Five Civilized Tribes – "friendly" eastern tribes such as the Cherokees and Seminoles – to exchange their lands for territory to the west. The Five Tribes proceeded to create five nations in Oklahoma, each with its own government and its own capital. All this was ended by the Civil War. To "punish" the Indians for siding with the Confederate South, the victorious United States Government took away the western portion of their lands, settling them with various tribes from other areas, many of them bitter enemies.

The image most people have of an "American Indian" is of a Sioux, a warrior on horseback in war paint and a feathered bonnet, as depicted in the film *Dances with Wolves.* It was the nomadic tribes of the Sioux who suffered most notably at the hands of the U.S. Government.

Currently, many Native American tribes are trying to get their own names back; the word "Sioux" is Chippewa for "adder;" white settlers presumably learned it from Chippewa guides (similarly, "Apache" is the Zuni word for "enemy"). The Sioux call themselves the Dakotas. "Navajo," for instance, is a Spanish word meaning "People of the Plowed Fields," and that tribe would rather be known by their own name for themselves, "Dineh," "the People."

The pueblo tribes of the Southwest have been able to retain more of their heritage. New Mexico's nineteen pueblos are some of the oldest settlements in North America. Remains of the adobe and brick buildings of prehistoric tribes – in Canyon de Chelly, Chaco Canyon, and other sites – don't look very different from Acoma, Taos, or other pueblos inhabited today. Also in the southwest are the Navajo, the largest Indian tribe (numbering some 200,000); they started out as wandering sheep herders, but adopted many pueblo customs and crafts when they settled in the area. Pots, jewelry, rugs and kachina dolls made by Pueblo tribes are sold throughout the Southwest. Some of these crafts were in fact developed after the advent of white settlers.

Today, there are almost 2 million Native Americans (0.2% of the U.S. population), struggling to keep their cultures alive in the face of overwhelming difficulties. Alcoholism is a terrible problem on many reservations, partly because of the limited opportunities for young people. Despite government reservation schooling, many children have to leave the reservation to get a high-school education; some of them don't come back. Increasing numbers of young people are unable to speak their own tribal languages.

Attempts are being made to reverse this trend; there was no system for writing it down until very recently. Today, scholars have produced Navajo dictionaries, and are trying to build up a body of Navajo-language publications so that Navajo can be taught in schools.

Native American tribes have moved into the 20th century in other ways. Common tribal businesses today are gambling casinos and ski resorts. The Navajo have a number of industries: a sawmill, power plants, oil wells.

But tribal governments are not exempt from the kind of power politics and corruption common to governments the world over. The tremendous power tribal chiefs have over their constituents has led to excesses: former Navajo chief MacDonald is today in jail for embezzling tribal funds.

Meanwhile, tradition has moved into the present as well. Annual events in many parts of the United States are powwows, which are at once competitions for costumed native dancers and meeting places for the members of the widely scattered tribes. Everyone is welcome at these festivals, which are a happy compromise between catering to the tourist trade and adhering to traditional ways of life which the dances of the powwow help to keep alive.

SPORTS IN AMERICA

Some Europeans stereotype America as a country of 250,000,000 semi-educated, overweight materialists whose lives revolve around fast food and who tend to ignore the rest of the world. But this leaves out one major point: sports. Americans are proud of their Big Mac and of living in the good ol' U. S. of A., but an even greater source of national – or local – pride are the country's professional athletes. Due to popular demand, the national media offers even couch potatoes unparalleled access to a wide variety of sports – baseball, basketball, hockey, golf, skiing or surfing competitions – nearly every day.

"Purest" of these is the quintessentially American game of baseball. Baseball, like cricket in Britain, may be a game you have to grow up with truly to understand.

Above: Sport shapes the heroes of the nation. Right: One who desires to be a cheerleader must begin early to practice.

Aficionados crave the leisurely pace of a summer afternoon doubleheader (that's two games played back to back): outfielders waiting for the ball to come their way, runners sweating in the sun, and spectators coming and going for beer and ice cream at the concession stands. To the uninitiated, this whole process may just seem hot and boring.

But it's worth giving the game a second chance, if only because baseball, since Abner Doubleday invented it in 1839, has become a kind of American experience nothing else can quite emulate. Baseball, unlike football or hockey, is a literary sport, a setting for countless American novels and movies. Perhaps one reason so many baseball players have become American popular heroes – Babe Ruth, Joe DiMaggio – is that the game, although a team sport, rises and falls with each individual on the field.

Basically, what happens in a baseball game is that a lone "pitcher" throws a ball at speeds of up to 100 miles an hour at a "batter," who tries to hit it. The pitcher can throw the ball in a number of ways: a "breaking ball," for example, comes toward the batter at one level, and then curves sharply downward before it reaches him. Confronted with this, a batter often swings and misses – a "strike." Three strikes and he's out. If he hits the ball within the designated playing field zone, however, he runs to first base; a player must run to all four of the eponymous "bases" to score a point for his team. The farther you hit the ball, the more bases you can run; and if you hit the ball out of the park altogether, you can circle all four bases in a triumphant "home run."

Beyond baseball, there's only one sport Americans crave: football! Each Sunday in autumn, football games attract crowds of 70,000 in the stands and several million more watching on television. In a listing of the highest-rated TV shows in the history of the world, the annual

championship known as the Super Bowl holds five of the top ten spots: some 38,000,000 households watch this January spectacle.

Where baseball is elegant and literary, football is tough and down-to-earth – literally so, in fact, since most of the plays seem to end up in a huge tangle of bodies piled atop each other on the field. Each team tries to fight its way past the other team and carry the elliptical leather ball, or "pigskin," across the goal line for a "touchdown" (6 points). For a sport called "football," there's not much footwork involved, although players do occasionally get to try to kick the ball high over the goal posts for a "field goal."

The winter member of the trio of great American sports is basketball (although hockey, too, has its passionate followers). While most professional sports in the States have become increasingly color-blind since the first African-American was allowed into baseball's major leagues in 1947 – Jackie Robinson, a star of the then-Brooklyn Dodgers – basketball is particularly the province of fine African-American athletes. Most inner-city districts in America boast outdoor basketball courts – no more than a cement surface with a hoop at each end – and for many gifted young players the sport has been a ticket out of the ghetto and into the limelight. Or the footlights, in the case of the show team The Harlem Globetrotters, who tour the world, not so much competing as performing their remarkable, quasi-acrobatic on-court antics.

It's not only pro sports that are popular in America. One reason sports are such a part of the national fabric is the widespread enthusiasm for college ball, at least football and basketball. College and university competitions get as much TV and media coverage as professional ones. And it isn't only college: go to any small town in America on a fall Friday night and you'll find most of the town's population turned out for the local high school football game – particularly if there's a crosstown rivalry with another local school.

PREPARATIONS

The U.S.A. in statistics

Population: 253 Mio. *Area:* 9,4 Mio qkm. *Ethnic groups:* 80% Whites, 12 % Blacks, 9% Hispanics, 3% Asians, 0,8% Indians, 4% others. *Religion:* 79 Mio. Protestants, 55 Mio. Roman Catholics, 6 Mio. Jews, 4 Mio. Eastern Churches, 0,8 Mio. Old Catholics, 0,1 Mio. Buddhists.

Climate

A rule of thumb is that the high season, that is the summer months from mid-July through September, is in many ways not the best for European tourists. Usually all prices are about 50 percent higher than during the rest of the year, and many of the best sights, notably the National Parks, are completely overrun by American tourists between the end of May (Memorial Day) and the beginning of September (Labor Day). In contrast, during the rest of the year (with the exception of California) National Parks and nature in general are fairly empty.

Europeans might also have difficulty coming to grips with the extremely high temperatures of the southwestern U.S. Beware of the desert and its burning heat, keep enough water around for yourself and your car (which should be in top working condition before attempting crossings of Death Valley). On the other hand, in much of California and parts of the Pacific Northwest the climate is sunny and mild most of the year.

For winter vacations the Rocky Mountains are ideal. The area around Aspen, Colorado, is a great ski destination; so are Vail, Taos (New Mexico), and a host of others.

When traveling in the U.S., bear in mind that nature is often a good deal more violent here than elsewhere in the world. Pay attention to radio warnings about heavy storms, tornadoes, hurricanes and floods. This applies especially to Texas around the Gulf of Mexico. The wooded areas of the West are also renowned for dangerous forest fires.

Money Matters

One basic rule is to carry as little cash around with you as possible. Between 100 and 200 US$ should be purchased before entering the country. Avoid carrying anything larger than a 50-Dollar bill. Foreign currencies can only be changed in larger cities, and that only at some banks. Hence, do not bother carrying wads of foreign currency around with you, it's of no use.

Better and safer are traveler's checks from American Express (which can be transferred to a partner) or from Visa. They can be used in all shops and hotels, or cashed at any bank.

Even safer and handier are credit cards. Anyone with a Mastercard (Eurocard in Europe), a Visa card or an American Express card will be welcome anywhere, anytime. For car rentals and in some hotels a credit card is sometimes required! If you don't already have a credit card, it is advisable to get one before going. Special offers for them sometimes include a very basic form of travel insurance.

Travel Expenses

The cost of traveling in the United States depends primarily on one's expectations and needs. There are, of course, certain basic considerations that can lessen the expense of a trip to the U.S.

Besides choosing the right time of year to travel, pre-booking of a car and hotel room from Europe is generally cheaper. On top of that, the price levels vary greatly on the West Coast, in the southwestern states and in the Rocky Mountains.

One rule of thumb in the West is that the farther east you travel (toward the prairies, that is), the cheaper life gets in general. The most expensive areas are the big cities of San Francisco and Los Angeles. At any rate California is more expensive than Texas or the Northwest. The northern states (Idaho, Wyoming, Montana, Oregon, Washington and Nebraska) are all relatively inexpensive destinations for the European tourist. Arizona and New Mexico are also fairly well priced. Colorado, especially around the big and famous resorts, and the more popular National Parks also experience spontaneous inflation when the tourists show up.

Travel Insurance

Traveling in the U.S. without travel insurance can be a passport to financial ruin! European and other social standards are in their infancy if born at all. Illness is considered a personal responsibility and the victim thereof is asked to come up with the cost of the repairs.

Many private insurance companies cover 80 to 100 percent of the doctors' bills and hospital bills abroad, as well as medication. If you are in doubt ask your regular insurance company for information, or find out more at a travel agent; but whatever policy you take, make sure you are covered 100 percent while in the U.S.! The travel insurance often included with a credit card is generally not enough.

In any case doctors' and hospital bills in the U.S. have to be paid right away either in cash, travelers checks or by credit card. And never forget, that in the land of unlimited opportunity, doctors are also interested in getting upward and along in life. Some will even refuse treatment if there is any doubt as to how it's supposed to be paid.

Travel planning and information

Before choosing one of the routes described in this book, give careful thought to which itineraries or sights genuinely appeal to you. Brochures and further information are readily available at any of the tourist offices of the United States, or at well-stocked travel agencies. Some in-dividual states even have offices abroad where you can find more specific materials. You'll find additional addresses and telephone numbers listed later in this chapter under "Practical Tips from A to Z", (p. 249).

Embassies and Consulates abroad

AUSTRALIA: **Embassy at Canberra**, Moonah Pl., Canberra, A.C.T. 2600, tel. (6) 270 5000. **Melbourne**, 553 St. Kilda Rd., PO Box 6722, Melbourne, Victoria 3004, tel. (3) 526 5900. **Sydney**, 59th Fl., MLC Centre, 19-29 Martin Place, Sydney, N.S.W. 2000, tel. (2) 373 9200. **CANADA**: **Embassy at Ottawa**, 100 Wellington St., K1P 5T1, tel. (613) 238 5335. **Calgary**, Suite 1050, 615 Mac leod Trail, S.E., Calgary, Alberta, T2G 4T8, tel. (403) 266 8962. **Halifax**, Suite 910, Cogswell Tower, Scotia Square, Halifax, Nova Scotia, B3J 3K1, tel. (902) 429 2480. **Montreal**, PO Box 65, Postal Station Desjardins, H5B 1G1, PO Box 847, Champlain, NY 12919-0847, tel. (514) 398 9695. **Quebec**, 2 Place Terrasse Dufferin, C.P. 939, G1R 4T9, PO Box 1547 Champlain, NY 12919-1547, tel. (418) 692 2095. **Toronto**, 360 University Ave., M5G 1S4, PO Box 135, Lewiston, NY 14092-0135, tel. (416) 595 1700. **Vancouver**, 1095 West Pender St., V6E 2M6, PO Box 5002, Point Roberts, WA 98281-5002, tel. (604) 685 4311.

GREAT BRITAIN: **Embassy at London**, 24/31 Grosvernor Square, W1A 1AE, tel. (71) 499 9000. **Consulate General at Belfast**, Queen's House, 14 Queen St., BT 1 6EQ, tel. (232) 32 82 39. **Consulate General at Edinburgh, 3 Regent Terrace, EH7 5BW, tel. (31) 556 8315.**

NEW ZEALAND: **Embassy at Wellington**, 29 Fitzherbert Terrace, Thorndon, Wellington, PO Box 1190, tel. (4) 472 2068. **Auckland**, 4th Floor, Yorkshire General Bldg., Auckland, tel. (9) 303 2724.

SOUTH AFRICA: **Embassy at Pretoria**, 877 Pretorius St., Arcadia

0083, PO Box 9536, Pretoria 0001, tel. (12) 342 1048. **Cape Town**, Broadway Industries Centre, Heerengrecht, Foreshore, tel. (21) 214 280. **Durban**, Durban Bay House, 29th Floor, 333 Smith St., tel. (31) 304 4737. **Johannesburg**, 11th Floor, Kine Center, Commissioner/Kruits Sts., PO Box 2155, tel. (11) 331 1681.

Visas

Tourists from England or the Commonwealth entering the U.S. no longer need a visa stamped in their passport, as long as they are not staying more than three months in the country as visitors, have a return ticket, and have sufficient funds to keep themselves during the length of their stay (see also "Customs"). On a tourist visa it is strictly prohibited to work (as an au-pair, for example), or even study. Should that be your wish, you will need a special visa from a U.S. Consulate in your country of departure.

Should you be traveling to the U.S. without a return ticket and/or be staying between three and six months (the maximum allowed), you will have to send a registered letter to the consulate applying for a visa, or appear there in person. Generally the visa is issued quickly and without too much burocratic mumbojumbo. During the high season, before summer vacations, for example, a waiting period should be expected.

Visa application forms should be filled out carefully according to the best of one's knowledge to avoid any later problems and misunderstandings. A tourist visa is seldom rejected, and then only in the case of a criminal record or drug offences. Should you want to stay longer than six months in the U.S.A., you can resort to a simple trick that is tacitly accepted by the authorities, namely traveling for a brief spell to Canada, making sure your exit is stamped in your passport, and then reapplying for an entry visa at the nearest American consulate.

To be absolutely sure of this method, you should prove you have enough money to survive on and be in possession of a return ticket.

ACCESS

Airlines

The large airline companies, such as United, offer a variety of special or one-time rates. One thing is sure, however: the rates between mid-August and mid-May or mid-June are considerably lower than rates during the summer holiday season (from mid-June to mid-August). Paying the holiday rate during the high season allows the tourist (intending to stay over seven days and under six months) to pick and choose point of arrival and point of departure in the States from the list of airports serviced by the airline. In the light of this, if traveling to New England, you may consider Northwest Airlines, one of the specialists in the area (in spite of its name!).

The difference in price between the various larger airlines is minimal. Currently, the combined route system of German airline Lufthansa, American company United Airlines and Canadian Airlines is the best bet for any traveler heading from Europe to North America. Offering the most expanded flight schedule, the Lufthansa-United alliance is the only of all major partnerships between airlines that links both continents with 300 flights daily to more than 70 destinations, thus covering the whole continental US and Canada.

Among those flights are typical tourist destinations such as California or Florida, as well as flights to the Midwest, the South or Canada's remote regions. If you are a member of a frequent flier program (Lufthansa Miles & More or United Mileage Plus, for example), the partner airline will credit you with the points. In addition, many other partner firms such as car rentals and hotel chains will give you refunds on your miles. If you want to travel around the country a bit, you might consider the kind of special stand-by ticket available to European residents from several American airlines, such as United. For a rather low flat fee, you can fly an umlimited amount within a 30- or 60-day period – although there's no guarantee you'll get on your first-choice flight. Also recommendable are coupon flights offered by United: you pay for a specific number of predetermined flights (up to twelve), which can be changed for a minor fee. You usually pay a base rate and then, depending on the number of coupons, subsequent fares.

Each of these offers assumes that the flights are within continental America and that the ticket be reserved in your country of origin.

Customs

Every traveler to the U.S. is given two forms in the airplane that must be filled out before reaching customs. The immigration form (so-called I94W, green in color, for tourists without a visa, and the white I94 for those with a visa) is for the usual bits of information about yourself. It also asks you for names and addresses of friends or family in the U.S., the reason for your visit, and whether you are a member of a prohibited organization or political party. The lower part of the form, bearing date and place of entry in the United States, is attached to your passport by the immigration official. On leaving the U.S. the slip is removed from your documents, generally by members of the airline staff. Be careful not to lose this bit of the I94.

There are seldom problems at immigration or customs. The officials are not particularly friendly, but very efficient in processing the passengers of incoming flights. Occasionally one of them will collar a traveler and ask how much money he or she is carrying, and what is his or her destination in the U.S. Anyone with enough money in the form of cash or travelers checks should have no problem getting through. Officials do get a little suspicious if your passport has a great deal of stamps from Communist countries such as North Korea and Cuba, or from certain Arab states such as Libya, Syria, Iraq, and Iran. Even in that case, they usually just ask a few questions, and a return ticket plus sufficient ready funds is enough to quiet them down.

A warning to those entering the country as tourists and then finding work as au pairs. If the immigration watchdogs find out about your idea, you will be on the next plane back at your own expense.

After clearing the minor hurdle of immigration, you come to the customs part. If you are flying in from a western or central European state, then the procedure is usually a simple paper-stamping. This is where you show the second form you filled out in the airplane. It requires you to list various taxable items (the quantity), that usually are irrelevant for the tourist. Importing dollars (in the form of cash or travelers checks) must be declared if the sum exceeds 10,000 US$. Importing fresh foods such as sausages, ham, bread, vegetables and fruit is not allowed.

You might also be asked if you spent time recently walking around on a farm. If you take medication regularly, ask your doctor or hospital to provide a written explanation in English prior to departure from your home country. This will prevent an official from confiscating the stuff in question during a routine search because it violates American laws on narcotics.

TRAVELING IN THE U.S.

Airlines

All U.S. and European (and other) airlines keep offices in larger towns and at airports. As with much of the shopping done in the U.S., bookings and payment can be taken care of by telephone using a credit card. All airlines are accessible for free using their 800-numbers:

American Airlines (AA): 1-800-433-7300. **Continental Airlines** (CO): 1-800-525-0280. **Delta Air Lines** (DL): 1-800-221-1212. **Northwest Airlines** (NW): 1-800-225-2525. **Southwest Airlines** (WN): 1-800-435-9792. **Trans World Airlines** (TWA): 1-800-221-2000. **United Airlines** (UA): 1-800-241-6522. **USAir** (US): 1-800-428-4322.

Buying a Car

If you are traveling for more than a month in the United States, you might consider the possibility of buying a used car. It's basically fairly easy. You need an international driver's license, or better yet an American one (easily available in one day by producing your international license and doing a test), an address in the state where you are, and the title of the car. Don't forget that in several states when a car changes owners it must be taken to an inspection at a certified garage. This should be taken care of *before* signing the purchase order.

Whether the seller is asking too much for the car can be checked in the Blue Book which is available in every garage. We recommend you purchase a *Collision Damage Waiver* in order to avoid ruinous expenses in the case of an accident. Another thing to remember is the horrendously high insurance costs that are determined not only by type of car, but rather according to the age, sex, residence and status of the owner. Insurance can be about 300 US$ cheaper with a US license than with an international document!

Car problems

If you run into problems with a rental car, the first thing to do is call the rental agency. Another possibility is to get help from the American Automobile Association (also known as foreign AAA or

Triple-A), Tel: 1-800-HELP. AAA also has contracts with foreign automobile associations, so you might also check what services or wares (maps, brochures, etc) are available to you for free.

Car Rental

The rule of thumb is that it is generally cheaper to book your car from abroad than actually rent it in the U.S. The price of the big rental agencies such as Avis, Budget and Hertz seldom differ greatly, but you should check on the special offers, because they sometimes grant big discounts. To rent a car the client must be at least 21 years of age and have a valid driver's license. Some companies require an international driver's license even for rental periods of under four weeks. That is available at the automobile club in your country of departure.

When booking a rental vehicle, you should find out about all the side expenses which are seldom mentioned anywhere. Among these are the insurance costs, the deductibles, the mileage limit (generally free miles is the deal) and the cost for returning the car, should you be ending the trip in another part of the country.

Find out more from your travel agent about fly-and-drive packages which include a car for a week with your flight, a very good deal indeed.

Once you are in the U.S., you can make calls to the following agencies free of charge (shopping for prices is an acceptable practice in the U.S.!):

Alamo Rent-A-Car: 1-800-327-9633. **Avis Reservations Center**: 1-800-331-1212. **Budget Rent-A-Car**: 1-800-527-0700. **Dollar Rent-A-Car**: 1-800-4000. **Hertz Corporation**: 1-800-654-3131 or 1-800-654-3001 (in Canada). **National Car Rental**: 1-800-CAR-RENT. **Thrifty Rent-A-Car**: 1-800-367-2277.

Another inexpensive way of getting hold of a car is the so-called driveaway service. You drive a car from say New

York to San Francisco in a certian time period that amounts to about 400 miles a day. In addition to a fee, the driveaway service requires usual insurance. For more information call the **Driveaway-Service**, Tel: 1-800-621-4155, or check the yellow pages of large cities under *Driveaway-Service* or *Auto-driveaway.*

Campers and RVs

A number of rental agencies offer campers and RVs, or recreational vehicles as they are known in America. Several states, however, Massachusetts among others, have banned them from the rental agencies. They tend to be quite expensive and are not easy to handle for the inexperienced driver. Still, only a class three license is needed to drive one.

Driving in the U.S.

Driving in the U.S. is a lot simpler and a lot more relaxing than in Europe. The roads are wider, in rural areas they are more often than not quite empty, and Americans usually follow the rule of "safety first." They drive defensively, politely, and a good deal more reasonably than in, say, Germany or Italy. Perhaps one reason for this is that the car in America is by and large not a status symbol or an object to boost one's self-confidence, but rather a tool to be used regularly to get from A to B. Public transportation out in the provinces is notoriously weak. Another reason for this careful driving is the fact that many Americans only have the lowest legal insurance coverage of 20,000 US$ per person, which is nothing compared to the cost of hospitalization.

Many of the daily plagues of European highways (flashing high beams on the slower drivers, tailgating and driving over the speed limit) are considered sheer rowdiness and rude in the U.S. Highway patrols are quick and efficient in dealing with such behavior. Americans expect civilized driving from their fellow Americans and from tourists, especially in the cities. Big city traffic, for example, flows fairly easily because most drivers stick to the speed limit and don't block up the intersections by impatiently going through the orange signal.

Should you be stopped by a patrol car stay calm, keep your hands on the wheel until asked for your papers, and then get them calmly out of your pocket. American police are not necessarily trigger-happy, but they can never be sure whom they just pulled over.

Parking is regulated by corresponding signs. Watch out for hydrants: keep at least 12 feet from them. Towing can be expensive.

In America it is expected that you stop at pedestrian crossings to let people cross. A stop sign means full stop. The reward for all this is the courtesy of other drivers: if trying to pull out into traffic from a difficult parking space, for example, you can rest assured that someone very soon will let you have the right of way. In Germany or Italy you would have to wait for the next snowfall.

Driving in America is on the right. The speed limit in towns and villages is 25 mph (40 km/h) unless otherwise marked. Since December 1995 each state is responsible for controlling its own speed limits on Highways and Interstates. These limits are by and large stuck to in America, as moving violations such as speeding are not only punished by a hefty fine but also by an increase in insurance premiums.

Overtaking is generally on the left, but passing on the right is also tolerated. This is the rule for the large highways and interstates. Stick to your lane and expect to be overtaken on both sides.

Stop signs (Stop all the way) regulate traffic at intersections. If two cars stop at the same time, it's the car which comes to a complete stop first which has the right of way; when in doubt, this is the driver on the right.

Lights turn from green to a long orange phase then to red, and then from red immediately to the green. Unless otherwise stated, one can turn right on red. At many signal lights the right or left lane turns into another street or ends after the light (Right Lane Must Turn Right). Pay attention to school busses. When one stops and flashes its red lights, traffic in *both directions* must come to a full stop and wait until the bus driver switches off his or her lights.

Two road signs are unknown to Europeans: the U-turn, which allows you to perform that otherwise prohibited maneuver; and the "Crossover," which allows the same on a highway.

Xing means *crossing*, so if you see "Gator Xing" it means that alligators like to cross the road at this point.

Multilane streets in some of the larger cities are marked *HOV-2* or *HOV-3*, standing for *High Occupancy Vehicle*. Only cars with two or three people in them are allowed to use these lanes during rush hour.

Greyhound Busses

A good way to get around, rub elbows with everyday America, and see quite a lot of highway and countryside, is to use Greyhound busses, which service the entire U.S.

The busses themselves are not particularly comfortable, but are sometimes equipped with movies and always a toilet. Foreigners can purchase an Ameripass in their country of origin before traveling to the U.S. This is a fairly cheap way of getting around. Smokers beware: there is no smoking on the busses, and the trips can sometimes be egregiously long.

Motorbiking

Experiencing America on a motorbike, preferably a Harley Davidson, is the ultimate biker's dream. Harleys (or other species) are available for rent at many lo-

cations. Should you want to buy a bike, you will have to buy insurance directly from the insurance company (i.e. not via agent), for example: **Dairyland Insurance Company, Berglund Insurance Company**, 5625 E. Indian School Rd., Studio B, Phoenix / Arizona 85018, Tel: 1-602-949-1034, Fax: 1-602-994-0321. You will need a credit card. Once the money has been transferred you will receive your policy. Don't forget to request the application from. Should you be traveling to the US with your own bike, you will also need this insurance.

Road Networks

The American highway and road system has been conceived in a simple and logical fashion. They usually consist of two- or four-lane overland roads, whereby a highway usually applies to any four- or more-laned road. The wide roads leading from one state to the next are logically called interstates. On many highways, be they turnpikes, freeways, parkways or expressways, there are tolls. Keep your handy for speedier processing, especially during rush hour.

The number allotted to an interstate is not haphazard. Even numbers indicate an interstate running east-west. Odd numbers indicate a north-south course. Three numbers (such as the I-405 near Los Angeles) indicate either a highway leading into or around a city. If the first number is even, then it leads into the city, if it is an odd number then it circumnavigates the place. The last two digits indicate the highway or interstate it is coming from.

In many American cities, orientation is relatively easy, even for a first-time arrival. This is because streets are often organized in a grid beginning at the edge of town with either the last letter of the alphabet or a high number: W Street or 99th Street, for example. The closer you get to A or the lower the number, the closer you are to the center of town. House numbers are often given according to the length streets: Number 5605 is a house between 56th and 57th Streets.

Gas stations are frequent in the US, many stay open all night or have at least automatic credit card service. Usually at night you will have to pay first and pump later.

Railways

In comparison to Europe, America's railroad network is poorly developed. The trains themselves are not particularly comfortable either. If you wish to make use of its service, however, find out more about prices, specials and the Amtrak Rail Pass at your local travel agent. Smokers be warned: there is no smoking anywhere on the trains.

A very special kind of travel are small trips on historic or narrow-gauge tracks. Among the great old-timer rides is the *Durango & Silverton Narrow Gauge Railroad,* Durango CO, Tel: 1-303-247-2733, Fax. 1-303-259-9349. It runs from end of April to end of October. The 3 1/4-hour trip costs US $ 43 (1995), half price for children. The *Grand Canyon Railway* in Arizona runs 2 3/4 hours, costs US $ 50 for adults. Tel. 1-800-843-8724, or 1-602-635-4000.

PRACTICAL TIPS FROM A TO Z

Accommodations

Even in the peak season, finding accommodations should not be a problem. Motels, hotels and B&Bs are in heavy supply. The only crunch might come around the favorite National Parks or during particularly busy weekends in such places as Yellowstone National Park. That's why booking ahead of time is recommended if you are traveling, say, around July 4, Labor Day or Memorial Day.

Even the cheaper motels offer two beds (double, king- or queen-size), color television with cable, and often a swimming pool. If you are cooking for yourself ask for a room with a kitchenette. Travelers over 55 years of age should ask

for the senior rate, which means a discount of up to 20 percent. Families can accommodate children under 12 years of age free of charge in some places, or even let them eat for free in the hotel restaurant. Larger groups might also ask for a discount if staying in one room.

The following 800 numbers (toll-free) can be used for information or for making reservations.

LUXURY (over 120 US$): **Hilton Hotels Corp.**, tel. 1-800-HILTONS. **HYATT Corp.**, tel. 1-800-228-9000. **Ritz-Carlton**, tel. 1-800-241-3333.

EXPENSIVE (90-120 US$): **Days Inn**, tel. 1-800-325-2525. **Holiday Inn**, tel. 1-800-HOLIDAY. **Mariott Hotels**, tel. 1-800-228-9290. **Sheraton Hotels & Inns**, tel. 1-800-325-3535.

MODERATE (60-90 US$): **Best Western**: tel. 1-800-528-1234. **Comfort Inn:** tel. 1-800-228-5150. **Howard Johnson**, tel. 1-800-654-2000. **Quality Inn**, tel. 1-800-228-5151. **Radisson Hotel Corp.**, tel. 1-800-333-3333. **Ramada Inns**, tel. 1-800-2-RAMADA. **Rodeway Inns**, tel. 1-800-228-2000.

BUDGET (under 60 US$): **Budget Inns**, tel. 1-800-4-BUD-HOST. **Econo Lodges of America**, tel. 1-800-446-6900. **Hampton Inn**, tel. 1-800-HAMP-TON. **Red Roof Inns**, tel. 1-800-843-7663. **Super 8 Motels**, tel. 1-800-843-1991/1-800-8000. **Travellodge International**, tel. 1-800-255-3050.

Alcohol and Cigarettes

For many Americans, alcohol is something to be scorned. This has to do not only with the Puritan past, the excesses of Prohibition and the current drug problem, but also with the exaggerated cult of fitness. The Dry Martini, the Daiquiri and other cocktails, though still available, have given way to vitamin pills, enzymes and other aids. Alcohol, like tobacco, is simply considered unhealthy.

Anyone out for a drink has to be 21 years of age or older. ID cards are requested by bartenders. In fact the same applies to those wanting to go into a bar or disco where alcohol is served. In some states, alcoholic beverages may only be purchased in special stores, "Liquor Stores" or "Package Stores." But at any rate, the salespeople are supposed to ask for an ID.

Consuming alcoholic beverages in public is strictly forbidden, which is why beer or whiskey or whatever is wrapped up in a brown paper bag. Drinking in a car is absolutely forbidden, so never leave a bottle lying around; lock it up in the trunk for safety's sake. Carrying alcoholic beverages onto an Indian reservation is forbidden as well.

Driving "while under the influence," or DWI, is treated as a misdemeanor. Penalties are heavy and sometimes ingenious. (One judge had the defendants tour high schools to give lectures on DWI!) Each state has its acceptable level, so the best bet is to avoid drinking and driving altogether. In an accident, the first thing the police do is administer a breathalyzer test or blood test. Breaking the law on this issue can land even a tourist in the local jail.

As for smokers, they will have a hard time in the U.S. Busses, trains, public buildings, most cafés and many restaurants simply prohibit it. Smoking sections in restaurants and bars are small. During the intermission at the theater you will have to step outside to enjoy a smoke.

Banks

Most banks are open between 9 am and 4 pm. They are closed on national holidays. To cash traveler's checks or take out cash on a credit card, you should always have an ID with you and in some cases even a second one (such as a driver's license). Some banks also impose a limit on the amount of cash you can take out. Money machines offer the service as well. The international Eurocard does not extend to the U.S.

Business Hours

American shopping hours are generally from 9 am to 9 pm, Monday to Saturday. Most shops and grocery stores also will be open on Sunday and even national holidays. Business hours for banks (9 am to 4 pm) and post offices (8 am to 5 pm) are more limited; both will be closed on Sunday and national holidays.

Camping and Youth Hostels

America is a paradise for campers. The National and State Parks have established excellent camping grounds in the midst of the most pristine nature. Sites are usually available on a first-come-first-served basis. You generally pay a basic fee for a spot (5 US$ to 15 US$, or sometimes free of charge), regardless of the number of people. Barbecues, showers, toilets and washing machines are the norm at camping sites. The camping places in the National Parks are generally fairly crowded in the summer months, so it is recommended you make reservations. Besides the telephone numbers mentioned in the guideposts at the end of each chapter, you can also try the toll-free 1-800-365-CAMP.

An alternative to the state-run camping sites are the private ones, though they are often more expensive (in some cases running up to 35 US$ per night!). On the other hand they offer motel-like luxury.

Youth hostels are not quite as widespread in the U.S. as in Europe, but they are nonetheless very cheap (in the range of 20 US$) and clean. Information and a complete directory can be ordered at the **American Youth Hostel Federation**, P.O.Box 37613, Washington, D.C. 20013, U.S.A.; or at the **Young Men's Christian Association**, the **YMCA**, 224 E 47th Street, New York, NY 10013.

Crime

Tourists in the U.S. should take the same precautions as in any other country they visit. Nevertheless, because of the high crime rate in the U.S. and the widespread availability and use of weapons, one should pay attention to certain unwritten rules.

Should your plane land at night, it is advisable to stay at a hotel near the airport and pick up your rental car the next morning.

Should you be purposely rammed on the highway or otherwise threatened, change lanes, keep driving, and accelerate. In cities pay attention to what locals say about certain areas, and avoid them during the day if possible, but especially at night. Hotel and restaurant personnel will give advice that should be followed, and if you are not sure about an area don't hesitate to ask. Americans live with crime and many know how to deal with it. At night some inner cities are completely dead. Inform yourself as to where nightlife is happening and drive or take a cab to that specific area or place.

Always make sure your car is locked and don't leave things lying about on the seats. On your strolls take only the necessary amount of money in your pocket (wallets are easy to steal for the professionals) and lock the rest away in the hotel safe. Should you own two credit cards, leave one elsewhere. If you should be mugged, forget Hollywood antics and let the mugger have your cash.

If you have lost your way in a big city ask the policemen or find the nearest hotel or restaurant and inquire there. If your car breaks down, park it by the side of the road, open the hood and wait in the car until the police or a tow-truck comes.

Avoid brandishing large sums of money or wearing expensive jewelry. Make sure you know who is knocking at your hotel or motel room door. If the person answers that he or she is personnel from the establishment, call the reception and ask if that is really the case.

Don't forget to keep the telephone numbers handy where you can cancel your credit cards or travelers' checks. The numbers and addresses of embassies and consulates are also important, as well as a photostat of your passport. Remember, too, that Americans themselves have become a little paranoid on the issue of crime. The free sale of weapons means that an unusually high number of regular citizens own firearms, and many of them are quite trigger-happy. If you must go to a house for help or address someone on the street, try to be non-aggressive.

While these precautions are important, we would like to add that there is no point in ruining your holiday by extreme fear. Crime in the U.S. is also fairly focused on poorer areas of big cities. In the sleepy, close-knit communities of villages and towns of the provinces, on the other hand, some people never even lock their cars (although such a feeling of security is on the wane of late). Travelers, of course, are well advised to lock their own cars at all times.

The number for the fire department, the ambulance and the police is 911.

Currency

The American dollar, or "greenback," as it used to be referred to, is not only the most important currency in the world, but also one with great symbolic value. It immediately calls to mind pure and unadulterated capitalism, rapid fortunes, wealth, financial daring.

The dollar is printed in bills of the same size (make sure you know which bill you just handed someone). It comes in denominations of 1, 5, 10, 20, 50, 100, 500, 1000, whereby most business transactions use only bills up to 50 US$. Some shops and restaurants, especially in rural areas, will balk at a 50-dollar bill, so it is advisable to keep break your big bills at a bank.

A dollar breaks down into 100 cents, minted in the following sizes: 1 (penny), 5 (nickel), 10 (dime), 25 (quarter), 50 (half-dollar, rare). Quarters and dimes are important for telephoning and for parking meters and other automats.

Some slang terms, past and present, for the currency are:

A buck . . . . 1 dollar;
. . . . . . ("It costs two bucks, bud!")
A fin: . 5 dollars. From the German *fünf*.
A fiver: . . . . also 5 dollars.
A sawbuck: . . . . 10 dollars.
A "C": . . . . 100 dollars.
A grand: . . . . 1000 dollars.
"Dough" is a common slang term for money in general.

Doctors, Drugstores, Emergencies

Any tourist with the proper health insurance coverage can visit any doctor, provided he or she can prove that the ailment is an emergency, and that he or she has enough cash on hand or a credit card. Payment must be made immediately. What percentage of the fee will be covered by the insurance must be cleared before the start of the trip.

Should a doctor refuse treatment, for whatever reason, try the local Medical Center. These organizations have several doctors working together, and they also provide a kind of out-patient emergency service. Those on medication, especially of the stronger type, should make sure their regular doctor gives them a letter confirming this (in English) for the customs officials. A doctor's prescription is also handy. Medication can be purchased at the Prescription Counter of drugstores and in some larger supermarkets, as well as in a pharmacy, although the latter are very rare.

Drugstores are more than just pharmacies in America. They include all sorts of other consumer goods including cookies and candy, stationery, cosmetics, sometimes even canned goods and the like. Some even have a lunch counter where one can get sandwiches, coffee, tea, doughnuts, Pain relievers, antacids and such are available on the shelves. A separate counter is reserved for prescription drugs.

The emergency telephone number for the police, ambulance or firemen is 911.

Electricity

Standard electricity in the U.S. is 110 volts, so European appliances will require a voltage adaptor that should be bought in your home country. Even though many modern appliances feature a voltage switch, you still need an adaptor because American sockets are smaller.

Embassies and Consulates

British Consulates are to be found in: **Houston** (Suite 1900, First Interstate Bank Plaza Building, 1000 Louisiana, Houston, TX 77002, tel. 713/659-6270); **Dallas** (813 Stemmons Tower West, 2730 Stemmons Freeway, Dallas, TX 75207, tel. 214/637-3600); **Denver** (c/o Davis, Graham & Stubbs, Suite 4700, 370 17th St, Denver, CO 80202, tel. 303/893-7300); **Los Angeles** (Suite 400, 11766 Wilshire Blvd., Los Angeles, CA 90025-6538, tel. 310/477-3322); **San Francisco** (Suite 850, 1 Sansome St, San Francisco, CA 94104, tel. 415/981-3030); **Seattle** (820 First Interstate Center, 999 Third Ave, Seattle, WA 98104, tel. 206/622-9255).

Australian Embassy, 1601 Massachusetts Ave., Washington, D.C. 20036, tel. 202/797 3000. **Australian Consulate Generals** are to be found in: **Houston** (Suite 800, 3 Post Oak Central, 1990 South Post Oak Blvd., Houston, TX 77056-9998, tel. 713/629 9131). **Los Angeles** (611 North Larchmont Blvd., Los Angeles, CA 90004-9998, tel. 213/469 4300). **San Francisco** (1 Bush St., San Francisco, CA 94104, tel. 415/362 6160).

Canadian Embassy, 501 Pennsylvania Ave., NW, Washington, D.C., 20001, tel. 202/682 1740. **Canadian Consulate Generals** are to be found in: **Dallas** (St. Paul Place, 750 North St., Paul St., Suite 1700, Dallas, TX 75201-3261, tel. 214/922 9806). **Los Angeles** (300 South Grand Ave., 10th Floor, Los Angeles, CA 90071, tel. 213/687 7432). **Seattle** (412 Plaza 600, Sixth and Stewart, Seattle, WA 98101-1286, tel. 206/443 1777).

South African Embassy, 3051 Mass-achusetts Ave. NW, Washington, D.C. 20008, tel. 202/232 44 00.

New Zealand Embassy, 37 Observatory Circle NW, Washington, D.C., 20008, tel. 202/328 4848. **New Zealand Consulate General**, 12400 Wilshire Blvd., Suite 1150, Los Angeles, CA 90025, tel. 310/207 1605.

Etiquette

Many European tourists, especially German and British, are considered excessively aggressive and rude in the U.S. This has to do with a misconception and misunderstanding of the different cultures. The apparently loose and informal American society in fact invites this kind of behavior.

On the contrary, however, social intercourse in the U.S. is governed by a slew of very subtle rules and regulations that are barely visible to the foreigner. In order to enjoy your holiday without any sudden and unpleasant experiences with Americans, here are a few tips on the correct behavior with your host country. You will be rewarded by an even broader smile.

Americans keep careful watch on physical distance, that means the moment you get closer than 50 cm to a stranger, or happen to walk very close by, you should utter an "excuse me." The answer will generally be a "hum" or some such noise. This rule can be applied universally, on the street, in the airplane, in shopping malls or in restaurants. If you want to get by someone you must call attention on yourself with another "excuse me."

Americans wait in line, and trying to cut in line is considered highly improper. Banks, post offices and other such places where lines are before counters, often have an ingenious funneling system to keep the first-come-first-served rule operating without hitches. Another rule that is obeyed naturally is to stand on the right while going up escalators.

Casual meetings seldom involve shaking hands, on the other hand a salesperson or businessperson may well insist on shaking your hand after a successful transaction. Greetings are otherwise fairly informal, involving a casual "Hi, how are you," which should be answered by a "Thanks, I'm fine, how are you." Even in department stores one finds this question being asked of customers, whereby a thorough and truthful answer concerning your state of being is neither expected nor desired.

Americans tend to talk loudly, a fact you will notice at the latest during your first visit to a restaurant. But they seldom raise their voices or use a cutting tone. Therefore, in case you have to complain about something, avoid becoming gruff and instead use a quiet, factual tone to register your complaint. Anything else would be seen as gratuitously aggressive and the reaction would be the same. In shops and restaurants, in businesses where you are the paying person, remember that the customer is *always* right. You will generally be treated with courtesy.

The general puritanism of American society extends to the whole issue of relations between the sexes as well. The established form of meeting up with someone of the opposite sex is to "date," which essentially implies an invitation to a restaurant, a movie, a cup of coffee, and so on. This highly contrived game is obnoxious to someone raised in Europe, but it should be played. If you are in business, and you are male, beware of making flirtatious remarks and giving the "eye" too much. There have been many cases of sexual harassment these past years, some apparently based on what some Europeans might consider perfectly normal intra-sexual behavior.

Food and Drink

America still has a reputation abroad for being a culinary backwater: hamburgers, steaks and chili is what the gourmet traveler expects when traveling the 50 states. Indeed, it is not the place for a major gastronomic tour, as opposed to say Germany or France. On the one hand the quality of the dishes is below the average European standard, on the other hand, for a gourmet meal in the U.S. you will have to fork out a considerable sum of money.

America's culinary forte is ethnic and local cuisine. Here it is without competition. This nation of immigrants offers countless restaurants offering ethnic food from every corner of the planet. Very common in just about every town of moderate size and over, are ethnic fast foods, from pizza parlors to taco joints (Mexican), from Indian food to Jewish delis (the birthplace of the American sandwich).

Driving along the highway, or approaching a town, you'll encounter dozens of outlets of the large fast-food chains such as McDonald's, Burger King, Checkers, Taco Bell, Popeye's, and so on, where you can either sit and "enjoy" your coke, hamburger and fries (or tacos); or you steer through the drive-in and have it all in your lap while cruising further on down the line. Another alternative is to find a friendly diner where the hamburgers will be tastier, and the menu will often include some local specialty or some solid home cooking. If time and money allows, try sampling some of the restaurants mentioned in the travel section or in the guideposts with their ethnic or regional specialties.

The American food day begins with a mighty breakfast, goes on to a light lunch, and ends in the evening with a warm dinner. Breakfast, which is seldom served in hotels, can be found at a coffee shop or a diner. It has many variations, but includes usually cereal (Cornflakes, oatmeal, müsli, with milk), freshly pressed orange juice, coffee (of a rather watery sort), eggs, bacon or ham, sausages, hashbrowns, home fries or pancakes (with butter and maple syrup). Fried eggs are either scrambled, sunny side up, or over easy (which is sunny side up briefly turned over so the yolk, or "sun," is "clouded"). Bread can be in the form of toast, rolls, or a bagel, a heavy, chewy, tasty doughnut-shaped roll.

Lunch consists often of soup and salad from a salad bar, or a sandwich at a local deli. Dinner is the main feast of the day.

Restaurant life is somewhat different than in Europe. Even in finer establishment one can arrive in informal attire unless otherwise indicated. The treatment of the clients is generally casual, and the clients for their part do not seek special treatment. (Many American women have no qualms about taking care of their make-up right at the table).

In most places you are greeted at the entrance by a host or hostess and subsequently led to a table. The usual question is "smoker or non-smoker?" Should no tables be immediately available, your name will be put on a waiting list and called out in due time. Usually there is a bar or lounge where you can enjoy an aperitif.

After sitting down the waitperson usually brings a menu and recites the specials of the day, including the price. A friendly gesture, that can become tiresome for the European used to formalities, is the "Hi, I'm (first name of the waitperson), I'm your waiter/waitress tonight." A busperson brings bread, butter and a glass of ice water.

American servings are fairly large, so unless you are voraciously hungry, you can skip the appetizer and go straight to the entrée. Things like coffee and soft drinks are often charged once with refills on the house or for a minor fee. If you want your drink without ice let the waitperson know. Also remember that a "regular" coffee is one with milk in it!

One way of reducing costs is by ordering the Special of the Day. Another way is to take advantage of the salad bar if there is one (whereby it usually comes together with an entrée). For industrial hunger find a place offering an all-you-can-eat special. For a single price the customer can benefit from a large buffet. Some American restaurants have specials for children, consisting of smaller portions and usually involving more health-conscious dishes.

What comes at the end of the meal is dessert. A word to the wise: Desserts in America can be very large, very filling, very sweet and very heavy. You may want to wait a little, take a walk and then find another place to enjoy the calories.

Should you not be able to finish what has been heaped on your plate, do not hesitate to ask for a doggie bag, another delightful American euphemism.

A word about drinks is also important. American beer is not always to the liking of European drinkers, because of its very low alcohol content. Not every restaurant offers import beers, however, so you may have to put up with an American brand. Some restaurants offer beers from the nearby microbreweries. These are usually very good. The wine lists are also frequently on the poor side. Once again, find out if there is a local wine worth a try at least. California, Washington State and Oregon also produce wines. Most Californian wines are a little stronger than their European equivalents.

On Sundays you might find that some places don't serve alcohol at all. In some of the Midwest communities and in the southern states no alcohol is served at any time, and restaurants have to offer alcohol-free beer and wine. Establishments that have no liquor license will advertise the acronym BYOB, which means bring your own bottle (or booze). Should you look as if you were under 21, you may be asked to produce an ID.

The check is presented after dessert, either directly at your table or at the register near the door. As soon as the check is paid you are expected to leave the establishment. Hanging around over a few drinks and chattering away is not appreciated. This is purely economic and should not be taken personally. Any nearby bar is the appropriate place to while away a few hours.

If you wish to avoid restaurants and find your own food, you will have to enter the world of the American supermarket. These huge establishments are frequently open 24 hours, and offer an enormous range of goods, and also run salad and sandwich bars, bakeries and small doughnut stores. Many also accept credit cards. Efficiency is the name of the supermarket game, so even if it seems filled to the brim with shoppers, you will seldom have to wait very long at the register. Bagging is done for the customer. Groceries, by the way, are by and large cheaper than in Europe, especially fruit and vegetables, beef and seafood.

For more personal service and better stocked in specialties, go to a delicatessen. These often have a better selection of salads, cheese and sausages. Vegetable stands are also a good source of food at good value. The "health food store" is the place to find organic vegetables, organic cheeses, special juices and the like.

Proper bread is difficult to find in the U.S., bakeries are far and few between. Pita bread, packaged pumpernickel, white rolls, French bread is generally available in supermarkets and delicatessens. Health food stores sometimes have a more serious selection. Here, too, there are regional differences. In more provincial areas the chance of finding healthy, organic stuff is remote, though every now and then one might come across a town that became a resort for hippies many moons ago, and has embraced the new health food gospel. Keeping your eyes peeled is important.

Hiking and Trekking

Most of the National Parks have extensive trails that can be explored alone or accompanied by a park ranger (who can tell you volumes about the park in question). These guided tours last anywhere from 20 minutes to several days and usually start daily during the summer months. Accommodation is either in camping sites or in simple huts that have to be reserved in advance either at the local Visitor Center or from the rangers of the National Park. For more information see page 232 of this guide.

Language

Volumes have been written about the American language and how it is spoken. The debate as to whose is better still rages on to this day between the old colonial master Great Britain and Americans, whereby the latter seem a lot more relaxed about the wagging of their tongues. In fact Americans are simply more relaxed when they speak, both in terms of pronunciation and grammar. As long as the meaning is out there, who cares what form it takes? At any rate, anyone wishing to find more information and thousands of linguistic tidbits should pick up a copy of H. L. Mencken's *The American Language*. Though written in the 1930s and 1940s, it gives the background to the development of euphemisms, of expletives, of surnames and place names, of cant and argot. It compares British and American English and examines (with typical Menckenian sarcasm) the differences between them.

The American language is very lively. New words appear out of the blue and spread across the country like wildfire. The student expression "to be psyched," for example, meaning prepared for or excited about something. Or "megabucks," meaning expensive. Some American words have even conquered the world. The best example is the famous OK, whose origins are the subject of philological debates. In American it has an unbelievable number of meanings. It can be a noun: "Congress gave its okay to a bill..." It can be a verb: "Congress okayed a bill...." It can be an adjective with contrasting meaning depending on intonation: "I'm okay" can mean yes, but not really, yes indeed, or so-so. It can signal approval.

Time is money, as Ben Franklin said, so things have to be shortened in America. The President is called the Prez, fabulous becomes fab, refrigerator is a fridge. Acronyms have a field day as well: BYOB = Bring Your Own Bottle (or Booze); SNAFU = Situation Normal All Fouled Up; PDQ = Pretty Damned Quick; ASAP = As Soon As Possible; SASE = Self-Addressed and Stamped Envelope; TLC = Tender Loving Care. And that is only the tip of the iceberg. Simplifying language also takes on another appearance. Through becomes thru, 4-sale means for sale, Ped Xing means Pedestrians Crossing, and Xmas is Christmas.

With all the linguistic freedom taken, however, Americans are beginning to suffer from the constraints of PC, which in this case means not personal computer but rather political correctness. In some cases the changes are indeed justified, but one must be careful not to offend a social group or minority by using the wrong word by accident or by habit. Syntactical acrobatics are now required to deal with the gender issue (he or she, waitpersons). Manning a telephone is a no-no. The list goes on. The result of all this is that the emotional quality of the language is beginning to disappear in certain quarters, to be replaced by objective sterility. And whether these mighty efforts are truly getting rid of discrimination is a wide open question.

Media

Foreigners traveling in America will realize without the shadow of a doubt just how insular this gigantic nation is. Television, radio and the print medium stick mainly to local topics, and world news is often given merely cursory treatment.

To stay in touch with international events you can turn to the Los Angeles *Times*, the New York *Times*, the San Francisco *Chronicle* or the *Wall Street Journal*. All others, even the most important print media, report almost exclusively on national topics. Even the main news magazines such as *Time*, *US News and World Report*, or *Newsweek*, are sold in their American version, which is different from the European one.

International newspapers and magazines are not easy to come by either, once you get beyond the big cities. Television offers little relief from the innate isolationism of the American media. The 99 percent private ownership of the broadcasting stations means that they have to sell their product as if it were shoes or doughnuts, and the American public, long used to using the media as means of switching off its gray cells, will not necessarily turn to news or news programs. As any bout of channel surfing with an American television set proves, the percentage of sheer bilge being broadcast on the major networks is extremely high.

Even the news programs, such as CNN and Dan Rather's evening news on CBS, has an overtone of perfectly contrived hype to it that removes a lot of its credibility. Somewhere and at some time, the networks got a message that their anchorpeople had to be more aggressive, and hence we have the image of a perfectly harmless fellow, Dan Rather in this case, performing such acts as cutting George Bush (then Vice-President) off of an interview, because he was talking too much about Irangate. The model here seems to be the talk show, during which such self-propelled high and windy priests as CNN's Larry King go about verbally bashing anyone in sight or earshot, usually by means of aggressive interruptions. It's part of the game of making information interesting by turning the anchors into stars and the news into show

biz. And, as already suggested, much of the news deals with national events. International events must either be of extreme importance and possibly with a tie to the U.S., or blood must be flowing or threatening to do so.

There are naturally some redeeming shows, even on CBS: *Eye on America*, makes an attempt at social commitment, and Ted Koppel on *Nightline* (ABC) has a more intelligent and profound way of conducting interviews. The best news show by far, however, is on PBS, the publicly funded network (Channel 13). Every weekday evening one can tune into the *MacNeil/Lehrer Report*, a one-hour news program on the British model. PBS should also be mentioned in connection with the public radio stations that cover the nation from Portland to Portland. No advertising is only one aspect of the relief. Their programming covers a wide range, from classical music, to news and public affairs. *Morning Edition* (in the morning of course), and *All Things Considered* in the evening give excellent coverage with good interviews. Some stations even broadcast a half hour of BBC World Service. Though conservative Americans constantly fire broadsides at PBS for its alleged liberal stance, in truth the views expressed are often quite balanced.

Finally, to be fair, one should mention CNN as a source of news as well. And if you are a news addict, or need to follow the daily life in your home country, we can only advise you purchasing a shortwave radio (see under "shopping").

The entertainment offered by the networks consists mostly of series, soaps, glossy shows that border on vulgarity, and lots and lots of advertisement. Movies are seldom shown, usually on Sunday nights. To get a good feel for American culture, tune into some of the specialties, such as *Late Night with David Letterman* on CBS or its forerunner on NBC, *The Tonight Show*, hosted by Jay

Leno, who took over from the legendary Johnny Carson. Then there are the countless talkshows that often start their drumfire in the morning. The stars are Oprah Winfrey, Phil Donahue and Geraldo, among others. They demonstrate how the public mind can be influenced and provide a deep view into the nature of the American psyche. They are also inadvertently comical.

Otherwise, American TV is characterized by great variety and by its technical proficiency. When booking a hotel room, ask if some of the movie channels are available in the room, HBO, Showtime or Movie, for example. These channels broadcast relatively recent films with few breaks for advertisement. If you are a sports addict tune into ESPN, a channel exclusively devoted to sports. Note, however, that the focus is on the U.S. Even during the World Cup soccer matches in America, ESPN favored baseball over some of the soccer games.

Post Offices

The American postal service is the only state-run operation in the US (barring the National Parks), and it functions relatively well, considering. Postage is also generally cheaper than in Europe.

Unfortunately there are not too many post offices around. Their business hours are basically from 8 am to 5 pm on weekdays, and from 8 am to midday Saturdays. Stamps are also available at supermarkets, in drugstores, in convenience stores (a small supermarket), and at hotel and motel receptions. Some stores also offer fax service, but fees to Europe can be quite high. A normal airmail letter to Europe currently costs 50 cents, a postcard 40. A letter within the U.S. costs 32 cents, a postcard 20.

Unlike many European states, the American post office has nothing to do with the telephone system. Coin-operated booths hanging on the walls are mere conveniences for the customers.

Public Holidays

Besides the usual holidays known to Europeans, America has several national holidays that have in part greater meaning to the general public than Christmas and Easter. This is true in particular for residents of the coastal cities, where Christians and citizens of European origin only form a part of a multicultural society. Government offices, post offices, banks, other public institutions and some businesses are closed during the following holidays.

January 1: New Year's Day.

Third Monday in January: Martin Luther King Day, celebrating the birthday of the great Civil Rights leader.

February 21: President's Day, celebrating the birthdays of George Washington, the first President of the U.S., and Abraham Lincoln (whose birthdays were formerly celebrated in consecutive February weeks).

Last Monday in May: Memorial Day, a day of national remembrance for Americans killed in foreign wars. The main vacation season begins after this day.

July 4: Independence Day, the most important national holiday, celebrates the signing of the Declaration of Independence. Parades and barbecues are the order of the day.

First Monday in September: Labor Day, the American equivalent of May 1 in Europe. It officially ends the vacation season and accordingly prices for tourists drop up to 50 percent.

October 12: Columbus Day, celebrating the discovery of America.

November 11: Veteran's Day, celebrates the veterans of the American army.

Third Thursday in November: Thanksgiving Day, a harvest feast, actually commemorates the Pilgrims' safe landing in America. It is second in importance to July 4.

December 25: Christmas Day.

Shopping

The U.S. is a paradise for consumers on the lookout for a good buy. Many items are a good deal cheaper than in Europe, though the quality can leave something to be desired. Shopping in America is also a great deal of fun. Firstly, the salespeople are very polite and helpful. Entering a store, you will immediately be greeted by (a sometimes nerve-wracking) "May I help you?" Secondly, there are no official closing hours, so shopping can be done during one's leisure time and therefore takes on the character of a pastime. Shopping is comfortable for the consumer, with large department stores, wide aisles, or generous malls with restaurants and cafés.

Besides the regional antiques and art and handicrafts recommended in the travel section, one should look into the purchase of electrical equipment (TVs, videos, CDs, cassettes), computers and PC paraphernalia, photographic equipment and clothing. All electronic equipment is on average 30 percent cheaper than in Europe. Make sure that the equipment can be switched to 220 volts and also function with a different Hertz frequency. The salespeople should know. Television and video equipment is of little use since the American TV system is not compatible with the European Pal-Secam. Videocassettes and taped videos can therefore only be used in the U.S. If you find a video camera or a camcorder, make sure that the cassettes it uses can be played back on a European machine. In the world of computers, notebooks and laptops are a lot cheaper than in Europe. Make sure that the maker has a subsidiary in your country of origin.

Far more simple is the purchase of photographic equipment. All major brands and their equipment are available in the U.S. at lower rates than in Europe. Los Angeles leads the pack in discounts. If you are staying longer in the U.S. and have a credit card and a permanent address, you can save even more by ordering by mail. The sales tax of the state of origin is then discounted. The item in question often takes just a week to reach you.

Buying clothing is only worthwhile if you are looking for an American product. Jeans and related clothing are cheaper (above all *Levis*). For shoes look for the brands *Timberland* and *Bass*, and in the sports department *Nike*, *Reebok* and *Converse all Stars*. American designer clothing is also a good deal cheaper: *Calvin Klein, DKNY, Katherine Hamnett, Ralph Lauren*. Some European brands, such as *Armani*, are a bit cheaper too. In some of the big department stores, such as Bloomingdale's, Macy's or Hecht's, you can find special discounts especially around holidays. An American specialty is the "outlet" or "factory store," where slightly damaged or imperfect clothing or collections from the previous year are peddled at minimal prices. Filene's Basement is particularly recommended for its inexpensive designer clothes.

Telephoning

No other country in the world has such a dense telephone and telecommunication network, and so many telephones available to customers that actually work. Furthermore the service is efficient and fairly inexpensive.

Before reaching for the receiver, note that the system is in private hands, and the service is taken on by several competing companies. There are area companies, regional ones, and long-distance companies. If phoning locally within an area code, just dial the seven digits. If phoning outside your area code, dial 1, then the area code where you are phoning to, followed by the seven digits. If phoning from a coin-operated telephone with coins, an operator will automatically come on to tell you how much you have to put into the slot and the duration of your call. Should you lose money in a coin-operated telephone, call the operator

(0) and give a U.S. address where the phone company can send the refund. Even a dime comes back!

Operators make life very easy, though using their services is a bit more expensive than direct dialing. If you're at a public phone that can't make international calls, an operator can help; they also perform such services as reversing charges.

The easiest and probably cheapest way of telephoning is to own a telephone card. Several companies offer them, AT&T, MCI and Sprint, for example. It costs nothing to get one, and the fees are charged either directly to your bank account or to a credit card. Furthermore, the companies offer special discounts for heavy phone users. If you have a great deal of phoning abroad to do, you can usually get a special discount. Just shop around for the best deal. The AT&T card, for example, has a number and a PIN (Personal Identification Number) that you should memorize. Dial an AT&T operator direct, or ask the normal operator to connect you. It's very simple and efficient. The service can be used in your hotel room to avoid high phone bills (you will be charged only for a local call, that is up to 75 cents). Operators can also charge your calls to a credit card. All of this eases the hassle of juggling with coins at a street corner.

Two other peculiarities of the American phone system that you might come across are pagers and voice-mail boxes. Pagers are known in other countries, but in America they are more widespread than elsewhere. The voice-mail box is a kind of answering machine service offered by the telephone companies. It switches on if no one answers the phone or the line is busy. Leave a message and the person will get back to you. All they have to do is pick up their phone and dial a number for the message to play back.

The 800 numbers are another American specialty. They are toll-free for the user. Sometimes they come with a com-

bination of letters, such as 1-800-345-ALEX. Look at any American telephone, and you will see letters next to each digit. The rest is a question of spelling. In the case of ALEX you would have to dial 1-800-354-2539.

Beware of the 900 numbers: They are very expensive for the user!

Directory assistance is 555-1212 nationwide. If you are in Manhattan and need assistance in, say, Western Massachusetts, you must dial 1-413-555-1212. All emergencies must be reported on 911.

Time Zones

The continental U.S. is divided into four time zones. On the east coast it's Eastern Standard Time (EST), which is 6 hours behind Central European Time (midday in Berlin means 6 am in New York). The next zone is Central Time (CT), one hour behind EST. Then comes Mountain Time (MT) and Pacific Time (PT), minus one hour respectively. At midday in New York it is 11 am in Chicago, 10 am in Colorado Springs and 9 am in San Francisco. Keep this in mind when telephoning across the continent.

Daylight Savings Time in America begins on the last Sunday in April and lasts until the last Sunday in October.

Departure and arrival times for flights are always given in local time.

Tipping

Service is not included in the bill at restaurants and in bars. Waiters and waitresses therefore expect quite a hefty tip, between 12 and 20 percent, which can be left as cash on the table or written into the appropriate slot on your credit card receipt. The reason for this rather large obulus is that the minimum wage for restaurant help is even lower than the already miserable national minimum wage, and waiters and waitresses live mainly from the tips. And theoretically at least a part of it has to be declared to the International Revenue Service. The by-product of this system is very polite and helpful waitpersons. Even if the service is poor and the food third rate, be a fair tipper and bring your complaints to the management.

Tipping is also appropriate for cabbies. Rounding off the fare to the next logical sum is usual ($ 6,35 to $ 7, for example, or if in doubt between 5 and 10 percent). For a great hackie (they can be very entertaining) you may want to give a larger tip. The same applies to extra services, such as waiting until you have entered your home at night.

Tipping at hotels can become expensive, and the more luxurious the place, the more one tends to give larger tips. This can become ruinous. For good service at a reception 10 to 20 Dollars at the end of a two-week stay is appropriate, more if the receptionist has really gone out of his or her way to do you favors. Less, of course, if the service was miserable and ill-humored. The bellboy might be rewarded with 2 Dollars per exertion. The doorman can be doused with quarters for his services hailing taxis etc.

Otherwise, tipping is not one of the great economic factors on a trip to the United States. Keep in mind, though, that it might leave a good impression with a particularly good guide or for a service rendered above the call of duty.

Tourist Information

The tourist in America is cared for in exemplary fashion. Besides dozens of visitor centers usually posted at the main sights, one can also make use of numerous toll-free telephone numbers to request more information or brochures. Here is a list:

WEST COAST: California, tel. 1-800-TO-CALIF. **Oregon**, tel. 1-800-547-7842. **Washington**, tel. 1-800-544-1800. **British Columbia**, (Canada) tel. 1-800-548-8016.

ROCKY MOUNTAINS: **Colorado**, tel. 1-800-433-2656. Idaho, tel. 1-800-635-7820. **Montana**, tel. 1-800-541-1447.

Nebraska, tel. 1-800-228-4307 (in state: tel. 1-800-742-7595). **Utah**, tel. 1-800-448-8355. **Wyoming**, tel. 1-800-225-5996. **SOUTHWEST: Arizona**, tel. (602) 542 86 87. **Nevada**, tel. 1-800-NEVADA-8. **New Mexico**, tel. 1-800-545-2040. **Texas**, tel. 1-800-8-8-TEX.

Weights, Measures, Temperatures

The metric system has made no impression on the U.S., even though in some places, especially near the Canadian border, kilometer distances are also given next to the miles.

LENGTHS:

1 inch (in. or ")	2.54 cm
1 foot (ft. or ') = 12 in. . . .	30.48 cm
1 yard (yd) = 36 in.	91.44 cm
1 mile (mi)	1,609 m

LIQUID MEASURES:

1 ounce (oz)	2.957 cl
1 pint = 16 oz	0.47 l
1 quart (qt) = 2 pints	0.95 l
1 gallon = 4 quarts	3.79 l

SOLID WEIGHTS:

1 ounce (oz)	28.35 g
1 pound (lb) = 16 oz	453.6 g

Note: British and Canadian weights and measures, though bearing the same names as American ones, do differ from them on occasion. A British gallon is 4.546 l.

TEMPERATURES:

Temperatures are given in Fahrenheit in the US. The formula for translation into Celsius is: °F - 32 x 9/5 = °C.

-4 °F	-20 °C
0 °F	-18 °C
15 °F	-10 °C
32 °F	0 °C
68 °F	20 °C
75 °F	23 °C
80 °F	27 °C
90 °F	32 °C
100 °F	38 °C

AUTHORS

Jürgen Scheunemann, a Berlin-based freelance journalist and translator, studied US history at the Free University of Berlin's John F. Kennedy Institute and taught American history at the University of Maryland. He was project editor of the *Nelles Guide to Berlin and Potsdam*. He wrote the chapters "A Journey through the Promised Land", "From Los Angeles to Las Vegas", "From Las Vegas to the Grand Canyon", "Through Navajo and Hopi Country", "From Los Angeles into Yosemite National Park" (with Arturo Gonzales), "From San Francisco to Seattle", "The Pacific Northwest", "From Seattle to Yellowstone National Park", "National Parks", "American Cuisine: Fast Food and Ethno" and "Immigration".

Arturo Gonzalez has worked for several U.S. magazines and newspaper for forty years. He wrote the chapters "From the Grand Canyon to Denver", "From Los Angeles to San Francisco", "From Los Angeles to Yosemite National Park", "From San Francisco to Salt Lake City" and "From Salt Lake City into Yellowstone National Park"

Sara Hare is a San Francisco-based journalist. She wrote the chapters "From Los Angeles to Phoenix" and "From Phoenix to Santa Fe".

Anita King, a former copy editor of the *San Francisco Independent*, contributed to Sara Hare's chapters.

Gary McKechnie, travel writer, wrote, together with Anne Midgette, the feature "Sports in America".

Anne Midgette lives in Munich and writes about music and the arts for the *Wall Street Journal, ARTnews, Opera News*, and other publications. Her published travel writings include a guidebook to Bavaria. She was also a co-author and project editor of the *Nelles Guide to New York*. She wrote the chapters "From Santa Fe to San Antonio", "From San Antonio to Houston", "The Native Americans" and "Sports in America".

PHOTOGRAPHERS

Explore the World

NELLES GUIDE

AVAILABLE TITLES

Australia
Bali / Lombok
Berlin and Potsdam
Brittany
California
  Las Vegas, Reno,
  Baja California
Cambodia / Laos
Canada
  Ontario, Québec,
  Atlantic Provinces
Caribbean
  The Greater Antilles,
  Bermuda, Bahamas
Caribbean
  The Lesser Antilles
China
Crete
Cyprus
Egypt
Florida
Greece - *The Mainland*
Hawaii
Hungary
India
  Northern, Northeastern
  and Central India

India
  Southern India
Indonesia
  Sumatra, Java, Bali,
  Lombok, Sulawesi
Ireland
Kenya
Malaysia
Mexico
Morocco
Moscow / St Petersburg
Munich
  Excursions to Castels,
  Lakes & Mountains
Nepal
New York - *City and State*
New Zealand
Paris
Philippines
Prague / Czech Republic
Provence
Rome
South Africa
Spain - *North*
Spain
  Mediterranean Coast,
  Southern Spain,
  Balearic Islands
Thailand

Turkey
Tuscany
U.S.A.
  The East, Midwest and
  South
U.S.A.
  The West, Rockies and
  Texas
Vietnam

FORTHCOMING

Corsica
Israel - with Excursions
  to Jordan
London, England and Wales
Portugal
Sri Lanka

Nelles Guides – authorative, informed and informative.
Allways up-to-date, extensivley illustrated, and with first-rate relief maps.
256 pages, appr. 150 color photos, appr. 25 maps
UK £ 8.95 USA US$ 14.95 AUS $A 21.95